THE EXECUTIVE SOURCEBOOK

Bert Darga

A STONESONG PRESS BOOK

SIMON AND SCHUSTER   NEW YORK

Published by Simon and Schuster
A Division of Simon & Schuster, Inc.

Simon & Schuster Building
Rockefeller Center
1230 Avenue of the Americas
New York, New York 10020

SIMON AND SCHUSTER and colophon are registered trademarks of Simon & Schuster, Inc.

Designed by Jennie Nichols/Levavi & Levavi

Manufactured in the United States of America

1   3   5   7   9   10   8   6   4   2

Library of Congress Cataloging in Publication Data

Darga, Bert.
The executive sourcebook.

Includes index.
1. Executive ability. I. Title. II. Title: Executive
source book.
HD38.2.D37   1985   658.4′09   84-27609

ISBN: 0-671-47772-2

FOR *BARBARA, JOHN* AND *MARGARET*

CONTENTS

INTRODUCTION

You've been promoted to a top position. With it comes the choice of furniture for your new office. Where do you begin the selection process?

The chief operating officer of your company asks you to suggest consulting firms for a study of a faltering division. Where do you look for information?

The CEO of your company decides that executives at your level must know how to use a personal computer. You must acquire a machine and the skills to use it. Where do you learn your options?

Your starting point is here, in these pages. They offer resources for answers in wide-ranging areas. More than ever, the effective and successful executive must either know the answers or know where and how to find them. *Knowing* is the key word.

For we are indeed in the midst of the knowledge revolution. The computer, of course, is both the model and the medium for the revolutionary changes that are taking place. It is the characteristic tool of our time, concentrating large masses of useful information for high-speed processing and access.

These pages provide a comparable tool. They concentrate information and resources for information. Entries detail the essential products and services that support the work of the executive. Reviews describe the books and periodicals that are vital resources for information and knowledge.

Section 1 catalogs the things that surround you in the office setting and it ranges through such categories as business and vacation travel and fitness and health. Your needs as an executive are many, but it is the quality of things in your life rather than quantity that is the focus here. From the elegant sheen of your teak desk to the fine craftsmanship of your attaché case, it is quality and style that define your personal image as an executive and leader. Samplings include pocket calculators and dictating machines as well as million-dollar jet aircraft 'for corporate travel.

A key element in your success as an executive will always be your ability to pinpoint specialists and use their services with efficient results. Section 2 supplies resources for your legal needs. Consulting services are highlighted. Resources include advertising and public relations and specialists in company relocation as well as relocation for the individual executive and his family and household.

Electronic technology is the subject matter of Section 3. The emphasis is on computer hardware and software, particularly the personal computer in its role as an executive tool. Reviews of books and periodicals provide a guide to reading that can give you an edge in the computer era. Resources here will inform your awareness of electronic possibilities, from massive data bases to telecommunications and teleconferencing.

Section 4 surveys a wide selection of reading resources on executive management. The practical and the theoretical appear side by side, in books, magazines, newsletters. Methods, strategies and skills come under close study by experts who know the world of the executive from the inside. Such areas as new-product development, marketing and sales receive special attention. Included are selections for the growing numbers of women executives.

The progress of your executive career is the concern of Section 5. Will you go for an MBA degree? Where can you get a degree in a part-time program? Here you will find resources for professional development. Included are the executive recruiters as well as the specialists in outplacement.

Section 6 rounds out the full scope of your career. Money and wealth are the subjects. These pages survey the wide range of services available to assist you in your investments and financial planning. Among the resources here are the newsletters that track the stock, bond and commodity markets. Included is essential information on buying and selling businesses, venture-capital sources and franchise operations.

The resources presented in these sections are samplings, of course. No single book could touch on all the material of use to the executive. Also appearing in these pages are samplings from the samplings—photos, drawings, book excerpts, quotations. The excerpts sample the success of authors dealing with complex subjects. They provide explanations, solutions and counsel. The quotations, on the other hand, share ideas and opinions with us. You may not agree with all of them, but they will, we hope, make this sourcebook stimulating as well as useful reading for you in your executive career.

Prices listed for products and services in these pages are subject to change, as are the products and services themselves. You should confirm prices with listed firms before mailing a payment. The inclusion of products and services in this book is not intended to warranty quality or performance.

We wish to thank the hundreds of publishers, manufacturers and other organizations and individuals who generously provided information, illustrations and assistance in the making of this sourcebook.

SECTION 1

Executive Style

OFFICE FURNITURE AND FURNISHINGS

GUNLOCKE: A TRADITION OF EXECUTIVE ELEGANCE

With eight decades of manufacturing behind it, the Gunlocke Co. offers a choice of both traditional and modern styles in office furniture. The firm markets a broad selection of fur-

Gunlocke's Executive Privilege line combines mahogany with a modern look.

Triad desk and credenza by Gunlocke feature simple lines and the richness of mahogany.

The elegance of mahogany is highlighted in the desk and credenza in the Élan styling by Gunlocke.

niture for open-plan office systems. Gunlocke also features mahogany furniture for the executive office which emphasizes the traditional look. Desks and credenzas in the Triad and Élan models, for instance, blend the richness of mahogany with simple lines of design. Mahogany also sets the tone in the more modern Executive Privilege style. For literature and dealer information, write:

Gunlocke Co.
1 Gunlocke Dr.
Wayland, NY 14572

FINE HARDWOOD BOOKCASES FROM HALE

The F. E. Hale Mfg. Co. specializes in bookcases crafted of oak, walnut or birch. The cases are available in a variety of styles and sizes. Model 754, for example, has glass doors and movable shelves. It stands 53 inches high and 41 inches wide, with shelves 11 inches deep. It is priced at $550 in oak and $480 in birch. For catalog, write:

F. E. Hale Mfg. Co.
Box 751
Herkimer, NY 13350

Hale bookcase model 754 is available in oak ($550) or birch ($480).

Imported by Scandinavian Office Design, this desk is solid, hand-carved teak. It has a leather top and a pull-out writing shelf. Measuring 72 inches by 36 inches, the desk is priced at $2,499.

A teak conference table by Scandinavian Office Design. It is 48 inches by 98 inches and is priced at $999. The teak armchair is $279.

EXECUTIVE ELEGANCE IN TEAK OR ROSEWOOD

Scandinavian Office Design markets imports from Denmark that offer elegant teak or rosewood furniture for the executive suite. The furniture includes desks, chairs, credenzas and cabinets, with selections for both your work area and your secretary's. For literature and further information, write:

Scandinavian Office Design
603 Worcester Rd.
Natick, MA 01760

IMPORTS FROM EUROPE FOR THE EXECUTIVE SUITE

Atelier International, Ltd., markets a selection of European designs in desks, credenzas, seat-

Executive furniture by Scandinavian Office Design features the richness of teak. The 72-inch desk is priced at $1,199. The cabinet and credenza are each $999; the chair is $599.

Desk designed by Giovanni Carini is marketed by Atelier International. The price ranges from about $3,500 to $5,000, depending on size.

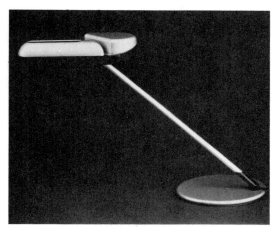

Available from Atelier International, the Ring desk lamp is an import from Holland. The price is about $375.

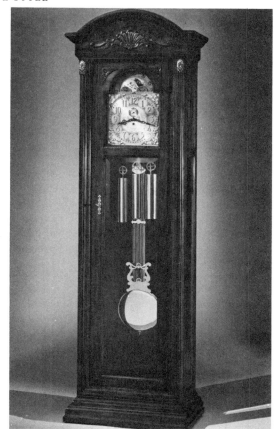

The Ellington model grandfather clock by Seth Thomas is priced at approximately $1,750.

ing, computer-support furniture and lighting for the executive office. The firm features such celebrated designers as Le Corbusier, Rietveld and Mackintosh, with emphasis on modern styling. For literature and further information, write:

Atelier International, Ltd.
595 Madison Ave.
New York, NY 10022

SETTING A TRADITIONAL STYLE WITH A GRANDFATHER CLOCK

If your office is decorated in a traditional style and you want to add an elegant tone, you might consider a grandfather clock from Seth Thomas. Several models are available, all crafted from select hardwoods and veneers with brass-finished fittings. The clocks stand over 6 feet tall and have eight-day weight-driven movements with chimes. Prices range upward from $1,000. For brochure, write:

Jomarr Distributing Co.
Box 175
Inwood, NY 11696

Woodcuts ceiling panels by Armstrong are available with a walnut, oak or mahogany finish.

Fabric-covered acoustical panels by Armstrong include the Soundsoak line for walls and the Soft Look line for ceilings.

The Prelude model grandfather clock by Ridgeway has an oak cabinet and stands over 6 feet tall.

CLOCKS THAT ADD WARMTH TO AN OFFICE

If your office is furnished in a traditional look, a grandfather clock might fit in well. Ridgeway Clocks markets a wide selection of models that feature fine wood cabinetry and chain-driven or cable-driven chimes. Cabinets are available in oak, cherry, elm or mahogany, and metalwork is brass. For brochure and price information, write:

Ridgeway Clocks
Box 407
Ridgeway, VA 24148

ARMSTRONG: PANELING IDEAS FOR EXECUTIVE OFFICES

Armstrong is a name well known for floor coverings as well as paneling for walls and ceilings. Its extensive line of products offers some elegant options for the executive office. The firm's Woodcuts ceiling panels, for instance, are wood veneers with walnut, oak or mahogany finish. The panels are 2-feet square and are oiled to enhance their rich graining. The firm also markets a wide selection of fabric-covered acoustical panels in its Soundsoak line for walls and its Soft Look ceiling panels. For literature, write:

Armstrong World Industries, Inc.
Box 3001
Lancaster, PA 17604

BUILDING EXECUTIVE STYLE INTO THE OPEN-PLAN OFFICE

JG Furniture Systems markets furniture and panel components for open-plan offices. Its Illuminated Open Plan (IOP) system, for instance, is based on panel components featuring wiring, acoustical and lighting options. At the same time, the system uses natural woods and fibers to enhance appearance, particularly in the executive office. In the Upholstered Panel System (UPS), all panels are fully upholstered in a design emphasizing acoustical performance. For brochures, write:

JG Furniture Systems
Burlington Industries
Quakertown, PA 18951

The IOP system by JG Furniture Systems features natural woods and fabrics and offers fine styling for the executive office.

OPEN OFFICE PLANNING
John Pile
1978/207 pp./$19.95
Watson-Guptill Publications
1515 Broadway
New York, NY 10036

The "open space" design approach has become more common in recent years, accommodating and adapting even the traditional work space of the executive. This book offers an introduction to the concept of enhancing communication by using open space for office layouts and it details the many planning elements that are involved. It is a handbook for professional designers, but it provides a useful reference resource for the executive.

FACILITIES DESIGN & MANAGEMENT
$30/9 issues per year
1515 Broadway
New York, NY 10036

What will be the next new look in office design? What changes are technology and automation bringing? How about the executive suite? If you want to keep well ahead of change, here is a magazine that will show you trends and styles as they develop. Included in both articles and advertising are examples of the latest in furniture and decoration for the executive office. (Your management position may qualify you for a free subscription to this controlled-circulation magazine.)

Free-standing panels and modular units by West-inghouse, used here in reception and conference areas.

OFFICE DESIGN IDEAS FROM WESTINGHOUSE

Westinghouse Furniture Systems uses free-standing panels and modular units to organize office work areas. Some of this furniture is especially adaptable to executive areas. Of particular interest is a selection of adjustable tables for use with computer equipment. The firm also offers a wide range of ergonomically designed chairs. For brochures and dealer information, write:

Westinghouse Furniture Systems
Box 8829
Grand Rapids, MI 49508

THE EXECUTIVE OFFICE AS EXECUTIVE WORK STATION

Herman Miller, Inc., furnishes today's office in the modern, technological style. Colors are vivid; materials range from wood and metal through plastics and man-made fabrics. The

An adjustable computer table from Westinghouse Furniture Systems.

Herman Miller furnishings and furniture in an executive work station. The panel units are finished in oak with chrome trim. The free-standing conference table and the surface at the right are alternative work areas for the executive.

look is that of pure utility combined with crisp elegance. Miller is well known for its designers and for its systems that transform open spaces into offices with panels and modular units. Even the company president's office is a work station in this environment, but it is in high style. If you have not looked into this style, ask for the full-color brochures *Managing the Work Environment* and *Furnishing the Interior Environment.* For literature and dealer information, write:

Herman Miller, Inc.
8500 Byron Rd.
Zeeland, MI 49464

THE OFFICE OF DISTINCTION WITH MAHOGANY FROM DUNBAR

For a look of distinction in the executive office, Dunbar offers the Bankers Edition, a line of mahogany furniture available in four shades of the wood finish. The line includes desks with either wooden or leather top as well as a wide selection of tables and cabinets. For literature and dealer information, write:

Dunbar
601 S. Fulton St.
Berne, IN 46711

WOODEN TRESTLE-LEG DESIGN FOR A COMPUTER WORKTABLE

Cargo Furniture markets a wooden table in a trestle-leg design for use with personal computers. Finished in natural wood stain, the worktable is 27 inches high, 38 inches wide and 24 inches deep. It can be used with or without its removable top shelf. Price is $98. For literature, write:

Cargo Furniture & Accents/USA
Box 18400
Fort Worth, TX 76118

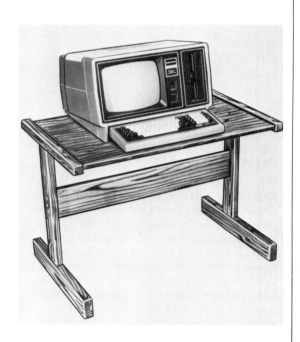

A trestle-leg wooden worktable for use with a personal computer.

Smokador's System 600 electronic desk pad has a built-in clock, calendar, calculator and telephone center. The price is about $1,000.

DESIGNER ACCESSORIES FOR THE EXECUTIVE OFFICE

Smokador specializes in imported designer accessories for the executive suite. Its products include ashtrays, vases and items for serving hot and cold beverages. The firm also markets the System 600 electronic desk pad. The pad's work surface measures 38 by 24 inches and comes in black or brown leather. The unit includes clock, calendar, calculator and telephone center. The phone features automatic dialing for 100 twenty-digit phone numbers, and there are jacks for recording phone conversations. For further information, write:

Smokador
470 W. 1st Ave.
Roselle, NJ 07203

Stainless-steel coffee service is imported from Denmark by Smokador. Price is about $260, with four china cups and saucers.

IMAGE AND ITS ROLE IN CAREER SUCCESS

What is your image? Quite simply, it is the sum total of the parts that you present to the world. On its more basic level (and the way that most people consider its meaning), it is the way you look—your dress, hair, makeup and overall physique. But also, it's your day-to-day business style—how you communicate your ideas, your "performance" at meetings, how you create visibility and your command of "corporate finesse." And on a more subtle level, it's how you handle a variety of challenging situations that executives face—office politics, business entertaining and travel, and interviewing for new jobs and promotions.

If you master all of these areas, you have a strong chance of career success, because as far as the rest of the world is concerned, you are your image. And no matter how competent or intelligent a person you are inside, your success in the business world will depend on what is perceived on the outside.

From: *The Extra Edge: Success Strategies for Women,* Charlene Mitchell with Thomas Burdick (Washington: Acropolis Books, Ltd., 1983)

Included in the Radius Two collection of desk accessories by Smith Metal Arts are elements of matte sandstone, upper left, and polished marble.

DESK ACCESSORIES IN METAL AND STONE

The Radius Two collection of desk accessories produced by Smith Metal Arts offers a wide variety of elements. Included are calendar, digital clock, phone index, pen base, paper clip holder. Designed by William Sklaroff, the elements are modular and can be assembled in many combinations. The collection is available in six metal finishes, in melamine plastic and in polished marble and matte sandstone. The firm also markets a broad line of traditional desk accessories. For literature and further information, write:

Smith Metal Arts
1721 Elmwood Ave.
Buffalo, NY 14207

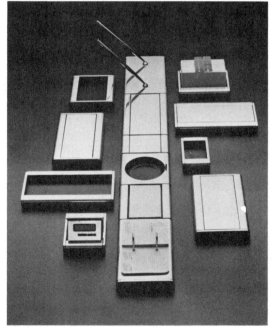

The Radius Two collection of desk accessories by Smith Metal Arts is available in six metal finishes.

DESK ACCESSORIES IN WALNUT AND OAK

Artistic Office Products markets a selection of wooden accessories for the executive office. With finishes in either walnut or oak, there are desk trays, pen stands, bookracks and wastebaskets as well as matching desk pads. For catalog and price information, write:

Artistic Office Products
721 E. 133rd St.
Bronx, NY 10454

TELEPHONES AND ANSWERING MACHINES

AT&T: SPECIALISTS IN PHONE EQUIPMENT

AT&T markets a wide variety of telephones, including the cellular mobile phone for use in your car. Of particular interest to the executive is the Genesis Telesystem, a modular phone unit with features that can be added by means of cartridges. Among the features are automatic dialing and an electronic telephone directory with an average memory of 75 names and phone numbers. With the electronic re-minder cartridge, you can program up to 40 messages that will appear on the phone console display on a date and at a time you specify. The company also markets its System 1000 cellular telephone for automobile use. The phone is offered in two models, one with the dial in the handset and the other with the dial in the phone base. For literature, write:

AT&T Consumer Products
5 Wood Hollow Rd.
Parsippany, NJ 07054

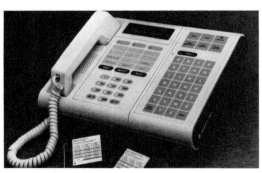

The Genesis Telesystem by AT&T offers add-on features in a modular telephone unit. The Genesis console is priced at $349.95.

The AT&T System 1000 cellular telephone unit for use in a car is available at prices ranging from $2,249 to $2,549.

Code-A-Phone model 2570 answering machine includes an automatic dialer and sells for $279.95.

TELEPHONE AUTOMATION FROM CODE-A-PHONE

The Code-A-Phone Corp. specializes in automated equipment for telephone communications. The firm markets a full line of telephone answering machines. The model 2570 system, for instance, features remote control and has its own built-in telephone. Computerized, the unit includes an automatic dialer that will program and store up to 10 different phone numbers (up to 16 digits long) for easy dialing with the press of just two buttons. The machine is priced at 279.95. Other equipment marketed by the firm includes the model 2597 call diverter ($695). Programmable for various functions, this unit will, for instance, permit your customer to dial a local number in a call that will automatically be forwarded to your offices via your firm's WATS or other long-distance service. The Code-A-Phone call controller ($3,153), an even more sophisticated computerized system, controls and monitors your long-distance lines by requiring employees to use a code number for access and by routing calls over the least expensive lines. For literature and further information, write:

Code-A-Phone Corp.
Box 5656
Portland, OR 97228

AUDIO SECURITY AND THE VULNERABLE TELEPHONE

The most basic of communication instruments in our society, the common telephone represents the major portion of the total audio security threat. It rests within easy reach of nearly every sensitive business or personal discussion, whether in an office, hotel, conference room or residence and offers the *maximum* opportunity for reliable audio penetration. With a few simple modifications to the earpiece or mouthpiece, the telephone provides easy concealment and ready access to electrical energy for powering listening devices and audio-sensing microphones.

As a threat, the telephone is suspect in three areas:

1. Taps—the most easily understood, wherein the actual conversation is overheard.
2. Use of the telephone line—for listening devices such as the infinity transmitter.
3. Audio compromise—wherein the telephone receives and transmits room audio while it is not being used.

From: *Corporate and Industrial Security*, A. Lewis Russell (Houston: Gulf Publishing Co., 1980)

The telephone is still under-used. How many times have you read something and said to yourself, "I need to talk to him"? You may never meet him, but chances are you can talk to him. Pick up the phone. Now.

From: *Further Up the Organization*, Robert Townsend (New York: Alfred A. Knopf, 1984)

TELEPHONES AND ACCESSORIES FROM A MAIL-ORDER SOURCE

Communications Corner is a mail-order outlet that specializes in telephones, phone accessories and related products. Included in the firm's catalog are answering machines, automatic dialers and cordless phones. Also included are systems for automatic tape-recording of phone conversations. Write for catalog:

Communications Corner
9 E. 37th St.
New York, NY 10016

PHONE-ANSWERING MACHINES AND CORDLESS PHONES FROM SANYO

The Sanyo line of telephone accessories includes two automatic answering machines, both of which feature a call-screening function. The model TAS 3000 also features a pocket-size remote-control unit that allows the user to access the machine by phone and play back, rewind and erase recorded messages. The firm also markets two cordless extension phones, both of which have ranges up to 700 feet. The model TH 2000 features a pocket-size hand unit that weighs only 8 ounces. For literature and dealer information, write:

Sanyo Business Systems Corp.
51 Joseph St.
Moonachie, NJ 07074

DICTATING EQUIPMENT

DICTATING AND TRANSCRIBING EQUIPMENT FROM SONY

Sony markets a broad selection of dictating and transcribing systems, with both portable and desktop units. The firm's pocket-size microcas-

The Sony model BM-550 Micro Dictator weighs just under 7 ounces.

sette dictating units offer indexing features designed for ease of use and efficient transcribing. The model BM-550 Micro Dictator weighs just under 7 ounces. Sony's desktop dictating-transcribing units feature a variety of hand and foot controls for smooth operation. For brochures and dealer information, write:

Sony Corporation of America
Sony Dr.
Park Ridge, NJ 07656

PORTABLE AND DESKTOP DICTATING UNITS FROM SANYO

Offering a wide variety of models, the Sanyo line of microcassette recorders features compact pocket-size design. The model TRC 5410, for instance, weighs only 7.4 ounces. The firm also markets a line of desktop dictating-transcribing units that include such features as electronic cueing and foot controls. For brochures and dealer information, write:

Sanyo Business Systems Corp.
51 Joseph St.
Moonachie, NJ 07074

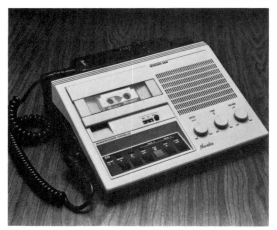

The model 510 Norelco recorder/transcriber has a suggested retail price of $495 (photo courtesy Norelco Dictation Systems, Philips Business Systems, Inc.).

The Norelco 895 portable dictation unit features an appointment reminder and elapsed-time counter. The suggested retail price is $389 (photo courtesy Norelco Dictation Systems, Philips Business Systems, Inc.).

PORTABLE AND DESKTOP DICTATION FROM NORELCO

The Norelco line of dictation equipment offers a wide variety of choices. Portable recorders are available in seven models that range in suggested retail price from $119 to $389. All the models feature a sophisticated indexing system that cues the transcribing secretary to the executive's instructions and to the location of specific dictation on the cassette. All the mini-cassette models are pocket-size and one micro-cassette model weighs only 5½ ounces and will fit in a shirt pocket. Five desktop models (at suggested retail prices from $395 to $650) serve as both recorders and transcribers, with foot control of fast-forward scan as well as automatic search and stop. Norelco also markets a central dictation system called the Intelli-

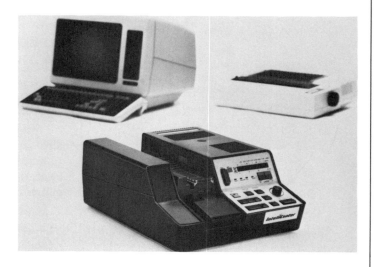

A multi-user central dictation system from Norelco, the IntelliCenter has a suggested retail price of $3,395 (photo courtesy of Norelco Dictation Systems, Philips Business Systems, Inc.).

Center, a multi-user system that takes dictation over the phone from distant points. The unit has a suggested retail price of $3,395. For brochures and detailed information about operating features, write:

Philips Business Systems, Inc.
810 Woodbury Rd.
Woodbury, NY 11797

MEMOCORD MINIATURE DICTATING UNIT

Part of the Memocord line manufactured in Austria, the model K177 Mini weighs 10 ounces and fits in the palm of the hand. The unit is capable of 90 minutes of recording and it features an audible end-of-tape signal and a visual battery-life indicator. It is priced at $259.

TECHNIQUES FOR GIVING MORE EFFECTIVE DICTATION

When you dictate, the person or persons who are to receive your message are not present. Usually, when you speak, you are face-to-face with your listeners, or they are on the other end of a telephone. Communicating with someone you don't see or hear can make you feel awkward. It's a little like the first time you dial a friend's telephone number and, unexpectedly, are answered by a recorded message. Fortunately, it is not a major hurdle and, after a comparatively short period of practice, it is overcome.

Not seeing or hearing the person you are directing your message to also shapes the situation. In conversation, what you say is usually responded to by the listener. That response, in turn, may influence what your next utterance will be. When you dictate, the burden of developing a self-sufficient message rests entirely with you. What you say must be clear, logical and understandable on its own terms.

When you're dictating a letter to John Smith or a memo to Mary Jones, it helps to visualize them as you speak. The message tends to become more of an actual exchange, more clearly directed toward the person.

Even if you don't know the recipient (it may be a letter to a person you've never met, a memo to a newcomer in the organization), it is still possible to develop an image of a person, starting with the name, the organization to which the individual belongs, a title and so on.

From: *Mastering the Art of Dictation*, Auren Uris (Houston: Gulf Publishing Co., 1980)

Other units in the Memocord line include desktop dictating recorders and transcribing equipment for the secretary. For further information, write:

Niktek, Inc.
Box 599
Montville, NJ 07045

◀ *The Memocord K177 Mini dictating unit weighs 10 ounces.*

SONY'S TYPECORDER—IT TYPES, RECORDS AND FITS IN YOUR ATTACHÉ CASE

For the executive who wants a handy choice between typing notes and letters or dictating them, Sony offers the Typecorder. Book-size and weighing only 3 pounds, the unit is a miniature word processor combined with a recorder. A single-line 40-character display provides for text review and editing. To print text, the unit is linked with a typewriter, printer, computer or word processor in a direct interface or over a telephone line. The unit's microcassette tape holds 60 minutes of dictation or up to 100 pages of text, or a combination of both. For literature and dealer information, write:

Sony Corporation of America
Sony Dr.
Park Ridge, NJ 07656

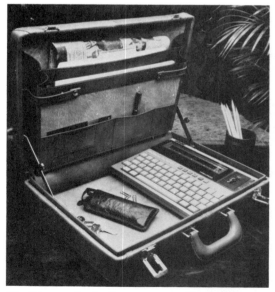

The Typecorder by Sony is a portable unit that combines typing and dictation functions on microcassette tape.

POCKET CALCULATORS AND DESKTOP COPIERS

POCKET CALCULATORS FROM RADIO SHACK

Radio Shack markets a wide selection of slim-line calculators designed to fit in pocket or purse. The model EC-407 for men and model EC-404 for women are both priced at $19.95 and each is solar-powered to eliminate the need for batteries. The man's model folds into a wallet, and the woman's model closes up to resemble a compact. The model EC-306 fits in a checkbook case. Also priced at $19.95, the calculator has three separate memories for checking and credit-card balances. See your Radio Shack dealer or write for catalog:

Radio Shack
1 Tandy Center
Fort Worth, TX 76102

Radio Shack calculator models EC-407 for men and EC-404 for women are both solar-powered and each is priced at $19.95 (photo courtesy of Radio Shack, a division of Tandy Corp.).

The HP-15C pocket calculator features built-in mathematical and scientific functions (photo courtesy Hewlett-Packard Co.).

PROGRAMMABLE POCKET CALCULATOR

Hewlett-Packard's electronics products range from pocket calculators to computer systems. Its HP-15C pocket calculator is a programmable multi-function unit. It features built-in mathematical and scientific functions as well as 448 lines of continuous program memory. For literature, write:

Hewlett-Packard Co.
Box 10301
Palo Alto, CA 94303

PORTABLE COMPUTER SYSTEM THAT FITS IN AN ATTACHÉ CASE

Another example of computer miniaturization, the Olympia portable computer system is designed to fit in an attaché case. Among seven peripheral components are an adapter for using a TV set as a display, an interface unit for connecting with a second computer, and a modem for using the computer on a phone line. The computer unit itself, with built-in display and

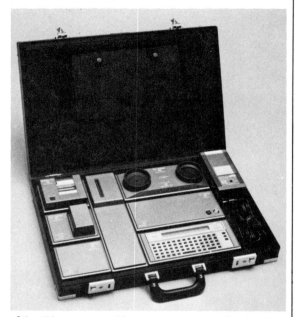

The Olympia portable computer system features compact design. The computer and its components fit snugly in an attaché case.

keyboard; weighs only 21 ounces. Its internal memory is expandable up to 52K. For literature, write:

Olympia USA, Inc.
Box 22
Somerville, NJ 08876

COMPACT COPIERS FROM MINOLTA

Minolta markets three compact tabletop copiers. The three units are plain-paper copiers, and they can copy from sheet, book or three-dimensional originals. The model EP 300 operates at 12 copies per minute and is priced at $2,195. Priced at $3,295, the EP 300RE has the additional feature of reducing and enlarg-

The Minolta model EP 300 tabletop copier operates at the rate of 12 copies per minute.

ing copies. The EP 320, priced at $3,995, operates at a rate of 18 copies per minute. For literature and dealer information, write:

Minolta Corp.
Business Equipment Division
101 Williams Dr.
Ramsey, NJ 07446

COMPACT COPIERS FROM TOSHIBA AMERICA

Toshiba markets two compact copier designs, both for tabletop use. The model BD-3701 is a high-performance unit that produces 12 copies per minute. It handles both letter and legal-size copies and is priced at under $2,000. The model BD-4511 offers such features as built-in reduction from oversize originals. Priced at under $4,000, the unit produces 15 copies per minute. For literature, write:

Toshiba America, Inc.
2441 Michelle Dr.
Tustin, CA 92680

TABLETOP COPYING MACHINES FROM 3M

The 3M Office Systems Division markets two compact copying machines. The units require minimal space and provide valuable convenience in the executive office. The model 273, the smaller of the two, requires the space of a standard office typewriter. Priced at $1,095, the

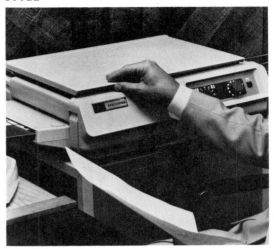

The 3M model 273 copier requires the space of a standard office typewriter and is priced at $1,095.

The 3M model 526 copying machine features compactness and is priced at $2,595.

machine produces 6 copies per minute on paper 8½ by 11 inches or 8½ by 14 inches. The larger model 526 is a plain-paper copier. It produces 12 copies per minute in either letter or legal size and is priced at $2,595. For brochures and further information, write:

3M Office Systems Division
3M Center, Bldg. 220-10E
St. Paul, MN 55144

PENS, PENCILS
AND STATIONERY

DIARY-PLANNERS
FOR TIME MANAGEMENT

Day-Timers markets a varied line of diary-planners for executives. A compact pocket edition is 3½ by 6½ inches in format, with two facing pages per day. Annual filler pages are $15.95, and leather wallets to hold the filler

Day-Timers pocket diary-planner has two facing pages per day. The format measures 3½ by 6½ inches.

pages range up to $40. Desk editions of the diary-planners are offered in sizes 5½ by 8½ inches and 8½ by 11 inches. The firm also sells a selection of personal-development cassette programs, a line of custom stationery and such items as imprinted report covers and binders. Write for free mail-order catalog:

Day-Timers, Inc.
Box 2368
East Texas, PA 18046

ELEGANT PENS, PENCILS
AND DESK SETS FROM CROSS

The A. T. Cross Co. markets ball and fountain pens, pencils and desk sets that are designed with an elegance that says much about the owner's style. The pens and pencils are offered in finishes that range from chrome to gold-filled and from sterling silver to 14-karat gold. Prices range from as low as $10 to as high as $1,000 (for a pen and pencil set in 14-karat gold). The wide variety of designs and prices provides many gift possibilities. Look for Cross

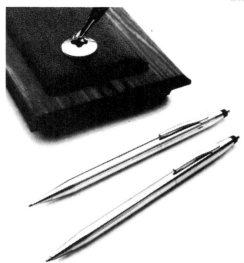

With a walnut and leather base, the desk set by the A. T. Cross Co. matches a 10-karat gold-filled ball pen and a mechanical pencil. The set is priced at $200.

FINE PENS AND STATIONERY FROM SHEAFFER EATON

Sheaffer pens and pencils and Eaton stationery present a broad selection to choose from. The Masterpiece model fountain pen and ballpoint pen are made of 18-karat gold and are priced at $3,500 and $2,500, respectively. Sheaffer also offers a lacquer-finished line of pens and pencils, with prices from $65 to $120. Its Targa pens and pencils range from $10 to $130. Stationery by Eaton provides a wide choice of letter and note papers as well as the At-a-Glance line of appointment books and planning calendars. For literature, write:

Sheaffer Eaton
75 S. Church St.
Pittsfield, MA 01201

Fountain pen by the A. T. Cross Co. is offered in a 10-karat gold-filled model ($80), a sterling silver and 14-karat gold-filled version ($100) and in 14-karat gold ($800).

The Parker Arrow ball pen and pencil set has a gold-filled finish and is priced at $80.

pens and pencils at better stores in your area or write for dealer information:

A. T. Cross Co.
1 Albion Rd.
Lincoln, RI 02865

PARKER: A FINE OLD NAME IN PENS AND PENCILS

Whether for a few dollars or a few hundred dollars, Parker pens and pencils have a long-standing reputation. They speak well of their

From the Parker Premier Collection, these pens are, from the top, a roller ball for $160, a ball pen for $140 and a fountain pen for $200.

owner—or their giver when they become a gift. The pens and pencils range from the inexpensive Jotter styles, priced at $10 and under, through the Classic and Arrow styles that are priced as high as $70. A special Premier Collection includes an 18-karat gold fountain pen priced at $2,500, as well as other pens in gold-plated, sterling silver or Chinese lacquer finishes. For catalog, write:

Parker Pen Co.
Box 5100
Janesville, WI 53547

A SELECTION OF PERSONALIZED BUSINESS STATIONERY

The Stationery House, Inc., specializes in personalized business stationery for executives. A wide variety of papers, colors, type styles and letterhead designs are available for letter and memo paper, envelopes and business cards. The firm also offers the Executive Monarch line of personal stationery. For catalog and prices, write:

The Stationery House, Inc.
1000 Florida Ave.
Hagerstown, MD 21740

BUSINESS GIFTS AND OTHER RESOURCES

GIFT IDEA: CRYSTAL FROM STEUBEN GLASS

Makers of fine crystal, Steuben Glass offers many candidates for the perfect gift. Perhaps a gift to yourself, something to add a distinguishing touch to your office. Among Steuben's collections is a series of works in glass that celebrate such sports as tennis, golf, skiing and fishing. Many of the works are suitable as commemorative awards, and inscription engraving is available. Prices range from a few to several hundred dollars. For brochures, write:

Steuben Glass
715 5th Ave.
New York, NY 10022

Created by Steuben Glass, this blown bowl is 8 inches in diameter and is derived from a design made in silver by Paul Revere. It is priced at $395.

A work of art by Steuben, the Eskimo, made of silver, spears fish engraved in the glass. Priced at $2,950, the work stands 6½ inches high.

Seiko desk unit features four display clocks regulated by a single master quartz movement. Each clock is set to a different time zone.

BUSINESS GIFT
IN A BOTTLE

Liquors, wines, champagnes and liqueurs can make the choice of a business gift quite easy. Yet getting the gift delivered can be a chore. Nationwide Gift Liquor Service, Inc., provides a handy solution. You give the firm your order by mail, or by phoning 1-800-CHEER UP. The firm contacts a local dealer, who gift wraps the order, encloses your message and delivers the package. Delivery is subsequently confirmed by mail. For brochure with gift selection and prices, write:

Nationwide Gift Liquor Service, Inc.
Box 32070
Phoenix, AZ 85016

GIFT IDEA: STEAK AND LOBSTER
FOR TWO, READY TO COOK

Smith Packing International offers a gourmet-food gift service that makes tasteful giving easy. You place your order from the firm's brochure and they assure delivery of gift-boxed food. The frozen food is triple-sealed and packed with dry ice for shipment. Selections include breast of chicken, beefsteak and lobster, in assortments that range in price from $31.95 to $53. The King's Pride package ($51.95) offers two 12-ounce strip-loin steaks, two 6-ounce lobster tails and two 6-ounce chicken breasts Florentine. For literature, write:

Smith Packing International Corp.
Box 446
Utica, NY 13503

SEIKO: TIMEPIECES
THAT MAKE TELLING GIFTS

Seiko markets a broad line of quartz wristwatches and clocks that can make fine business gifts and prized incentive awards. The timepieces in the firm's Continuity Collection range in price from $95 to $225. Seiko's products include elegant items designed for the executive as well. A desk unit, for instance, combines four display clocks regulated by one master quartz movement. Each clock is set to a different time zone. The clocks are mounted in a handsome rosewood base with brass metalwork at its corners. The unit is priced at $195. For literature, write:

Seiko Time Corp.
640 5th Ave.
New York, NY 10019

GIFT ITEMS FROM YOU
AND YOUR COMPANY

The many-bladed Swiss Army Officer's Knife made by Victorinox is offered in many models and has become a popular business gift. Imported by the R. H. Forschner Co. along with

The Bijou model Victorinox pocket knife for men and women has nail file, scissors and tweezers.

other Victorinox pocket knives, these products can be imprinted with your company's name or logo. Prices for Army models range from $15.70 to $44.65 for orders of 100 to 249 knives. Other Victorinox knives designed for use by both men and women are available at prices from $7.15 to $44. The Bijou model, for instance, includes a nail file, a knife and scissors. It is priced at $13 per knife for orders of 100 to 249 knives. Prices vary with smaller- and larger-order quantities. For illustrated catalog, write:

R. H. Forschner Co., Inc.
Box 846
Shelton, CT 06484

BUSINESS GIFTS THAT CARRY THE COMPANY NAME

Execu-Time Systems, Inc., markets a wide line of items to be imprinted with company name or logo and used in promotions or as business gifts. The items range from a line of Pierre Cardin diaries and planners to a variety of luggage, clothing, drinking cups, pens, wrist-

watches, digital clocks and pocket calculators. For a catalog, write:

Execu-Time Systems, Inc.
Box 631
Lake Forest, IL 60045

TIPS FOR GIFT GIVING OVERSEAS

It is bad form in the Arab world to offer a businessman a gift for his wife or wives. A Japanese will generally prefer scotch over bourbon. These valuable bits of advice are among many in a booklet of tips titled *International Business Gift-Giving Customs.* The booklet is published by the Parker Pen Co. and is available for $1 (to cover postage and handling). Write:

Parker Pen Co.
Box 5100
Janesville, WI 53547

SHOWING THE COMPANY COLORS

Hampton Hall specializes in custom-designed ties, scarves and blazer badges that carry your company's logo and colors. Minimum quantities are 150 for the ties and scarves, while as few as six blazer badges can be ordered. These items have a variety of uses, including presentation as incentives or as gifts. Write:

Hampton Hall, Ltd.
220 5th Ave.
New York, NY 10001

GIFT-GIVING PRACTICES FOR THE TRAVELER IN JAPAN

The Japanese appreciate and enjoy both giving and receiving gifts on every possible occasion, and visitors to Japan should go prepared with a number of small gifts to be presented to most of the people whom they will meet. Small souvenirs are quite acceptable and it is not necessary to buy expensive presents, except perhaps for very senior executives, but it is important for all gifts to be attractively wrapped. If books are given—and illustrated books about one's own countryside are always welcome—a suitable inscription should be written inside for the benefit of the recipient. If a visitor also happens to be an author and has written a book or technical paper, this—suitably autographed—makes an ideal gift. Such gifts are never opened in the presence of the giver, except by special permission.

A gift made by a Japanese is usually accompanied with some belittling remark about its smallness and general unworthiness, with which, of course, the recipient must strongly disagree, and the same procedure adopted by a Westerner when making a gift would be appreciated. It is considered polite when receiving gifts to hold them in both hands, even when one hand would do just as well, which is a custom originating from the desire to handle things carefully and thus show that they are of value. If a gift is received from a Japanese colleague, it is important to ensure that his gift is reciprocated sometime during your stay in his country.

From: *The Business Traveler's Handbook*, Foseco Minsep (Englewood Cliffs, NJ: Prentice-Hall, Inc., 1983)

THE SECRETARY
$12/9 issues per year
2440 Pershing Rd.
Kansas City, MO 64108

An association publication of Professional Secretaries International, this magazine offers you a window onto the work and concerns of today's secretary. It could be useful to you to read it from time to time. If your secretary does not already get the magazine, you might provide a subscription as a gift.

THE SECRETARY'S QUICK REFERENCE HANDBOOK
Sheryl L. Lindsell
1983/282 pp./$3.95
Arco Publishing, Inc.
219 Park Ave. S.
New York, NY 10003

This handy guide will provide maximum assistance and take a minimum of space—in your secretary's desk or your own. The book covers grammar, punctuation, capitalization and spelling. There are lists of commonly misspelled as well as commonly confused words. There is a full listing of abbreviations. Formats for letters, memos, reports and minutes are illustrated. The book also includes such other useful information as postal, telephone and telegraph services. (If ordering by mail, add $1 for postage and handling.)

SHORTER SENTENCES MAKE BETTER READING

Short sentences are characteristic of good modern writing. Today's average sentence of 20 words contrasts with the 60 words of a few centuries ago. Experts insist that short sentences are more understandable, and evidence indicates that readers prefer them.

Long sentences usually result from our failure to *think* before writing. We plunge into a sentence with an idea and then stumble along, adding exceptions, qualifiers and incidental remarks. We create a verbal maze for our readers.

Perhaps the problem stems from our concern that each sentence must express a complete thought. As soon as we state an idea, we realize that it isn't complete without some background information or qualifying remarks; or our original idea branches in several directions. Our "complete thought" becomes bogged down by its own weight.

Coherence may be a better criterion in shaping sentences. Let the words between two periods express a unified idea—but not everything there is to say about a given subject.

From: *Better Letters*, Jan Venolia (Berkeley, CA: Ten Speed Press, 1982)

MASTERING THE ART OF DICTATION
Auren Uris
1980/146 pp./$9.95
Gulf Publishing Co.
Box 2608
Houston, TX 77001

The author provides very detailed and useful coaching aimed at dictating proficiency. His advice is designed to help the reader polish technique and thus save time and improve communication skills. The book covers dictation both to secretary and into recording equipment. A separate chapter deals with how to take full advantage of word-processing systems.

WRITE RIGHT!
Jan Venolia
1979, 1982/126 pp./$3.95
Ten Speed Press
Box 7123
Berkeley, CA 94707

This small book will fit in a corner of your desk or briefcase, and even if you use the language with great polish, there will be times when these pages will rescue you. The author deals with punctuation, grammar and style and the pitfalls thereof. Special sections provide selections of confused and abused words as well as frequently misspelled words.

BETTER LETTERS

Jan Venolia
1981/173 pp./$5.95
Ten Speed Press
Box 7123
Berkeley, CA 94707

This book will serve you or your secretary very effectively as a working reference. The author gives guidance for good style, advice for smooth composition and directions for correct format. Specific kinds of business letters are covered in detail, word-processing methods are spelled out and a special section deals with sexist language. Especially useful is a separate chapter on dictation to a secretary or into a machine.

SUMMARY ENDINGS IN MEMO WRITING

In a memo of two pages or less, a summary ending should not be necessary, especially if the recommendation or conclusion is visually highlighted by bullets or underlining at the beginning of the memo.... In fact, in a very short report, you insult a reader's intelligence by summarizing. In a long report, however, the ending should summarize your thinking on the subject—it should reinforce the major points you want the reader to remember. This is your last chance to get your message across.

From: *Writing for Decision Makers*, Marya W. Holcombe and Judith K. Stein (Belmont, CA: Lifetime Learning Publications, 1981)

WRITING EFFECTIVE BUSINESS LETTERS, MEMOS, PROPOSALS AND REPORTS

Samuel A. Cypert
1983/309 pp./$8.95
Contemporary Books, Inc.
180 N. Michigan Ave.
Chicago, IL 60601

The author presents a complete manual on effective writing for business communication. He covers every aspect of the subject, with an emphasis on very practical how-to directions. Included are chapters on research and information sources, on editing your own writing, on organizing material and preparing outlines as well as techniques for making your writing interesting. Separate chapters deal with the various kinds of communications in detail, and the author provides very helpful text examples to illustrate his coaching.

REVISED STANDARD REFERENCE FOR SECRETARIES AND ADMINISTRATORS

Margaret H. Thompson and J. Harold Janis
1972, 1980/763 pp./$14.95
Macmillan Publishing Co.
866 3rd Ave.
New York, NY 10022

Both you and your secretary will find this handbook a valuable resource. It is exhaustive

```
┌─────────────────────────────────────────────────┐
│                    MEETING                       │
│                                                  │
│ Group _____ Date _____ Time ___ to ___│
│                                                  │
│ Room _____ Reservation made (date) _____ No. of persons ___│
│                                                  │
│ Seating Arrangements   ☐ Regular                 │
│                        ☐ Special (If special room layout is required, send│
│                                  diagram to Building Dept. and file copy│
│                                  in folder.)     │
│                                                  │
│     Equipment Required          Refreshments     │
│                    Ordered                Ordered│
│  ☐ Blackboard       _____    ☐ Coffee     _____  │
│  ☐ Pad and easel    _____                        │
│  ☐ Lectern          _____    ☐ Tea        _____  │
│  ☐ Public address                                │
│    system           _____    ☐ Soft drinks _____ │
│  ☐ Neck microphone  _____                        │
│  ☐ Slide projector  _____    ☐ Danish     _____  │
│  ☐ Overhead projector _____                      │
│  ☐ Movie projector (_ mm.) _____  ☐ _____ _____  │
│  ☐ Screen                                        │
│  ☐ Place cards      _____    ☐ _____ _____       │
│  ☐ _____      _____                        │
│  ☐ _____      _____    ☐ _____ _____       │
└─────────────────────────────────────────────────┘
```

A checklist for planning meetings (from Revised Standard Reference for Secretaries and Administrators).

ate. The system will handle collections of pages up to three inches thick. Covers are available in a variety of colors and with customized lettering and decoration. See your retailer for prices, or write:

Velo-Bind, Inc.
650 Almanor Ave.
Sunnyvale, CA 94086

in its collection of how-to directions and useful information. A chapter on meetings, for instance, includes detailed arrangements as well as the basics of parliamentary procedure and proper preparation of minutes. There are separate chapters on letters and reports, editing, correct English usage and punctuation. Various office procedures and services are detailed, including how-to tips for increased efficiency. Especially useful are a comprehensive listing of standard abbreviations and a dictionary of business terms.

COVERS THAT ADD A PROFESSIONAL TOUCH

Using a special plastic binding strip, the Velo-Bind system puts a soft or hard cover on reports, presentations and proposals. The binding is done in a machine that is about the size of a typewriter and requires no training to oper-

Adding protection and impact, the Velo-Bind system puts reports into colorful soft or hard covers.

The Kroy 80K keyboard lettering system produces headlines and titles for your reports and presentations. The unit is priced at $3,795.

ADDING A PROFESSIONAL LOOK TO REPORTS AND PRESENTATIONS

With the Kroy 80K keyboard lettering system, your secretary can produce lettering for headlines and titles in your reports and presentations. The unit consists of a standard typewriter keyboard and a system that prints lettering on tape, with 29 different typefaces available. The lettering tape is then put in place with typed material for reproduction with a copying machine or in a printing process. The lettering can also be employed in reproducing newsletters and brochures and with projected transparencies. For literature and dealer information, write:

Kroy, Inc.
Scottsdale Airpark
Scottsdale, AZ 85261

KELLY SERVICES: FILLING THE NEED FOR TEMPORARY HELP

Kelly Services is a leader among the companies that regularly bail out executives who need temporary help. Your executive secretary is suddenly hospitalized or your office staff is swamped with a series of reports: Kelly can provide a temporary secretary or a whole team of secretarial help. The firm can also supply technical and light-industrial workers. In the marketing area, Kelly can provide trained personnel for conventions, trade shows, product demonstrations and surveys. Many permanent staff members have developed from temporary assignments. Direct contact with a local source of temporary help can often save the day. For literature and a directory of local offices, write:

Kelly Services
999 W. Big Beaver Rd.
Troy, MI 48084

OTHER MAJOR TEMPORARY SERVICES

Below are listed the main offices of four other major temporary services. These firms provide a variety of trained personnel. Write for literature and detailed information.

Manpower, Inc.
5301 N. Ironwood Rd.
Milwaukee, WI 53217

Olsten Corp.
Merrick Ave.
Westbury, NY 11590

Personnel Pool of America, Inc.
303 S.E. 17th St.
Fort Lauderdale, FL 33316

Uniforce Temporary Services
1335 Jericho Turnpike
New Hyde Park, NY 11040

ANOTHER KIND OF TELECOMMUNICATIONS

One of the major courier services, Emery Worldwide offers same-day and next-day door-to-door delivery of letters and documents, packages and commercial cargo. The company covers the U.S., Canada and Europe. Emery and its competitors work wonders in communications. For literature and directory of local offices, write:

Emery Worldwide
Old Danbury Rd.
Wilton, CT 06897

OTHER MAJOR COURIER SERVICES

Below are listed the main offices of five other major courier services. While all these firms provide door-to-door delivery, the extent of their services varies. You may add to this listing the Express Mail program of the U.S. Postal Service, which offers its delivery services through branch offices.

Archer Courier Systems
855 Avenue of the Americas
New York, NY 10001

Brink's, Inc.
Thorndal Circle
Darien, CT 06820

DHL Courier Service
1818 Gilbreth
Burlingame, CA 94010

Federal Express Corp.
Box 727
Memphis, TN 38194

Purolator Courier Corp.
3333 New Hyde Park Rd.
New Hyde Park, NY 11042

ELECTRIC WASTEBASKET DESKSIDE PAPER SHREDDERS

The Electric Wastebasket Corp. markets a selection of several small paper shredders in its Destroyit line. The Executive model is a com-

The Executive model paper shredder by Electric Wastebasket Corp. is housed in a teakwood cabinet.

Electric Wastebasket Corp. offers a free brochure,
Records Retention Timetable.

pact deskside unit mounted on casters and housed in a teakwood cabinet. It handles up to seven sheets at a time and it accepts paper clips and staples without damage to the unit. The machine starts and stops automatically and it has a removable wastebin. It is priced at $735. The firm offers a useful resource in its free brochure, *Records Retention Timetable*, which charts various retention periods. For literature and dealer information, write:

Electric Wastebasket Corp.
145 W. 45th St.
New York, NY 10036

DOCUMENT SECURITY
WITH A PAPER SHREDDER

The Cummins-Allison Corp. markets its compact model 500 paper shredder for use by office personnel. The unit requires minimal space and has built-in casters for easy movement. Shredded material is ejected into a disposable plastic bag in a cabinet beneath the cutters. The unit may also be used as a tabletop model, with shredded material ejected directly into a wastebasket. For literature and price and dealer information, write:

Cummins-Allison Corp.
891 Feehanville Dr.
Mt. Prospect, IL 60056

The Cummins-Allison model 500 paper shredder requires minimal space and has built-in casters for easy movement.

MORE THAN 35,000
TOLL-FREE NUMBERS

The *Toll-Free Digest* lists more than 35,000 phone numbers in categories of products and services, much like the yellow pages. Published

annually and priced at $10.95, the directory contains more than 500 pages. Included is an alphabetical listing of companies as well as a special section for hotel and motel listings. The listings also include federal and state government toll-free numbers as well as those of public-service agencies.

Toll-Free Digest Co., Inc.
Box 800
Claverack, NY 12513

DIRECTORY ASSISTANCE AT YOUR FINGERTIPS

The *National Directory of Addresses and Telephone Numbers* ($24.95) provides almost 900 pages of valuable data. The listings include 50,000 U.S. corporations and institutions, presented both alphabetically and within 300 standard industry categories. A separate section lists 3,000 toll-free numbers, which include all the major airlines, hotel and motel chains, and car rentals. There are also separate sections for such services as law firms, advertising agencies, banks and brokerage firms. Included are media and information sources, associations, and federal government offices. Write:

Concord Reference Books, Inc.
135 W. 50th St.
New York, NY 10020

TRAVEL

BUSINESS TRAVELER'S REPORT

$60/12 issues per year
10076 Boca Entrada Blvd.
Boca Raton, FL 33433

Emphasizing ways to control the costs and increase the quality of business travel, this newsletter reports on transportation and accommodations. It features detailed coverage of hotels and restaurants as well as places of entertainment.

TRACKING THE AIRLINES
FOR THE FLYING EXECUTIVE

Official Airline Guides, Inc., publishes a variety of material for travelers. Its Pocket Flight Guide series is updated in monthly issues and offers airline schedules in separate editions for North America, Europe and the Middle East, and the Pacific. Comprehensive versions of the guides are available in North American and Worldwide editions, which are also combined in a data base version that you can access by telephone lines for display on your computer or terminal. Along with its Travel Planner in two

editions as well as two editions of its Cruise and Tour Guide, the firm also publishes the monthly magazine *Frequent Flyer*. The magazine provides useful know-how in its articles and regional reports. In a one-year subscription package priced at $39.52, you receive *Frequent Flyer*, the *North American Pocket Flight*

Guide and the semiannual *Pocket Travel Planner* with hotel and restaurant listings. For brochures, write:

Official Airline Guides, Inc.
2000 Clearwater Dr.
Oak Brook, IL 60521

TRAVEL SMART FOR BUSINESS
$96/12 issues per year
40 Beechdale Rd.
Dobbs Ferry, NY 10522

Providing both hard data and practical advice, this newsletter aims for optimum transportation and accommodations at the best possible prices. There are city-by-city guides to hotels, for instance. Each issue includes an updated listing of the best airline fares as well as the best rental-car rates city by city. This newsletter is a prime resource for the individual executive as well as the company as a whole.

YOUR TRAVEL AGENT: A CONSUMER'S GUIDE
Americana Hotels
1979/159 pp./$1.95
Dorison House Publishers, Inc.
824 Park Square Bldg.
Boston, MA 02116

This handbook provides helpful guidance for dealing with travel agents, both for business and for personal travel. Especially useful is a section on selecting a travel agent. The book presents consumer-protection information as well as practical advice for various travel situations.

AIRPORT INFORMATION FOR YOUR PARIS FLIGHT

The international airports for Paris are Charles de Gaulle (Roissy), 20 miles from the city; Orly, 11 miles; and Le Bourget, just over 15 miles from the city center and mostly used for charter flights. Buses leave the airports for the terminals at Porte Maillot (for Charles de Gaulle) and Les Invalides (for Orly) every 15 minutes. The fare is F20 from Charles de Gaulle and from Orly. There is a connecting service between the three airports, with departures every 20 minutes; the fare is F35, free to connecting airline passengers. A rail link is available at Orly as part of the new suburban high speed train system. Departures every 15 minutes at F14 for several Paris stops. Taxis are also available: fares to the city center are around F100 during the day, F120-150 at night, from Charles de Gaulle and F80 from Orly. Tip porters F1 for every piece of luggage. All airports have duty-free shop and hotel reservations counter. Car rental counters are at all the airports. If you are flying to the Riviera, you will land either at Marignane Airport, 18 miles from Marseilles, or at Nice–Côte d'Azur Airport, 3 miles from town.

From: *Pan Am's World Guide*, Pan American World Airways (New York: McGraw-Hill Book Co., 1982)

A TRAVELER'S TELEPHONE DIRECTORY

Business Traveler's Hotline is a pocket-size 24-page directory of phone numbers for domestic and foreign airlines, U.S. hotel and motel chains and major car rentals. Where available, toll-free numbers are listed. Priced at $6.95 and updated frequently, the booklet is offered by:

Newsletter Management Corp.
10076 Boca Entrada Blvd.
Boca Raton, FL 33433

THE TRAVELING WOMAN
Dena Kaye
1980/398 pp./$11.95
Doubleday & Co.
245 Park Ave.
New York, NY 10017

This very readable book is crammed with practical advice for travelers. It covers both vacation and business situations and it pays particular attention to tips for the woman who is traveling alone. The author focuses on specifics and pinpoints ways to add ease and pleasure to traveling. A special section presents weather charts for more than 200 cities around the world.

WORLDWIDE DIRECTORY OF DELUXE HOTELS

An association of deluxe hotels, The Leading Hotels of the World represents more than 180 hotels in more than 40 countries around the world. The organization's annual directory ($2) provides detailed listings of the member hotels, with facilities, rates and reservation information. Write:

The Leading Hotels of the World (Dept. ESB)
747 3rd Ave.
New York, NY 10017

SOME TRAVEL TIPS FOR WOMEN EXECUTIVES

If you are arriving late at night or very early in the morning, arrange to have a limousine or radio cab meet you. You must weigh the possible expense against the anxiety of a woman arriving alone at off-hours in an unfamiliar airport and city. If you have to rent a car, you might want to rent in town to avoid navigating your way in from the airport and finding the hotel. In fact, carefully assess the merits of renting a car at all. You're facing one-way streets, topography and parking spaces, with the added pressure of having to be places at a specific time. Ask your hotel or your business associates about the practicality of public transport (a subway in Manhattan is sometimes the only way to go), or the possibility of getting a car and driver. The cost is rarely prohibitive. Your choice is not an indulgence but an intelligent business decision to help you do the best job possible with the least personal fuss.

From: *The Traveling Woman,* Dena Kaye (Garden City, NY: Doubleday & Co., 1980)

PREFERRED HOTELS: A SELECTION OF THE WORLD'S FINEST

Preferred Hotels Worldwide is an association of more than 50 independent luxury hotels located in major cities around the globe. Thirty-one of the hotels are in U.S. cities, including New York, Chicago, Boston, Dallas and Washington, D.C. Among the members of the organization are the Beverly Wilshire in Beverly Hills, the Breakers in Palm Beach, the Dorchester in Longon and the Hotel Le Bristol in Paris. For a directory of the hotels, with facilities, rates and reservation information, write:

Preferred Hotels Worldwide
1919 S. Highland Ave.
Lombard, IL 60148

RAMADA INNS: HOSTING BUSINESS WORLDWIDE

With 600 locations around the world, Ramada Inns, Inc., has become a standby for the traveling executive. The chain also caters to company needs, with meeting rooms that feature audiovisual rental equipment as well as food and beverage service. Ramada's accommodations are on three levels: inns in large numbers, its system of hotels and its newly developed chain of Renaissance Hotels. The *Ramada Worldwide Directory* details facilities at all lo-

cations and is available free. Also available at no charge is membership in Pacesetter, a service for frequent travelers, which can smooth reservations and offer advantages in room rates. For literature and further information, write:

Ramada Inns, Inc.
Box 590
Phoenix, AZ 85001

RADISSON SPECIAL SERVICES FOR FREQUENT TRAVELERS

Radisson offers first-class accommodations in a chain of more than 20 hotels concentrated largely in secondary cities in the eastern half of the U.S. Of interest to the traveling executive are the special services of the Radisson Plus program. Included in the program are guaranteed reservations, discounts, check-cashing privileges, and express check-in and check-out. For literature and further information, write:

Radisson Hotel Corp.
12805 State Hwy. 55
Minneapolis, MN 55441

HOLIDAY INNS: MORE THAN 1,700 LOCATIONS AROUND THE GLOBE

You will find the familiar Holiday Inn sign at more than 1,700 locations in more than 50 countries. Services of special interest to executives range from video teleconferencing to the Holidome physical-fitness facilities. Particularly at the chain's Crowne Plaza hotels, exclusive services are offered on the Concierge Floor. Included is a private lounge with honor bar as well as the concierge, who handles such needs as travel reservations. With the Priority Club, frequent travelers can earn points toward reduced-price or free room accommodations. The Preferred Corporate Traveler Card permits you to charge all expenses at your lodging, including room, food and entertainment. A detailed directory of all the Holiday Inn locations is available free, as is a separate directory that lists those that feature tennis, golf and running facilities. For literature and further information, write:

Holiday Inns, Inc.
3742 Lamar Ave.
Memphis, TN 38195

HYATT'S SPECIAL SERVICES FOR TRAVELING EXECUTIVES

Hyatt Hotels offer a wide variety of services for the executive. Regency Club accommodations provide deluxe rooms or suites in a separate part of the hotel and are available in many of the Hyatt hotels in the U.S. The accommodations include a private lounge with bar as well as a concierge who will arrange secretarial services and handle reservations. Telex service is available at all Hyatts in the U.S. and 16 provide a boardroom that can accommodate up to 12 people for meetings. For frequent guests, the Gold Passport program provides a variety of special services that include upgraded accommodations, check-cashing privileges and complimentary weekends. Many of the more

than 100 Hyatt hotels in the U.S. and foreign countries offer such physical-fitness facilities as jogging tracks and health clubs. The 32-page *Hyatt Spirit of Sports Directory* lists sports and exercise facilities and major spectator sports at or near its hotels in the U.S., Canada and Mexico. For literature and further information, write:

Hyatt Hotels Corp.
9700 W. Bryn Mawr Ave.
Rosemont, IL 60018

HILTON'S TOWERS: SPECIAL EXECUTIVE ACCOMMODATIONS

With more than 300 hotels around the world, Hilton is a name well known to the traveling executive. A special accommodation for executives is the Towers feature in some selected hotels, offering exclusive services. Included is a private lounge with honor bar and continental breakfast as well as a concierge to attend to dining, entertainment and travel arrangements. Other amenities include private elevators and registration desk at some hotels. Towers services are available at hotels in Chicago, New York, Washington, New Orleans, Atlanta, Los Angeles and Miami. For literature, write:

Hilton Hotels Corp.
9880 Wilshire Blvd.
Beverly Hills, CA 90210

MARRIOTT'S SPECIAL SERVICES FOR FREQUENT TRAVELERS

For the executive who travels frequently, Marriott offers special services at its more than 100 hotels and resorts in the U.S., Mexico, Central America, the Caribbean, Europe and the Middle East. Membership in the Marquis Club provides guaranteed reservations, rapid check-in and check-out, check-cashing privileges and use of health-club facilities. Frequent guests earn points toward awards of free accommodations, air travel and rental cars. At some hotels, separate floors are set aside for business travelers. Called the Concierge Level, these floors offer such special features as a private lounge, honor bar and complimentary continental breakfast as well as a concierge who provides personal assistance. Along with swimming pools and other recreational facilities, most hotels have specialized exercise rooms. A corporate rate is available to business travelers. For directory and further information, write:

Marriott Corp.
1 Marriott Dr.
Washington, DC 20058

THE HIDEAWAY REPORT
$45/12 issues per year
Box 300
Fairfax Station, VA 22039

If you are looking for secluded retreats for business meetings or vacations, here is a newsletter that specializes in such resorts both in the U.S. and overseas. The accommodations vary from country inns to ancient castles, with an emphasis on privacy and fine food and service. The selections offer opportunities for small executive conferences and seminars free from distraction.

VACATION EXCHANGE: SWAP YOUR HOME FOR A CHALET IN THE SWISS ALPS

The Vacation Exchange Club is part of a network of organizations in countries around the world. It publishes an annual directory of those wishing to exchange residences: you and your family spend your weeks in a chalet, for instance, while a Swiss family lives in your home. For a subscription fee of $22.70, you are listed in the directory and receive a copy in which to seek out an exchange partner. For $15 you can buy the directory without listing yourself. Write:

Vacation Exchange Club
12006 111th Ave., Unit 12
Youngtown, AZ 85363

DEAK-PERERA: CURRENCY SERVICES FOR THE TRAVELING EXECUTIVE

With branch offices in major U.S. cities, Deak-Perera buys and sells currencies from over 120 foreign countries. The firm sells U.S. and foreign traveler's checks and provides fund-transfer services. A dealer in precious metals, the firm also offers a storage program for investors. *Getting Around Overseas*, a free 32-page guide to travel in Europe, lists the firm's branch offices. Write:

Deak-Perera
677 S. Figueroa St.
Los Angeles, CA 90017

MAIL-ORDER HELP FOR TRAVELERS

Traveler's Checklist is a mail-order house that specializes in travel accessories. One of the firm's more popular items is the Money Exchanger ($19.95), a pocket calculator that computes currency equivalents (you enter the exchange rate in the unit's memory). Other items include voltage converters, personal ap-

Offered by Traveler's Checklist, the pocket-size Money Exchanger computes currency equivalents.

pliances such as a miniature clothes iron, money belt, pocket flashlight and luggage straps. A pocket-size battery-powered Personal Security System ($49.95) serves as a smoke, fire and break-in detector. Write for catalog:

Traveler's Checklist
Cornwall Bridge Rd.
Sharon, CT 06069

JET LAG AND THE ARGONNE LAB DIET

Few airline travelers escape the physical distress and general disorientation of jet lag after a long flight. Some, however, are learning to prevent the symptoms or at least speed up their recovery time. Their remedy is a diet plan developed at the U.S. Department of Energy's Argonne National Laboratory. The diet is the result of studies of natural body cycles, which are disrupted in long jet flights. The body normally needs one day of adjustment for each time zone crossed, but the diet can help make the recovery in a single day. The plan sets meal contents and timing for four days leading up to and through the flight in order to help reset the body's inner clock. A wallet-size card summarizing the diet is available. Send a stamped and self-addressed envelope to:

Anti-Jet-Lag Diet
Argonne National Laboratory
9700 S. Cass Ave.
Argonne, IL 60439

THE JET LAG BOOK
Don Kowet
1983/138 pp./$4.95
Crown Publishers, Inc.
1 Park Ave.
New York, NY 10016

The fatigue and confusion you experience on that first day of business meetings in London can be costly to you and to your company. Yet there is no miracle drug to counter the effects of jet lag. There are, however, steps you can take to ease the effects and even eliminate them. The author carefully explains what jet lag is and how it works on the mind and body. Then he details what you can do about it before, during and after your flight, including information on such factors as diet and exercise.

The author's anecdotal style makes easy reading out of what is often a harrowing experience.

AVIS: SPECIAL SERVICES FOR BUSINESS EXECUTIVES

Like its competitors in the car-rental field, Avis caters to the business traveler. You will profit from knowing about all the special services and options that are available to you and your company. Avis, for instance, offers a program of corporate discounts and also provides special President's Club services for top executives. For literature and further information, write:

Avis
900 Old Country Rd.
Garden City, NY 11530

THE STOPOVER REMEDY FOR THE JET-LAG LAMENT

Stopovers can help the body readjust gradually to a new time cycle and thus reduce the impact of jet lag. Birds seem to understand this fact instinctively. The Arctic tern crosses five time zones but breaks up its flight with frequent stops along the way. Again, modern man is proving to be just as clever as birds. IBM employees take a day's rest after passing through eight time zones, and Canadian government officials are entitled to a night's stopover after nine hours of flying. When President Richard Nixon embarked on his historic jaunt to China, the stops he made in Hawaii and Guam were not, as reported, to inspect our military bases. They were for Rest and Recreation, so that he would arrive at his destination in proper working order—mentally, emotionally and physically.

The best advice is: On any trip that takes you to the other side of the world (the worst situation for jet lag, since the more time zones you cross, the more upset your systems become), break up your journey with a one- or two-day stopover.

From: *The Jet Lag Book*, Don Kowet (New York: Crown Publishers, Inc., 1983)

THE BUSINESS TRAVELLER'S HANDBOOK

Foseco Minsep Group
1983/310 pp./$7.95
Prentice-Hall, Inc.
Englewood Cliffs, NJ 07632

This book is a concise compilation of etiquette and codes of behavior in 100 countries around the world. Originally prepared by and for its members, the book is the work of the Foseco Minsep Group, an international industrial firm. The information and advice here is based on firsthand experience, and the book is a valuable resource. Material is presented under such headings as introductions, correct forms of address, punctuality, conversation, language, clothing, entertainment, tipping, gifts, religion. In Algeria, for instance, wearing a tie is not obligatory, but tipping in advance is how you ensure good service.

THE RED CARPET CLUB AT UNITED AIRLINES

United's Red Carpet Club facilities are available at 18 major airports across the country. The clubrooms are hosted by receptionists who assist with check-in, seat assignments and last-minute travel arrangements. Services include cocktails and beverages and coffee and snacks. Phones and message services are provided.

Conference rooms are available for small meetings. The clubrooms are furnished for the traveler's comfort and they offer magazines, local newspapers, color TV as well as TV monitors for arrival and departure information. Annual membership fees are $110 for new members, $60 for renewing members and $20 for spouse membership. For brochures, write:

Red Carpet Club
Box 2247
Boston, MA 02107

THE IONOSPHERE CLUB AT EASTERN AIRLINES

With clubrooms at 28 airports along its routes, Eastern's Ionosphere Club offers its members comfort and convenience before, after and between flights. Eastern personnel in the lounges handle flight reservations and seat selection. The setting provides a place to meet with business associates or simply to relax. TV, newspapers and magazines are available. There is bar service as well as complimentary coffee and soft drinks. Annual membership fee is $75 (five-year fee is $225, and lifetime fee is $525). Membership for a spouse is available for a supplemental fee. In addition to its Ionosphere Club, Eastern offers a special registration program for traveling executives. The program is

Pan Am Clipper Club lounge at New York's JFK International Airport.

designed to facilitate reservations and provide other services. For brochures, write:

Eastern Ionosphere Club
Miami International Airport
Miami, FL 33148

HOSPITALITY FOR THE EXECUTIVE AT PAN AM'S CLIPPER CLUBS

Clipper Club facilities are available to its members at 26 airports along Pan Am's worldwide routes. Like comparable clubs offered by other major airlines, the Clipper Club lounges provide a haven for the business traveler beginning a trip or waiting between flights while en route. The lounges also provide privacy for meetings with business associates. Pan Am personnel host the clubrooms and handle seat selection. Phones and message services are available. The comfortable lounges offer complimentary cocktails, coffee and soft drinks. Annual membership is $65 ($175 for three years or $650 for a lifetime membership). There is a $25 initiation fee, and membership for a spouse is available for a supplementary fee. In addition to Clipper Club services, Pan Am offers business travelers its Clipper Class, a special section available on many of its flights. For brochures, write:

Pan Am Clipper Club
Pan Am Bldg.
New York, NY 10166

TWA'S AMBASSADORS CLUB: A PLACE TO REST EN ROUTE

TWA's accommodation for the traveling executive is the Ambassadors Club. This service offers members clubroom facilities at airports in 18 major cities in the U.S. and six cities in Europe. A place to relax or work while awaiting a flight, each clubroom provides bar service as well as the assistance of a receptionist. Conference rooms for small meetings are available at some of the airports. Annual membership is $85. Write:

Trans World Airlines, Inc.
605 3rd Ave.
New York, NY 10158

SWISSAIR: WORLDWIDE SERVICE AND RESOURCE FOR INFORMATION

With a long record of service for business executives, Swissair provides the traveler with a choice of either first-class or business-class accommodations on all its worldwide flights. The firm also offers the executive valuable information resources. Especially useful is a series of kits, organized by region, with concise and detailed pamphlets on individual countries. Included is information about language, currency, tipping, climate, social customs. The

Calendar of International Coming Events is a 342-page directory of trade shows, conventions, conferences and exhibitions. Another valuable publication is *Public Holidays Around the World*, a country-by-country directory to use in planning your business itinerary. For literature and further information, write:

Swissair
608 5th Ave.
New York, NY 10020

FLYING BUSINESS CLASS WITH ALITALIA AIRLINES

Alitalia's business-class service is another example of the options open to the traveling executive. The business-class cabin features roomy seating. There are separate check-in counters at airports, with pre-boarding lounges and complimentary cocktails. The service includes priority boarding and deplaning. Special accommodations in hotels and car rentals are also provided. Alitalia offers two useful booklets for the traveler, one a 79-page directory of world conferences and the other a 76-page collection of practical tips for airline travel. For literature and further information, write:

Alitalia Airlines
666 5th Ave.
New York, NY 10103

AIR FRANCE: THE CONCORDE, LE CLUB AND A TRAVEL GUIDE

For the executive traveling to Paris or elsewhere in France, the Concorde is perhaps the best-known service of Air France. The Concorde will take you to Paris from New York in so brief a trip that you can literally conduct business in France the same day. The airline's subsonic jets offer Le Club, a special class for business travelers in a separate cabin area offering especially comfortable seating. There are special check-in facilities as well as in-flight amenities. The *Air France Business Traveler's Guide* is yet another accommodation for the executive. The guide provides wide-ranging information about currency, shopping, taxis, postal service, cables, telexes and tipping.

There are lists of important business and government addresses as well as information about Paris restaurants and night life. Included are listings of the hotels of Paris and the Riviera. For the guide and other information, write (on your letterhead or attach your business card):

Air France
1350 Avenue of the Americas
New York, NY 10019

IAN KEOWN'S CARIBBEAN HIDEAWAYS
Ian Keown
1982/319 pp./$7.95
Crown Publishers, Inc.
1 Park Ave.
New York, NY 10016

Here are more than 100 small hotels and inns on the islands of the Caribbean. This guidebook tours 34 of the islands, seeking accommodations that offer quality and quiet. The hotels and inns are often secluded and are always apart from the giant resort hotels. The directory information is comprehensive, with detailed information about services, meals and costs. A special section covers the subject of charter yachts. The hotels and inns are spotlighted for their individual character, making this a valuable resource for planning a vacation or an executive conference.

IAN KEOWN'S EUROPEAN HIDEAWAYS
Ian Keown
1980/388 pp./$7.95
Crown Publishers, Inc.
1 Park Ave.
New York, NY 10016

If it is time for you to get away for a while, this guidebook offers vacation destinations to lure you on. More than 200 small hotels and inns in Western Europe are described, each with the distinctive details that make it unique. Many of these hostelries are in out-of-the-way places; some of them are medieval castles. The accommodations are described in detail, with specifics on services, meals and prices. In some instances the hotels and inns cater to corporate meetings.

EGON RONAY'S TWA GUIDE TO GOOD RESTAURANTS IN 35 EUROPEAN BUSINESS CITIES

Egon Ronay Organization
1983/256 pp./$6.95
Crown Publishers, Inc.
1 Park Ave.
New York, NY 10016

This pocket-size guidebook presents concise sketches of almost 300 fine restaurants in 18 European countries. The book is organized in sections, one for each of the 35 cities, with a city map showing restaurant locations. The individual restaurant entries list phone number, map directions, business hours, credit cards accepted and an average meal price. Restaurant cuisine and specialties are briefly described. The restaurants vary in style, size and prices, giving the traveling executive a broad selection to choose from.

PAN AM'S TRAVEL GUIDES TO THE U.S. AND THE WORLD

Pan Am markets two of the most comprehensive travel guides in print. The 26th edition of the *Pan Am World Guide* ($9.95) contains more than 1,000 pages of practical information and advice on travel in 139 countries. The *Pan Am U.S.A. Guide* ($8.95) offers 600 pages covering the 50 states, Puerto Rico, the Virgin Islands, Guam, Micronesia and American

Samoa. Whether for business or pleasure, the two guides will help you to a smooth trip and a comfortable stay. Write:

Pan American World Airways, Inc.
Pan Am Bldg.
New York, NY 10166

COMBINING QE2 AND CONCORDE FOR THE IDEAL EUROPEAN TRIP

Cunard's superliner *Queen Elizabeth 2* has been teamed with the British Airways supersonic Concorde to provide an ideal round trip to and from Europe. The service gives the traveler a five-day crossing from New York. After business or leisure time in Europe, you fly back on the Concorde. Round-trip fare is as low as $1,750, which is lower than the regular Concorde fare. Among the features of the *QE2* voyage is a computer center in which the executive can take seminar training in the use of personal computers. For literature, write:

Cunard Line
555 5th Ave.
New York, NY 10017

VACATION IDEA: A WEEK ON A YACHT

Yachting Worldwide, Inc., specializes in arranging vacations on fully crewed sailing and power yachts. The boats range in size from 40 to 150 feet and carry from two to 18 guests. The crew includes captain, chef, steward and deckhands. Yachting areas are Florida, the Bahamas, the Caribbean, Greece and the Mediterranean. Costs vary but are generally comparable to those of resort accommodations. Write:

Yachting Worldwide, Inc.
Box 22399
Fort Lauderdale, FL 33316

VACATION IDEA: YOUR OWN APARTMENT ON MONTEGO BAY

The Half Moon Club on Montego Bay, Jamaica, offers hotel, apartment and cottage accommodations along one mile of private beach. There are 62 apartments available, with optional maid/cook service. There are also 23 cottages, some with individual fresh-water pools. Facilities include an 18-hole golf course and tennis and squash courts. There are also meeting rooms and banquet facilities to accommodate business conferences. For literature and further information, write:

The Half Moon Club
Box 80
Montego Bay
Jamaica, W.I.

VACATION IDEA: A VILLA IN THE VIRGIN ISLANDS

The Point Pleasant resort on St. Thomas in the American Virgin Islands offers a vacation or business-conference site on one of the most beautiful islands in the Caribbean. Among the accommodations at Point Pleasant are efficiency and studio apartments, suites and villas. The rate for a villa for four persons for one week during the winter season is about $1,900 (about $1,300 during the summer season). The units all look onto the sea and have fully equipped kitchens. For literature and further information, write:

Point Pleasant
Box 496
Huntington, NY 11743

LOCAL COLOR: CITY MAGAZINES OF INTEREST TO EXECUTIVES

Many major cities have magazines that can be a big help to traveling business people or executives who like to keep up on new trends and regional activities, or who just want information on cultural and sports events, restaurants and entertainment when they are in town on business.

The following are among the top city magazines:

Boston Magazine
1050 Park Square Bldg.
Boston, MA 02116
Monthly
$1.75/issue, $15/year

Chicago
303 E. Wacker Dr.
Chicago, IL 60601
Monthly
$2/issue, $15/year

D [Dallas]
3988 North Central Expwy.
Suite 1200
Dallas, TX 75204
Monthly
$1.95/issue, $14/year

Los Angeles Magazine
1888 Century Park East
Suite 920
Los Angeles, CA 90067
Monthly
$2/issue, $20/year

New York
755 Second Ave.
New York, NY 10017
50 issues/year
$1.50/issue, $26/year

Philadelphia Magazine
1500 Walnut St.
Philadelphia, PA 19102
Monthly
$1.95/issue, $15/year

San Francisco Magazine
973 Market St.
San Francisco, CA 94103
Monthly
$1.75/issue, $16/year

The Washingtonian
1828 L St., N.W.
Washington, DC 20036
Monthly
$1.95/issue, $18/year

LUGGAGE AND ATTACHÉ CASES

FINE LEATHER GOODS FROM MARK CROSS, INC.

Mark Cross, Inc., specializes in fine leather products for the traveler. Among the firm's offerings is the Outback collection, a line of luggage made of fabric and leather. An example from the line is a small shoulder-strap bag, priced at about $200. Other items include a leather wallet for traveler's checks as well as a calfskin passport cover. For literature and further information, write:

Mark Cross, Inc.
645 5th Ave.
New York, NY 10022

This small shoulder-strap bag is from the Outback collection by Mark Cross, Inc. It combines fabric and leather and is priced at about $200.

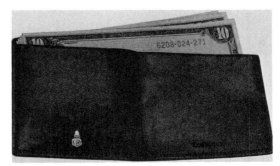

This leather wallet by Mark Cross, Inc., is designed for carrying traveler's checks.

LEATHER GOODS BY BUXTON

Buxton, Inc., markets a wide variety of personal leather goods for men and women. Of special interest to the executive is the firm's line of wallets that include a slimline calculator. The Cal-Q-Clutch for women includes both checkbook holder and calculator, comes in gray, navy, red or burgundy and is priced at $45. The Cal-Q-Traveler wallet includes the calculator as well as compartments for passport, credit cards, cash and other items. Priced at $57.50, it is available in black or mahogany leather. Another item of interest is a man's money belt called the Safe Place, priced at $16 and offered in black or brown. See your local retailer or write:

Buxton, Inc.
Box 1650
Springfield, MA 01101

RUGGED LUGGAGE
FROM SAMSONITE

Samsonite has a long-standing reputation for luggage that travels well. Its Silhouette III line of hard-side and soft-side cases, totes, bags and garment bags offers a stylish look along with durability. Several colors are available. Prices range up to $185 for the Jumbo Suiter Cartwheels model. See your local retailer or write for literature:

Samsonite Corp.
11200 E. 45th Ave.
Denver, CO 80239

LEATHER ATTACHÉS
FROM PEDRO

The Pedro Companies market a wide choice of leather attaché cases. A dozen models are available, at prices ranging from $150 to $375. The firm also markets a large selection of luggage, briefcases, portfolios and personal accessories, constructed of both leather and synthetics. Included are billfolds, key cases and checkbook covers. For catalogs, write:

The Pedro Companies
104 E. 10th St.
St. Paul, MN 55101

OLEG CASSINI LUGGAGE
FROM AIRWAY INDUSTRIES

Airway Industries, Inc., offers luggage and attaché cases by designer Oleg Cassini. The Elite collection of luggage consists of three suitcases and five other bags, all constructed of washable nylon with vinyl backing. Colors are brown, gray or black and prices range from $45 to $97. An Elite model 4-inch attaché case is covered

Oleg Cassini attaché case by Airway Industries is priced at $89.

The Grasshopper luggage collection by Atlantic Products offers a selection of eight suitcases and bags priced from $40 to $100.

in mahogany vinyl and is priced at $89. For brochures, write:

Airway Industries, Inc.
Airway Park
Ellwood City, PA 16117

LUGGAGE VARIETY FROM ATLANTIC PRODUCTS

The Atlantic Products Corp. markets a wide range of luggage models. The Grasshopper collection offers a choice of eight suitcases and bags, constructed of heavy-duty nylon and priced from $40 to $100. Included are three suitcase sizes, two of them with wheels. Colors

The Vista collection by Atlantic Products includes suitcase, garment carrier and two other bags, at prices from $72 to $129. ▶

available are gray and khaki-brown. The Vista collection offers a polycanvas suitcase and three bags, with a price range from $72 to $129. The firm also offers its Executive model 4-inch attaché case, covered in tan or cordovan vinyl and priced at $89. For brochures, write:

Atlantic Products Corp.
Airway Park
Ellwood City, PA 16117

LUGGAGE AND ATTACHÉ CASES FROM AMERICAN TOURISTER

Among the best-known names in luggage, American Tourister offers a wide selection of luggage as well as attaché cases and portfolios. The firm offers collections of luggage in matched sets of bags and suitcases. An example is the Saronno collection of seven pieces, available individually or as a set ($655). Another

Soft-Tech luggage collection by American Tourister includes garment bag (upper left, $90), shoulder tote (upper right, $55), club tote (center, $70), 26-inch suitcase with wheels (lower left, $115) and carry-on bag (lower right, $80). The luggage is available in black, gray, red or rose.

example is the Soft-Tech collection of bags and suitcases, made of nylon and available in a five-piece set for $410. The firm's selection of attaché cases and portfolios includes the LTL model 8803, an attaché finished in top-grain leather and priced at $175. For brochures, write:

American Tourister, Inc.
91 Main St.
Warren, RI 02885

BRIEFCASES, FOLIOS AND DATA ORGANIZERS

Boorum & Pease markets a wide selection of briefcases, notepad folios and organizers in its Royal line, all crafted of vinyl. Organizers in several sizes use the firm's Cardfolio system, in which note cards are lined up in pockets, with capacities of up to 72 cards. Included in the firm's selection of briefcases is the Royal Ambassador, a case with zippered center compart-

The Royal Ambassador briefcase by Boorum & Pease is made of vinyl and has a zippered center compartment and two side pockets. Colors are tan, light brown and burgundy. The price is $32.

ment and two side pockets. For brochures and dealer information, write:

Boorum & Pease
801 Newark Ave.
Elizabeth, NJ 07208

CORPORATE AVIATION

CORPORATE FLYING
WITH CHARTER AIRCRAFT

Pacific Executive Charter provides some cost figures for considering the use of charter aircraft instead of purchasing and maintaining a company plane. Hourly rates range from as low as $85 for a single-engine plane carrying up to three persons to $650 for a turboprop plane carrying up to eight passengers. Helicopter charter service is available at $395 per hour. For literature and further information, write:

Pacific Executive Charter
2733 E. Spring St.
Long Beach, CA 90806

EXECUTIVE AIR FLEET
Joseph Kleinpeter, Jr.
1978/135 pp./$4.95
Aviation Book Co.
1640 Victory Blvd.
Glendale, CA 91201

This survey of corporate aviation provides a source of useful information, particularly for a company contemplating purchase of its first aircraft. The author describes the various air-craft on the market and he gives advice on the purchase of both new and used planes. Included are such data as average salaries of corporate pilots and maintenance personnel.

MANAGEMENT SERVICES
BY EXECUTIVE AIR FLEET

The Executive Air Fleet Corp. provides air-craft-charter, brokerage and management services for corporate clients. The firm's management services include crew selection and training, budgeting, scheduling, catering, hangerage, flight planning, fuel purchase and maintenance. Its brokerage services include both purchase and sale of aircraft. For literature, write:

Executive Air Fleet Corp.
90 Moonachie Ave.
Teterboro, NJ 07608

THE CHOICE IS VARIED
AT CESSNA AIRCRAFT

Cessna markets a wide selection of business aircraft, varying from single-engine planes to

Cessna Skyhawk II has four seats and costs about $50,000.

twin-engine turboprops to twin-jet models. The single-engine Skyhawk II, for instance, has four seats and costs about $50,000. The Conquest I is a twin-engine turboprop that carries up to six passengers and is priced at upwards of $1 million. Cessna's line of business jets includes the Citation II, which can accommodate from six to 10 passengers. This jet flies at speeds up to 420 mph, with a range of 2,100 miles. It is available with custom options that include telephones and executive desks. For literature and further information, write:

Cessna Aircraft Co.
5800 E. Pawnee
Wichita, KS 67201

The Cessna Conquest I seats up to six passengers and is priced at upwards of $1 million.

The Cessna Citation II is a business jet that can seat from six to 10 passengers and has a range of 2,100 miles.

The two-engine Falcon 100 model from the Falcon Jet Corp.

A Beechcraft Super King Air B200 shown in flight. The lower photo is a view of the plane's cabin.

CORPORATE AIRPLANES FROM BEECH AIRCRAFT

A well-known name in aircraft, Beech markets several models that are popular choices as company planes. One of the best known is the Super King Air B200, a jetprop plane that cruises at speeds up to 338 mph. With eight passengers, the plane has a range of 1,789 miles. A variety of cabin-furnishings options are available. For literature and price information, write:

Beech Aircraft Corp.
9709 E. Central
Wichita, KS 67201

EXECUTIVE JETS FROM FRANCE

The Falcon Jet line of executive aircraft is manufactured in France. The jets vary in size.

The two-engine Falcon 100 has seating for six and a range of more than 2,000 nautical miles. The three-engine Falcon 50 has seating for nine and a range of more than 4,000 miles. The cabin features such conveniences as fold-out tables and there are galley facilities. For brochures and price information, write:

Falcon Jet Corp.
Teterboro Airport
Teterboro, NJ 07608

DIRECTORY RESOURCE FOR HELICOPTER INFO

Whether you are interested in purchasing a helicopter as a company aircraft or in chartering one for local travel, Helicopter Annual ($25) provides a useful source of information. The publication features a directory of commercial operators, specifying their services. Current helicopter models on the market are presented with photos and performance data. Write:

Helicopter Association International
1110 Vermont Ave., N.W., Suite 430
Washington, DC 20005

BUSINESS FLYING: THE PROFITABLE USE OF PERSONAL AIRCRAFT
Paul E. Hansen
1982/253 pp./$22.50
McGraw-Hill Book Co.
1221 Avenue of the Americas
New York, NY 10020

While it focuses on the use of the private plane in a small business, this book is of value to the executive of the larger company interested in the practical advantages of such transportation. The author provides guidelines for assessing the business value of private flying. He also details the cost factors in owning and operating an airplane.

BUYING AND OWNING YOUR OWN AIRPLANE
James E. Ellis
1980/172 pp./$13.95
Iowa State University Press
2121 S. State Ave.
Ames, IA 50010

The author presents a detailed guide to everything you need to know about buying and owning your own small plane. Costs of all

THE BASICS OF BUYING A COMPANY AIRPLANE

An interested company can request a demonstration flight. The aircraft is flown to the airport nearest the company and officials may be taken on an actual business trip rather than a 10-minute spin around the airport. This enables company pilots to observe flight performance and passengers to try out the creature comforts of the aircraft. Sales procedures of this nature are standard.

Once the purchase is agreed upon, buyer and seller enter into a contract and a deposit is made. A corporation may choose to make a cash purchase or finance the aircraft. When construction is completed, selections of exterior paint, cockpit instruments and cabin interior must be made.

Cabin furnishings such as chairs and couches are not bought at the local furniture outlet. They are custom built to specification. There is also a wide range of options to review.

To offset the financial expense of owning and operating an aircraft, a company may choose to charter its aircraft to outside users when not in use. By doing this an aircraft is paying for itself even when not in use by the owner. Another popular arrangement is to purchase an aircraft and lease it to a management concern who in turn provides flight crews and mechanics. This usually costs more than having a company flight department, but it eliminates establishing and managing the department.

From: *Executive Air Fleet*, Joseph Kleinpeter, Jr. (Glendale, CA: Aviation Book Co., 1978)

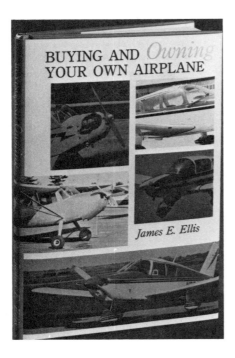

BUYING AND *Owning* YOUR OWN AIRPLANE

James E. Ellis

kinds are spelled out. Very specific directions take you through the process of buying a plane and there are separate chapters on maintenance and on engine operation. The author also provides an introduction to the small planes now on the market.

YOUR PILOT'S LICENSE
Joe Christy and Clay Johnson
1983/154 pp./$9.25
TAB Books, Inc.
Blue Ridge Summit, PA 17214

Flying a small plane can give you valuable mobility. If you contemplate becoming a pilot, this book will help you sort out your thinking. It is a basic and thorough introduction, beginning with flight-training options and costs. The book takes you through a step-by-step explanation of how a plane works and how you learn to fly it.

WHO IS IN CHARGE ON THE COMPANY PLANE?

The pilot is the captain and his decisions must be respected and followed. The pilot has to comply with all the federal and state aviation rules and follow tower instructions. It is up to him to gauge when and if he can take off and where and when he makes an emergency landing. In addition, his own experience and his expertise dictate when he thinks it is advisable for the plane to be airborne, when passengers must not smoke or when they should fasten their seat belts. Not even the chairman of the board or the president of the company can contradict or impose any changes in the pilot's orders.

From: *Corporate Etiquette*, Milla Alihan (New York: New American Library, 1974)

FLYING
$17.98/12 issues per year
1 Park Ave.
New York, NY 10016

If you contemplate learning to fly or simply want to gain some background about flying, here is a monthly that will serve your needs. A magazine for pilots of small planes, it reports on both the technology and the lore of flying.

EXECUTIVE FITNESS
AND HEALTH

Recently a study was done by several major corporations whose executives were on specific exercise training programs. The findings showed that strict adherence to the programs increased the executive's aggressiveness, performance level and ability to handle stress.

From: *The Businessman's Minutes-a-Day Guide to Shaping Up*, Dr. Franco Columbu with Lydia Fragomeni (Chicago: Contemporary Books, Inc., 1983)

a series of tests that are repeated every six months. A typical workout session lasts less than an hour and is repeated two or three times a week. Exercises include use of rowing machine, jump rope and treadmill. The annual fee of several hundred dollars is in most cases paid by the executive's company. For an illustrated brochure, write:

Cardio-Fitness Centers, Inc.
345 Park Ave.
New York, NY 10022

KEEPING FIT: EXERCISE
FOR A HEALTHY HEART

Cardio-Fitness Centers, Inc., a network of health clubs in New York City, is an example of a growing trend toward specialized exercise facilities for executives. Professionals trained in exercise physiology supervise individualized exercise programs that focus on maintaining a healthy heart. Membership requires medical clearance from your personal physician or company doctor and you begin your program with

EXECUTIVE HEALTH
$30/12 issues per year
Box 589
Rancho Santa Fe, CA 92067

This newsletter devotes each of its monthly issues to a single health topic. Written by physicians and other professionals, these in-depth studies are related to the needs and interests of executives. A listing of topics in back issues is available for ordering individual reports ($3).

EXECUTIVE TUNE-UP
Karl Albrecht
1981/210 pp./$6.95
Prentice-Hall, Inc.
Englewood Cliffs, NJ 07632

The author offers counseling for personal effectiveness. He focuses on such subjects as the dynamics of self-esteem and mood-control skills. His emphasis is on self-understanding and self-actualization and practical action. A separate chapter deals with managing stress and maintaining good health. Another very useful chapter is devoted to advice on developing an effective interpersonal style.

MUST SUCCESS COST SO MUCH?
Paul Evans and Fernando Bartolomé
1981/250 pp./$13.95
Basic Books, Inc.
10 E. 53rd St.
New York, NY 10022

Based on hundreds of interviews with executives, this book is a study of the interacting demands of corporate and private life. The research was conducted among successful European and American executives of varying ages. All were married men and in some instances their wives also participated in interviews. The authors report in detail on how their subjects cope with the stresses that shape their lives in the office and the home.

STATISTICAL BULLETIN
$25/4 issues per year
1 Madison Ave.
New York, NY 10010

This quarterly magazine will give you a broad perspective on health trends and medical-care developments. Published by the Metropolitan Life Insurance Co., the magazine reports on how Americans live as seen in various population studies.

EXECUTIVES UNDER PRESSURE
Judi Marshall and Cary L. Cooper
1979/150 pp./$27.95
Praeger Publishers
383 Madison Ave.
New York, NY 10017

This book reports on research conducted with a sample of British executives and their wives. The authors present extensive background material, including references to comparable studies made with executives in the U.S. The research findings are detailed and provide useful insights into the causes of and remedies for executive stress.

COPING WITH EXECUTIVE STRESS
Executive Health Examiners
1983/225 pp./$14.95
McGraw-Hill Book Co.
1221 Avenue of the Americas
New York, NY 10020

Based on the expertise of specialists in executive health, this book examines the effects of stress in the life of the executive. Physiological and medical aspects are clearly explained and a wide range of stress-related health problems are discussed. There are detailed presentations on such conditions as heart disease and ulcers, with an emphasis on countermeasures. The book's specific and practical advice for coping with stress makes it an especially valuable resource.

EXECUTIVE FITNESS
Executive Health Examiners
1983/210 pp./$14.95
McGraw-Hill Book Co.
1221 Avenue of the Americas
New York, NY 10020

Aimed at countering stress and increasing stamina and productivity, this book of exercise techniques offers a variety of options for a fitness program. The book details such aerobic exercises as walking, running, cycling, swimming and rope skipping. Also covered are such strength-building and stretching exercises as weight-lifting and calisthenics as well as yoga. There are also exercises that can be done in your office, even while sitting at your desk. Included is information on exercise for women

RELIEVING STRESS
AND THE PAIN IN THE NECK

On any day, and especially on a day full of stress, take a brief time out to elevate your shoulders. Bring them up close to your ears, then shake them down. Wiggle your shoulders up and around. Roll your head around, too, in gentle circles. In carrying out these movements, you are, of course, contracting muscles. But you are also causing the muscles to relax and the relaxation helps to prevent spasm.

If spasm-induced neck pain does appear, keep in mind that as the spasm triggers pain, the pain in turn leads to more spasms. The cycle must be interrupted as soon as possible. In addition to aspirin or another pain reliever . . . heat or cold can be applied to . . . the back of the neck.

Massage can be useful. With your fingertips, rub the area from the back of your skull down your neck and across the top of your shoulders, repeating the procedure several times.

From: *Coping with Executive Stress*, Executive Health Examiners (New York: McGraw-Hill Book Co., 1983)

executives, company fitness programs and weight-reduction techniques. The exercise directions are fully illustrated with photographs.

THE EXECUTIVE'S PERSONAL HEALTH ADVISOR
$49/12 issues per year
10076 Boca Entrada Blvd.
Boca Raton, FL 33433

Drawing on material from a variety of publications, this newsletter reports on a wide range of health matters. The latest findings on health care are covered and such factors as diet and exercise are highlighted.

HOW TO LICK EXECUTIVE STRESS
Robert Collier Page, M.D., F.A.C.P.
1961, 1981/159 pp./$6.95
Simon and Schuster
1230 Avenue of the Americas
New York, NY 10020

A physician and onetime medical director of Standard Oil, the author bases this book on his experience as advisor to hundreds of executives. He deals with both the physical and the emotional aspects of health and he examines stress factors in both business and personal life. Included is advice on such factors as nutrition and exercise as well as the use of alcohol and tobacco.

TIPS FOR STARTING A RUNNING PROGRAM

The first thing to remember about running or jogging (we use the words interchangeably because there is no clear distinction between the two) . . . is that it can be hazardous to your health. Running is a strenuous form of exercise and demands a great deal from the body. If you are not in good shape, running can be a punishing activity, but it does not have to be. If you use common sense and take the proper precautions, you will find that running can be an exhilarating, stress-reducing, safe and pleasurable experience.

Running presents a great potential danger to people with heart disease, which is why we strongly recommend that any executive over 35 have a complete physical examination including a stress test before setting out on a running program. Any executive under 35 who has been inactive for a long period of time should also have a physical examination before starting a jogging program.

With your doctor's consent, you can map out a running strategy. The first thing to do is to go out and spend a few dollars on a good sturdy pair of running shoes. The most important thing to remember as you begin is to start *gradually*, especially if you have been living a sedentary life. Running is such a jarring shock to the out-of-shape body that Executive Health Examiners urges all beginners to combine walking and running at first and then to work gradually up to a total running regimen.

From: *Executive Fitness*, Executive Health Examiners (New York: McGraw-Hill Book Co., 1983)

BUILDING GOOD HEALTH ON DIET AND EXERCISE

Combining a diet regimen with daily exercise, the Pritikin Longevity Center has gained national attention for its health program. The program is designed for both treatment and prevention of heart disease, diabetes, hypertension and overweight. Occupying an oceanfront hotel, the center offers a 13-day format ($2,985) and a 26-day format ($5,970). The program's low-fat diet is combined with an exercise regimen that emphasizes walking or jogging. Participants also take part in a series of educational sessions that relate living habits to health and cover such aspects of health care as diet cooking. The program is supervised by a staff of physicians. For further information:

Pritikin Longevity Center
1910 Ocean Front Walk
Santa Monica, CA 90405

EXECUTIVE NUTRITION AND DIET

Executive Health Examiners
1983/274 pp./$14.95
McGraw-Hill Book Co.
1221 Avenue of the Americas
New York, NY 10020

This book comes from a group of executive-health specialists and presents a detailed review of the medical and practical aspects of nutrition and diet. The basics of nutrition are clearly explained and advice on nutrition and weight control takes into account the executive lifestyle. The book examines the relationship be-

MODIFYING EATING HABITS FOR WEIGHT REDUCTION

Eat slowly and enjoy your food. Many studies indicate that when you make a deliberate decision to eat and then take the time to enjoy the eating thoroughly, you will experience a greater sense of satisfaction, even though you may be consuming fewer calories.

Eat slowly to give your appetite a chance to be satisfied. If you eat a meal in less than 20 minutes, you are eating too fast to enjoy it. Moreover, it takes about 20 minutes for the brain to register "Enough." Therefore, if you finish a meal in less time, you are more likely to reach for seconds because you still feel hungry.

Put your fork or spoon down after each bite and wait until you have swallowed before taking another forkful or spoonful of food.

Concentrate on your eating. Avoid watching television or reading.

Even at home, avoid "family-style" eating and, instead, have food portioned on plates before it is brought to the table. Keep serving platters and bowls in the kitchen.

Develop a tolerance for mild hunger. Think of it as a positive feeling.

Make deliberate decisions to eat; don't eat absentmindedly.

Plan in advance to indulge yourself occasionally—and to make up for it by eating less of something else.

From: *Executive Nutrition and Diet*, Executive Health Examiners (New York: McGraw-Hill Book Co., 1983)

Expect to see physiological changes in three areas: strength, flexibility and cardiovascular endurance. Don't be surprised if these change your entire life, though, because they add up to just one thing: improved self-image. Call it personal power, or self-worth, or self-actualization or anything you want; you're going to feel an inner strength you haven't felt before. It's the one thread that runs through every woman's account of her Nautilus training experience.

From: *Nautilus Fitness for Women*, Michael D. Wolf, Ph.D. (Chicago: Contemporary Books, Inc., 1983)

tween nutrition and cardiovascular diseases as well as the effects of alcohol and caffeine. Especially useful are guidelines for menu planning and healthful eating habits.

MEDICAL EXAMS AND PREVENTIVE CARE

Executive Health Examiners specializes in periodic health evaluations for executives. Examinations are available in more than 400 cities in the U.S. and overseas. This organization offers both individual and corporate programs. Write:

Executive Health Examiners
777 3rd Ave.
New York, NY 10017

SMOKENDERS: SOME HELP FOR YOUR HEALTH

If you are a smoker and the time has come for you to quit, SmokEnders may be able to help you. This organization, which functions nationally, offers a supervised program for smokers. The program consists of eight weekly meetings, each about two hours long and held in your locality. For more information and the brochure *How to Stop Smoking for Good:*

SmokEnders
12255 DePaul Dr.
Bridgeton, MO 63044

MEDICAL ASSISTANCE FOR FOREIGN TRAVEL

Intermedic, Inc., is a medical referral service for travelers overseas. Its annual directory for members lists English-speaking physicians in more than 200 foreign cities. An information service answers queries about immunizations and medications. Annual membership in the service is $6 ($10 for a family group). For brochure and application, write:

Intermedic, Inc.
777 3rd Ave.
New York, NY 10017

JOINING UP WITH THE COUNTRY'S JOGGERS

The American Running & Fitness Association offers information services that can be useful in an individual's fitness program. Membership is $20 annually and includes *Running & Fitness,* a tabloid published every two months. The newspaper covers such health aspects as diet, nutrition and injury prevention and treatment and also provides motivational guidance for runners. Write:

American Running & Fitness Association.
2420 K St., N.W.
Washington, DC 20037

THE NAUTILUS BOOK
Ellington Darden, Ph.D.
1980, 1982/196 pp./$7.95
Contemporary Books, Inc.
180 N. Michigan Ave.
Chicago, IL 60601

The author, who is research director for Nautilus, the manufacturer of exercise equipment, presents a thorough review of its various exercise machines and their use. He gives a detailed

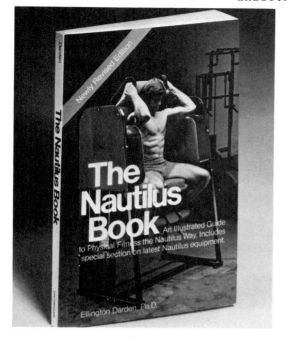

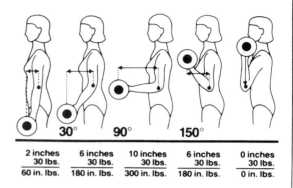

2 inches	6 inches	10 inches	6 inches	0 inches
30 lbs.	30 lbs.	30 lbs.	30 lbs.	30 lbs.
60 in. lbs.	180 in. lbs.	300 in. lbs.	180 in. lbs.	0 in. lbs.

The effect of the weight of a 30-pound barbell changes with position during a curling exercise (from Nautilus Fitness for Women).

introduction to the training principles that are involved and then explains the exercise routines used for the various parts of the body. The text is fully illustrated with photographs. Especially helpful is a section of questions and answers which covers all aspects of this popular physical-training equipment.

NAUTILUS FITNESS FOR WOMEN
Michael D. Wolf, Ph.D.
1983/186 pp./$7.95
Contemporary Books, Inc.
180 N. Michigan Ave.
Chicago, IL 60601

This book focuses on the use of Nautilus exercise machines by women. The author, who has been a researcher for the manufacturer, reviews each of the various machines, with emphasis on correct adjustment for women. Illustrated with detailed line drawings, the instructions show how the exercise routines concentrate on specific areas of the body for toning, reshaping and strengthening. Included are chapters on

nutrition as well as on the use of Nautilus training in combination with sports and other fitness exercises.

THE BUSINESSMAN'S MINUTES-A-DAY GUIDE TO SHAPING UP
Dr. Franco Columbu with Lydia Fragomeni
1983/187 pp./$16.95
Contemporary Books, Inc.
180 N. Michigan Ave.
Chicago, IL 60601

The authors offer exercise programs that are specifically designed for businessmen, including routines involving as little as 10 minutes a day. The programs consist of both weightlifting and calisthenics. The authors review equipment for use in either home or office gym and give guidance for selecting a commercial gym. The exercise programs are illustrated with photographs. The book covers both basic and advanced bodybuilding programs, and a separate chapter deals with nutrition.

THE COMPLETE BOOK OF EXERCISEWALKING

Gary D. Yanker
1983/266 pp./$8.95
Contemporary Books, Inc.
180 N. Michigan Ave.
Chicago, IL 60601

A deliberate regimen of walking exercise could be the beginning of your fitness program, particularly if it can fit conveniently into some part of your daily schedule. The author explains how walking can function as a conditioning exercise. He shows how walking can be transformed into disciplined routines as well as how to measure and evaluate the benefits of such exercise. Illustrated with both photos and line drawings, the book is a valuable resource in its detailed information and advice on all aspects of the subject.

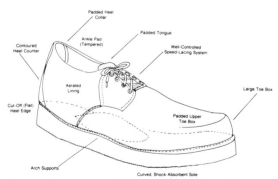

Design features needed in a good walking shoe (from The Complete Book of Exercisewalking).

USING WALKING FOR FITNESS EXERCISE

There are really two basic types of walking: natural and dynamic. Both can be forms of exercise providing fitness and health benefits. Natural walking is the kind we all do without regarding it as exercise. We just do it for fun or function. The speed of the natural walker falls between one and three miles per hour. It's the art of walking if we take a walk for its own sake without any particular destination. It's functional walking if it gets us to a place we want to go. Either form is just what comes naturally.

Dynamic walking is walking with a greater level of metabolic expenditure than natural walking. It's the kind of walking we do to get into shape for a particular purpose. The speed of the dynamic walker is often above 3 mph and up to 10 mph. But it's not only speed that makes the difference—duration of the walk, incline of the walking surface and work effort also add metabolic expenditure to the walking activity. Some dynamic walkers go slowly but carry a big weight load. Other dynamic walkers travel up inclines, and still others raise their legs higher (to walk on sand, snow or rocky terrain, for instance).

From: *The Complete Book of Exercisewalking*, Gary D. Yanker (Chicago: Contemporary Books, Inc., 1983)

UNIVERSAL FITNESS EQUIPMENT FOR HOME AND OFFICE GYMS

The Universal Fitness Products Co. markets a wide selection of gym equipment and accessories produced by Universal Gym Equipment, Inc., and other companies. Products include single-station and multi-station exercise machines, motorized and manual treadmills, exercise bikes, rowing machines, exercise benches, weight-lifting equipment and a variety of meters and scales. The firm also offers training aids, literature and films, as well as training courses for fitness instructors. While much of this equipment is appropriate for the home

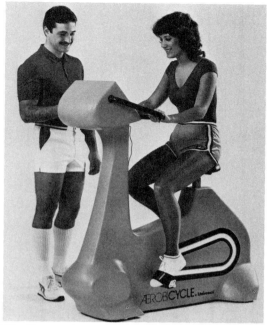

gym, this firm specializes in designing and out-fitting company gyms as well as commercial and institutional fitness centers. Free consulta-tion is available and the firm offers an intro-ductory booklet titled *How to Develop a Company Fitness Program*. The booklet in-cludes sample gym layouts, with equipment specified and prices indicated. For the booklet, catalog and other literature, write:

Universal Fitness Products Co.
20 Terminal Dr.
Plainview, NY 11803

The Universal Aerobicycle features programmed exercise modes, with digital display of readings for pedal speed, work load, calorie expenditure, pulse rate and elapsed time. Unit is priced at $2,160.

This gym facility is based on equipment from Universal Fit-ness Products. At left is the Power Pak 400 exercise ma-chine ($4,417); at right is the Monark exercise bike ($465).

The Marcy Bodybar 2000 is designed to provide a complete exercise program in a minimum of space.

GYM EQUIPMENT FOR HOME OR OFFICE

The Marcy Gymnasium Equipment Co. markets a wide variety of units ranging from compact designs to larger units suitable for a company gym. The Bodybar 2000 model, for instance, is designed to provide a complete exercise program in a minimum of space. It comes with 100 pounds of weights, with an eight-position lifting arm. On a larger scale, the 3-Station Master Gym model 1303 requires a floor space of 8 by 12 feet. The firm also offers treadmills, exercise bikes and a variety of accessories. For catalogs and further information, write:

Marcy Gymnasium Equipment Co.
2801 W. Mission Rd.
Alhambra, CA 91803

TYPICAL EQUIPMENT FOR THE EXECUTIVE GYM

The variety of equipment available for the executive gym is extensive and careful selection is essential. From the Universal Fitness Products Co. comes the following suggestions for a basic gym facility using the firm's products.

The exercise room's layout is based on a floor area 12 feet by 18 feet in size and is calculated to accommodate four to eight people per hour. The central unit in the room is a six-station exercise machine (Power Pak 400, $4,417). Also in the room is a motorized treadmill (Tredex model, $6,685), as well as two exercise bikes (Monark model, each $465). Other equipment includes two pulsemeters (each $129), indoor jogging unit ($149), physician's scale ($239) and a large pace clock ($325). Total cost is $13,003.

A second suggested gym layout is scaled upward to accommodate 15 to 25 people per hour. The room area is 20 feet by 24 feet. Replacing the six-station exercise machine is a 10-station unit ($7,400). Added are two single-station machines ($2,595 and $1,625) as well as an exercise bench ($620). Total cost is $20,826.

BODY CONDITIONING
IN HOME OR OFFICE GYM

The West Bend Co. markets exercise systems designed for complete body-conditioning programs. The Pro and Plus Pro systems are compact units, both of which can be freestanding or wall-mounted. The Pro system ($359) provides nine resistance levels for exercise, while the Plus Pro system ($499) offers 11 resistance levels. For literature and dealer information, write:

West Bend Co.
400 Washington Ave.
West Bend, WI 53095

ASSESSING NAUTILUS FOR FITNESS EXERCISE

The reason Nautilus revolutionized physical conditioning was, in one word, efficiency. Nautilus training was much more efficient than traditional methods of exercise. Earlier methods of conditioning had centered around long programs of exercise. To obtain a high level of fitness, an individual had to spend a minimum of 90 minutes a day on stretching for flexibility, jogging for heart-lung endurance and lifting barbells for strength. The average fitness enthusiast might spend from 5 to 10 hours a week on such exercise programs.

If Nautilus machines required the same amount of time as traditional methods and produced slightly better results, that would still be a worthwhile contribution. But if Nautilus machines produced three times the results in one-tenth of the time, that could only be described as revolutionary. And that is exactly what Nautilus produced: three times the results in one-tenth of the time!

From: *The Nautilus Book*, Ellington Darden, Ph.D. (Chicago: Contemporary Books, Inc., 1982)

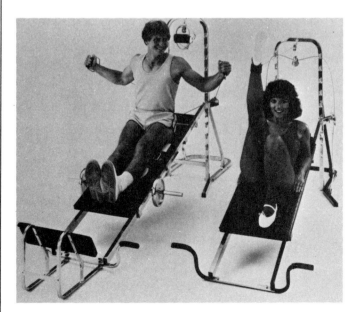

West Bend exercise systems include the Plus Pro ($499), left, and the Pro ($359).

The Fitness Master exercise unit is made of chrome-plated steel and weighs 68 pounds.

FITNESS MASTER: SKIING EXERCISE WITHOUT SNOW

Fitness Master, Inc., uses a cable and pulley system in its model XC-1 exercise unit to simulate the rhythmic motion of cross-country skiing. It is designed so that legs and arms move in a natural motion, with adjustable resistance in both forward and backward directions. The unit is made of chrome-plated steel, weighs 68 pounds and is designed to fold compactly for storage. It requires an operating space just under 5 feet long. The unit is priced at $479. Also available is a battery-powered meter ($105) for monitoring pulse rate and exercise time. For literature and further information, write:

Fitness Master, Inc.
12 Haverhill
Jonathan, MN 55318

GUIDELINES FOR SELECTING YOUR FITNESS DIRECTOR

Good leadership is essential to the success of your [company] program. Ideally, your fitness director will have studied physiology and physical education at the college level and will have experience with exercise physiology and modern conditioning methods. A graduate student at a nearby college or university might fill your requirements perfectly.

You may elect to hire a knowledgeable fitness director on a part-time or full-time basis, or you may discover that a suitable candidate is already on the payroll. Some qualifications to look for are:

- Experience with exercise stress-testing
- Practical background in leading adult fitness activities
- Knowledge of behavior modification techniques and awareness of other lifestyle habits that can affect employee health, such as nutrition, smoking, stress and use of alcohol
- Qualified to practice and teach CPR (cardiopulmonary resuscitation)
- A creative personality to assist in inspiring employees. Should be familiar with the use of music and a variety of special equipment and innovative approaches to working with different people.
- Personal appearance that will help to encourage his or her fitness classes to slim down and stay fit. A fat director just won't do.
- A sense of humor

From: *How to Develop a Company Fitness Program*, Universal Gym Equipment, Inc. (Cedar Rapids, IA: Universal, 1981)

The NordicTrack exercise unit duplicates the body movements of cross-country skiing.

NORDICTRACK: KEEPING FIT WITH A SKI MACHINE

NordicTrack is an exercise unit that duplicates the body movements of cross-country skiing. Roller-supported skis in the unit's frame permit smooth striding, while the upper body is exercised with arm movements on a tension-adjusted cord mechanism. The compact exerciser requires an operating space 2 feet wide and 7 feet long. The unit is priced at $470, with an optional battery-powered meter for digital readout of both pulse and elapsed time for $108. Write:

NordicTrack
124 Columbia Court
Chaska, MN 55318

THE SPA BOOK
Judy Babcock and Judy Kennedy
1983/278 pp./$14.95
Crown Publishers, Inc.
1 Park Ave.
New York, NY 10016

The health spa continues to be a popular place to find the benefits of an organized program of nutrition and exercise. A few days of seclusion can give you a soothing rest as well as a fresh start toward fitness. This book is a directory of more than 60 spas and is designed to help you select one that will work well for you. The listings specify costs and accommodations, describe special features and identify those spas that cater to men as well as to women.

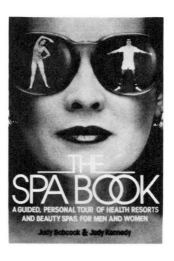

CLOTHING, STYLE AND TASTE

THE EXECUTIVE LOOK
Mortimer Levitt
1981/181 pp./$16.95
Atheneum Publishers
597 5th Ave.
New York, NY 10017

Writing from his expertise as a men's clothing designer, the author dresses the reader to project an executive style. He spells out basic standards and then, in text and photos, he shows the many combinations and variations that enhance appearance. The book focuses on suit, shirt and tie, but it also covers all the major elements of wardrobe.

THE EXTRA EDGE
Charlene Mitchell with Thomas Burdick
1983/207 pp./$14.95
Acropolis Books, Ltd.
2400 17th St., N.W.
Washington, DC 20009

A guide to considerations of image, style and career strategies, this book for women executives offers counsel and direction in such aspects as attitude, clothing, health and beauty care. By way of guidance for the reader, the authors present the results of a survey of women graduates of the Harvard Business School. Especially useful are chapters on business entertaining and travel.

**THE EXECUTIVE LOOK
IN BUSINESS SUITS FOR MEN**

The name Palm Beach has a special reputation in suits for men, and the Palm Beach Menswear Group adds to its luster with the Gant, Haspel, Evan-Picone and John Weitz labels. Gathered together, these fine names offer a broad selection of styling and fabrics. Their suits favor the traditional look and cut a figure that fits in elegantly in the boardroom setting. While Palm Beach and Haspel have long been recognized especially for their summer-weight suits, they and the others in this group provide wardrobes for all seasons. For further information, write:

Palm Beach Menswear Group
1290 Avenue of the Americas
New York, NY 10104

Single-breasted suit by Palm Beach is a worsted blend called Palm Paca, which combines wool, alpaca and polyester. About $230 (Palm Beach Menswear Group).

Suit by John Weitz is a slate gray with an overplaid weave of subtle coloring. About $210 (Palm Beach Menswear Group).

This navy-blue pinstripe suit by Evan-Picone is a blend of worsted wool and polyester. About $235 (Palm Beach Menswear Group).

Crisp and cool for summer, tan poplin suit by Gant is a blend of combed cotton and polyester. About $175 (Palm Beach Menswear Group).

Blending cotton and polyester for summer wear, this suit by Haspel has the texture of a worsted wool. About $205 (Palm Beach Menswear Group).

The double-breasted navy-blue blazer is a classic design. This tropical-weight wool blend by Palm Beach combines polyester and worsted wool. About $145 (Palm Beach Menswear Group).

Professional style is more than the result of a person's clothes—it involves grooming, physical presence, posture and manner. It's the unmistakable confidence that comes from knowing how to handle any situation. It's an aura of vitality and energy. The executive who has it commands attention at meetings, speaks with confidence and authority, and moves with self-assurance through the corporate corridors.

From: *The Extra Edge: Success Strategies for Women*, Charlene Mitchell with Thomas Burdick (Washington: Acropolis Books, Ltd., 1983)

FINE BUSINESS SUITS BY WAY OF A CATALOG

Saint Laurie, Ltd., specializes in business suits for men and women, in classic tailoring and a wide variety of fabrics and colors. The wool, cotton, linen, silk and polyester fabrics include imports from Europe and the Far East. Suit prices range up to $400. You make your selection from a fully illustrated catalog and a collection of fabric swatches. Suits are shown in color photographs, and drawings and size charts guide your choice. For catalog and swatches, write:

Saint Laurie, Ltd.
897 Broadway
New York, NY 10003

HARTMARX: NAMES THAT MEAN FINE SUITS FOR MEN

Hart Schaffner & Marx is a label that has long stood for fine suits for men. The Hartmarx Corp. adds several other celebrated names to form a menswear group. Included are such labels as Austin Reed of Regent Street, Chris-

---

WARDROBE GUIDELINES FOR THE CLASSIC LOOK

A plain, tightly woven tweed suit, along with a gray flannel suit, should be the backbone of your business wardrobe. Strongly patterned tweed sport jackets and loosely woven or coarse tweed suits should be reserved for weekends.

Unpatterned tweed suits, along with gray flannel and brown hopsacking, gabardine, twill, glen plaid and saxony weaves, are all appropriate for everyday business. The navy blue suit is appropriate for any social occasion. Dressier fabrics (sharkskin, pinhead, unfinished worsted, pinstripe) are appropriate for important business meetings.

All men look good in gray suits, but your best colors depend on your coloring. Men with blue eyes will look good in blue. Men with brown eyes will look good in brown. . . . In addition to eye color, it is desirable to take into account hair color and skin tone; taken together, they account for the fact that a man will look his best in one color, and his worst in another color.

You need a minimum of one navy blazer and one strongly patterned tweed jacket. There is a difference between a blazer and a sport jacket. The blazer, like the full-dress uniform of a naval officer, has gold buttons. The sport jacket, in contrast, has bone buttons. . . .

A dinner jacket is black with satin or grosgrain lapels and a matching stripe on the outside of each trouser leg. The traditional evening shirt has a pleated bosom of white broadcloth with a voile or batiste body cloth for cooler comfort.

From: *The Executive Look*, Mortimer Levitt (New York: Atheneum Publishers, 1981)

Pinstripe suit by Hart Schaffner & Marx has natural-shoulder tailoring and is a blend of polyester and wool worsted. Prices in the line range from $335 to $450.

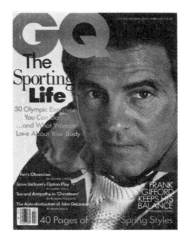

tian Dior, Hickey-Freeman, Pierre Cardin, Nino Cerruti and Johnny Carson. A wide variety of styling and fabrics are offered. Prices range from $450 down to $150. See your retailer for selections, or write:

Hartmarx Corp.
101 N. Wacker Dr.
Chicago, IL 60606

GQ—GENTLEMEN'S QUARTERLY

$18/12 issues per year
350 Madison Ave.
New York, NY 10017

GQ is a quarterly in name only. However, its monthly issues are a reliable resource for keeping track of styles in men's clothing. The male executive does not have many options in this respect, while a woman can find fashions pictured in many media. GQ is for the male executive who wants fresh ideas for his wardrobe.

THE SUCCESS IMAGE: A GUIDE FOR THE BETTER-DRESSED BUSINESSWOMAN

Vicki Keltner and Mike Holsey
1982/78 pp./$5.95
Gulf Publishing Co.
Box 2608
Houston, TX 77001

This book focuses on wardrobe and how it can enhance a woman executive's business image. Author Keltner is a management consultant and author Holsey is a custom tailor who specializes in clothes for women. They provide very specific advice about wardrobe selection, with heavy emphasis on suits. Styling details are spotlighted and sketches illustrate the text.

WORKING WOMAN

$18/12 issues per year
342 Madison Ave.
New York, NY 10173

Focusing on career planning and building, this monthly offers counsel and practical coaching for the woman executive. There are articles about career opportunities as well as accounts

of successful careers. Regular monthly departments deal with various aspects of management. The magazine also spotlights such subjects as personal finance, fitness, wardrobe, travel and life-styles.

THREE GUIDELINES FOR CHOOSING COLORS

1. Always choose a color that will make your skin look its best. Color is powerful. It can make us look sad, depressed or even unhealthy. Likewise, wearing our best colors can help to smooth out facial wrinkles and can help make us look healthy.
2. Choose colors that will enhance your hair color. Of course, you want the color of your hair to look interesting rather than dull and drab. Medium-blond and gray-haired women, in particular, have this problem.
3. Select reds that will match and complement the rosy glow of your natural complexion. Your blood tone is the color that you blush, flush and sunburn. The blood tone is visible just inside the lower lip. Colors that clash with the red in your face will be devastating. Reds are versatile.

From: *The Success Image: A Guide for the Better-Dressed Businesswoman*, Vicki Keltner and Mike Holsey (Houston: Gulf Publishing Co., 1982)

A WOMAN'S GUIDE TO BUSINESS AND SOCIAL SUCCESS
Ruth Tolman
1967, 1982/431 pp./$18.20
Milady Publishing Corp.
3839 White Plains Rd.
Bronx, NY 10467

This guide is a primer on personal development and image for women. Much of the material here is basic, but the book is comprehensive and is illustrated extensively with line drawings. The author gives detailed coaching on poise as well as the basics of beauty care. A separate section is devoted to wardrobe, and the author offers individual chapters of coaching on posture, exercise routines and nutrition.

10 ORGANIZATIONS FOR EXECUTIVES

Listed below are 10 organizations of broad interest to executives. Not included are associations devoted to such professional specializations as law and accounting.

Administrative Management Society
2360 Maryland Rd.
Willow Grove, PA 19090

American Management Associations
135 W. 50th St.
New York, NY 10020

WOMEN EXECUTIVES AND THE BUSINESS SUIT

The business suit is right for all women because its design is classic. The classic look can be described as tailored, timeless, traditional and basic. Solid-colored suits chosen from smooth-textured fabrics such as gabardine or flannel are appropriate for business. Stripes, paisley and foulard designs are suitable for ties and scarves. Wearing the classic business suit helps women . . . to be taken seriously. Women who are fragile and delicate looking will look as if they can be given a responsible position and do a good job. The business suit is also correct for the woman who has the bold look. It helps them to appear confident without being threatening.

From: *The Success Image: A Guide for the Better-Dressed Business Woman*, Vicki Keltner and Mike Holsey (Houston: Gulf Publishing Co., 1982)

American Marketing Association
250 S. Wacker Dr.
Chicago, IL 60606

American Society for
    Personnel Administration
30 Park St.
Berea, OH 44017

American Society for
    Training and Development
600 Maryland Ave., S.W.
Washington, DC 20024

Business and Professional
    Womens National Federation
2012 Massachusetts Ave., N.W.
Washington, DC 20036

Industrial Management Society
570 Northwest Hwy.
Des Plaines, IL 60016

National Association of Manufacturers
1776 F St., N.W.
Washington, DC 20006

National Management Association
2210 Arbor Blvd.
Dayton, OH 45439

North American Society
    for Corporate Planning
300 Arcade Sq.
Dayton, OH 45402

ENCYCLOPEDIA OF NATIONAL AND INTERNATIONAL ASSOCIATIONS

The *Encyclopedia of Associations* is a five-volume reference resource. The basic volume is Volume 1, *National Organizations of the U.S.*, which provides more than 16,500 detailed entries in its 18th edition (1,930 pp. in two parts, $170). The encyclopedia's other volumes cover international organizations, offer a geographic and executive index and list new associations and projects as well as research activities and funding programs.

Gale Research Co.
Book Tower
Detroit, MI 48226

CONNOISSEUR

$19.95/12 issues per year
224 W. 57th St.
New York, NY 10019

A magazine about things elegant and beautiful, here is a resource for the search for style. Its pages will sharpen and test your taste with a variety that ranges from the fine arts to fine. wines. The coverage includes fashions, travel, architecture and interior design. The advertising is lavish with illustration. The collector and the traveler will find everything here.

SUNBELT EXECUTIVE
$20/4 issues per year
6666 Morrison Rd.
New Orleans, LA 70126

Life-style is as much in the spotlight in this quarterly as are the business interests of executive readers. The magazine reports on business news in the sunbelt states, but there is equal emphasis on such topics as furnishing the executive office, personal health and travel.

THE ETIQUETTE OF THE HANDSHAKE

The most established form of etiquette in our society is the handshake. It is absolutely an insult to refuse to shake hands with someone, especially in a business situation. Even if your right hand is broken or not shakable for some physical reason, you must offer your other hand, with an apology for not being able to perform the proper amenity.

There was a time when it was proper to wait for a woman to offer her hand to respect her preference. Now it is expected that both people will automatically put forth their hands together. It is not rude to forget to offer one's hand, but it is definitely bad manners not to accept a hand that is offered. Even business rivals are expected to perform this small courtesy with each other as an acknowledgment that our common humanity is more important than money.

From: *The New Office Etiquette*, George Mazzei (New York: Poseidon Press, 1983)

EXECUTIVE SECURITY

**CORPORATE AND INDUSTRIAL
SECURITY**
A. Lewis Russell
1980/275 pp./$16.95
Gulf Publishing Co.
Box 2608
Houston, TX 77001

This book provides a thorough introduction to security measures and technology. The author covers such subjects as corporate security programs, protection of company property and personnel, and safeguarding of company information. Especially useful are several checklists for security surveys.

SECURITY LETTER
$117/24 issues per year
166 E. 96th St.
New York, NY 10028

Covering all aspects of corporate security, this newsletter reports on such varied subjects as systems and products, services, financial controls, personnel evaluation and insurance strategy. Included are executive protection and computer security. The newsletter offers a continuing survey of what is happening in this field.

SECURITY LETTER SOURCE BOOK
Robert McCrie, Editor
1983/350 pp./$75
Butterworth Publishers
80 Montvale Ave.
Stoneham, MA 02180

Compiled by the staff of the *Security Letter*, this comprehensive directory is a guide to ser-

A good security program seeks to protect the company in all its parts and in all its activities— in an operational sense, then, security transcends all departments within a company. The program should protect personnel, plants, offices, equipment, material, operations, methods, procedures and ... even the company's reputation and good name.

From: *Corporate and Industrial Security*, A. Lewis Russell (Houston: Gulf Publishing Co., 1980)

vices, suppliers and manufacturers in the security field. Categories range from security consultants to sources of security products and systems. Company listings provide detailed background information.

LEGAL ASPECTS OF PRIVATE SECURITY

Arthur J. Bilek, John C. Klotter
  and R. Keegan Federal
1981/287 pp./$16.95
Anderson Publishing Co.
646 Main St.
Cincinnati, OH 45201

This handbook for security personnel provides a useful reference resource. The book covers such aspects of private security programs as

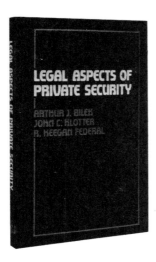

powers of detention and arrest as well as search and seizure. Of particular interest to executives responsible for company security are chapters on the criminal and civil liabilities of private security personnel.

EXECUTIVE PROTECTION MANUAL

Jan Reber and Paul Shaw
1976/282 pp./$39.95
MTI Teleprograms, Inc.
3710 Commercial Ave.
Northbrook, IL 60062

Prepared as a reference for security specialists, this guide covers all aspects of protecting executives from terrorist and criminal attack. Included are chapters on attack tactics, security surveys and checklists, and protection hardware and strategies. The authors also cover such topics as the use and training of bodyguards and the special problems of the executive's family.

EQUIPMENT FOR EXECUTIVE PROTECTION

CCS Communication Control, Inc., markets a wide selection of security equipment. Its offerings include devices for detecting wiretaps and bugs, bomb detectors, alarm systems and such personal protection equipment as bullet-proof vests. Among the firm's consulting services are security evaluations and training seminars. Write for catalog:

CCS Communication Control, Inc.
633 3rd Ave.
New York, NY 10017

TERRORISM: THE EXECUTIVE'S GUIDE TO SURVIVAL
Paul Fuqua and Jerry V. Wilson
1978/158 pp./$16.95
Gulf Publishing Co.
Box 2608
Houston, TX 77001

Security specialists, the authors present a guidebook on dealing with the threats of bombings, kidnappings and extortion. They focus primarily on bombings. Included are detailed descriptions of various bomb types, in-

These are the zones in conducting a bomb search (*from* Terrorism: The Executive's Guide to Survival).

cluding mail bombs, as well as methods for dealing with them. The authors cover evacuation and search procedures in detail. Chapters on kidnapping deal with both prevention and response to an abduction.

SPECIALIZED TRAINING FOR EXECUTIVE PROTECTION

Executive Security International offers training courses for executives as well as specialists in executive security. The training includes evasive driving, handgun shooting, hand-to-hand defense, demolition search, electronic security and emergency medical skills. The firm also sells a series of training manuals. For a kit of catalog and course information ($5), write:

Executive Security International, Ltd.
720 E. Hyman Ave.
Aspen, CO 81611

SECTION 2

Essential Services

LEGAL RESOURCES

**THE LIABILITIES OF OFFICE:
INDEMNIFICATION AND
INSURANCE OF CORPORATE
OFFICERS AND DIRECTORS**
Michael A. Schaeftler
1976/326 pp./$22.50
Little, Brown & Co.
34 Beacon St.
Boston, MA 02106

The author, an attorney, writes about the current legal status of the accountability of corporate officers and directors for their acts. Increasingly, suits by stockholders result in individual liability, causing officers and directors to seek the protection of indemnification and insurance. The author studies these measures in detail and provides background on all aspects of this subject.

At a time when physicians are alarmed over the number of malpractice suits and the high rates of insurance premiums, and attorneys and accountants face a rising tide of claims by dissatisfied consumers of their services, it is no wonder that directors and officers feel growing pressures for higher standards of performance and accountability and fear that stockholders' suits will result in individual liability.

> From: *The Liabilities of Office: Indemnification and Insurance of Corporate Officers and Directors*, Michael A Schaeftler (Boston: Little, Brown & Co., 1976)

**CORPORATE EXECUTIVE'S
LEGAL HANDBOOK**
John C. Howell
1980/132 pp./$5.95
Prentice-Hall, Inc.
Englewood Cliffs, NJ 07632

The author offers a basic introduction to the legal aspects of corporate organization and management and how they affect the executive. The book details the legal duties, obligations and responsibilities of corporate officials and it focuses on the liabilities they can face. While the perspective here is on the smaller company, the author presents a broad understanding of corporate law.

TALLYING THE PENALTIES OF ANTITRUST VIOLATIONS

Violations of the antitrust and trade regulation laws can be punished severely. . . . Violations of various provisions can result in dismemberment of a company, imprisonment of its officers and employees, cumulative fines, liability for treble damages to parties injured by violations, seizure of goods and a wide variety of decrees or orders narrowly regulating the future conduct of offending firms and individuals. And, as we shall see also, there are heavy indirect penalties for transgressions against these laws. Major antitrust litigation is notoriously long and notoriously costly. What promised to be a relatively uncomplicated deceptive practices matter before the Federal Trade Commission consumed 16 years from the time of complaint to final disposition by the courts. A major monopoly case may drag on for a genera-

tion. Even an unexceptional case in this area may consume two to five years. Large investments in time inevitably result in large outlays of money. Costs alone, not including attorneys' fees, easily can run into six figures in antitrust cases. When attorneys' fees and executive and employee time lost through file searches, preparation for trial and attendance at hearings are included, even a victory may evoke the old adage that "the operation was a success, but the patient died." To the sum of these costs must be added the frightful indirect costs in reputation and good will that may result from a well-publicized violation. In this age of public relations possible damage to reputation alone compels the prescient businessman to consider the applicability of the antitrust laws to every phase of his operations.

From: *An Antitrust Primer*, Earl W. Kintner (New York: Macmillan Publishing Co., 1973)

THE COMPLETE GUIDE TO BUSINESS CONTRACTS
John C. Howell
1980/147 pp./$5.95
Prentice-Hall, Inc.
Englewood Cliffs, NJ 07632

An attorney and specialist in corporate law, the author presents a primer on business contracts. He writes for the layperson, explaining both the theory and the practice of contracts. His premise is that the reader can negotiate and prepare many of the most common business contracts without the aid of an attorney. Included are sample contract forms. In an especially useful chapter, the author details the main parts of the Uniform Commercial Code. Another chapter deals with employment contracts, including a checklist of aspects to be considered for inclusion and a sample contract form.

WASHINGTON FINANCIAL REPORTS
$470/50 issues per year
1231 25th St., N.W.
Washington, DC 20037

This detailed weekly newsletter reports on federal regulatory developments that affect banks and other financial institutions. Coverage includes news summaries, special reports and complete texts of selected documents.

DAILY UPDATE FROM WASHINGTON

A comprehensive information service on regulatory, legislative and judicial developments, the *Daily Report for Executives* provides extended coverage from Washington. The annual subscription for the publication is $3,550. It presents both summary information and de-

LEGAL ROLES OF BOARD, MANAGEMENT, SHAREHOLDERS

Perhaps the most striking aspect of the received legal model is the distinctive position of management. Simple business organizations are managed either by the owners or by persons who are legally agents of the owners. Under the received legal model of the corporation, however, the officers are agents not of the shareholders but of the board, while the board itself is conceived of not as an agent of the shareholders but as an independent institution. For example, while the authority of an agent can normally be terminated by his principal at any time, directors are normally removable by shareholders only for good cause shown. Similarly, while an agent must normally follow his principal's instructions, shareholders have no legal power to give binding instructions to the board on matters within its powers. Any study of corporate structure must therefore consider two very different interfaces: that between the shareholders and the managerial organs taken together, and that between the managerial organs themselves.

From: *The Structure of the Corporation*, Melvin Aron Eisenberg (Boston: Little, Brown & Co., 1976)

tailed reports on a wide variety of subjects related to business and economics. Included are the texts of major legislation and court decisions as well as economic statistics. The publisher also offers a broad range of other reports and information services from the capital that cover business regulation, economics, legal matters, labor relations, environment and safety and tax management. Write:

Bureau of National Affairs, Inc.
1231 25th St., N.W.
Washington, DC 20037

FTC: WATCH
$396/22 issues per year
Box 2220
Springfield, VA 22152

Reporting exclusively on the Federal Trade Commission, this newsletter covers such aspects as mergers and acquisitions as well as antitrust enforcement. It covers all areas and stages of the agency's regulatory activities, including the rule-making process. Of particular interest are cases involving advertising claims. The publisher also offers a weekly newsletter titled the *FTC Freedom of Information Log* ($170), which lists requests for material from the agency's files.

HOW ARBITRATION WORKS
Frank Elkouri and
  Edna Asper Elkouri
1960, 1983/819 pp./$30
BNA Books
1231 25th St., N.W.
Washington, DC 20037

Formal arbitration of disputes has become a standard practice in labor-management relations and few executives do not have some contact with the process during their careers. This guidebook presents a comprehensive study of the workings of arbitration. The authors, both attorneys, use arbitration cases extensively to illustrate their text, and the book is designed as a resource for professionals and laymen alike.

MANAGEMENT CONSULTANTS

CONSULTING FOR ORGANIZATIONAL CHANGE
Fritz Steele
1975/202 pp./$8
University of Massachusetts Press
Box 429
Amherst, MA 01004

The author examines the social and psychological elements involved in the consulting process and the organizational changes it can produce. His advice is directed both to the professional outside consultant and to the "inside consultant," who can influence change within his or her own organization. Presenting much of this material in a humorous style, the author provides a very useful and readable perspective on consulting.

Consultation is not simply the mechanical tossing of expertise toward a painful client; it is an experience in shared resources. There is an appropriate place for technique, tactic and form. However, it is the substance and spirit in the helping process which gives consultation its unique humanness.

The core of the act of helping is the interaction of two or more people relating in order to improve some person, situation or thing. The quality of those dynamics determines if the encounter results in more help than harm, more joy than sorrow and more growth than death.

From: *The Client-Consultant Handbook*, Chip R. Bell and Leonard Nadler (Houston: Gulf Publishing Co., 1979)

THE CLIENT-CONSULTANT HANDBOOK
Chip R. Bell and
   Leonard Nadler, Editors
1979/279 pp./$17.95
Gulf Publishing Co.
Box 2608
Houston, TX 77001

This book on the client-consultant relationship is a collection of 23 articles by consultants. Their advice for executives ranges from how to choose a consultant to the ethical considerations involved in the process. The nature of the consulting relationship receives careful study, and the authors offer valuable counsel on how to make it most productive.

THE INTERNAL CONSULTANT
Denis J. Lovelace
1982/56 pp./$5
Exposition Press, Inc.
Box 2120
Smithtown, NY 11787

The author outlines the qualifications and functions of the internal consultant and the internal consulting team. Focusing on training and experience, the author shows how the internal consultant applies skills to management needs. He also examines the workings of a consulting team, pointing out pitfalls as well as indicating areas for optimum results.

HOW TO BE YOUR OWN MANAGEMENT CONSULTANT
Kenneth J. Albert
1978/207 pp./$22.95
McGraw-Hill Book Co.
1221 Avenue of the Americas
New York, NY 10020

The author's premise is that, by learning the consultant's approach, an executive can have comparable success in problem solving. A management consultant by profession, the author first explains the basics of the consulting process. Then he applies the approach to a series of common business situations such as strategic planning, acquisition evaluation and executive search. Included are chapters on setting up an internal consulting system as well as on buying outside services.

MANAGEMENT CONSULTANTS: FINDING YOUR WAY TO THE RIGHT ONE

Listing more than 700 firms in the U.S. and foreign countries, the annual *Directory of Management Consultants* is a valuable source of basic information. Included in each listing are address and phone number, a brief profile of the firm, names of principals, professional affiliations, services offered and industries served. Priced at $48.50, the directory also indexes the listings by the name of the key principal and by geographical location, as well as by services offered and industries served. The publisher also markets *100 Leading Management Consulting Firms in the U.S. Today* ($2), a concise listing showing only name, address and phone number. Write:

Consultants News
Templeton Rd.
Fitzwilliam, NH 03447

21 MAJOR MANAGEMENT CONSULTING FIRMS

Directories list several hundred management consulting firms in the U.S. Many of them concentrate their work in specific regions of the

Some consultants try to disguise and mystify their work, as if their results were somehow obtained by magic. But, in fact, no magic exists. Consultants solve business problems with a simple, pragmatic approach, and they successfully use the same approach for almost all problems, regardless of the problem's nature or type.

From: *How to Be Your Own Management Consultant*, Kenneth J. Albert (New York: McGraw-Hill Book Co., 1978)

country and some of them specialize in one or more aspects of management. Below, however, are listed 21 of the largest firms. All have branch offices in major cities and all offer a broad range of services (* indicates accounting firm with consulting services). Your inquiry letter will bring literature about services.

*Arthur Andersen & Co.
Management Information Consulting Div.
69 W. Washington St.
Chicago, IL 60602

Bain & Co., Inc.
3 Faneuil Hall Marketplace
Boston, MA 02109

Theodore Barry & Associates
1520 Wilshire Blvd.
Los Angeles, CA 90017

Booz Allen & Hamilton, Inc.
101 Park Ave.
New York, NY 10178

The Boston Consulting Group, Inc.
1 Boston Pl.
Boston, MA 02106

*Coopers & Lybrand
Management Consulting Services
1251 Avenue of the Americas
New York, NY 10020

Cresap, McCormick & Paget, Inc.
245 Park Ave.
New York, NY 10167

*Deloitte, Haskins & Sells
Management Advisory Services
1114 Avenue of the Americas
New York, NY 10036

*Ernst & Whinney
2000 National City Center
Cleveland, OH 44114

*Alexander Grant & Co.
3900 Prudential Plaza
Chicago, IL 60601

Harbridge House, Inc.
11 Arlington St.
Boston, MA 02116

The Hay Group
229 S. 18th St.
Philadelphia, PA 19103

A. T. Kearney, Inc.
222 S. Riverside Plaza
Chicago, IL 60606

Arthur D. Little, Inc.
25 Acorn Pk.
Cambridge, MA 02140

Management Analysis Center, Inc.
1430 Massachusetts Ave.
Cambridge, MA 02138

*McGladrey, Hendrickson & Co.
1699 E. Woodfield Rd.
Schaumburg, IL 60195

McKinsey & Co., Inc.
55 E. 52nd St.
New York, NY 10022

*Peat, Marwick, Mitchell & Co.
345 Park Ave.
New York, NY 10154

*Touche, Ross & Co.
Management Consulting Div.
1633 Broadway
New York, NY 10019

Towers, Perrin, Forster & Crosby
600 3rd Ave.
New York, NY 10016

Arthur Young & Co.
277 Park Ave.
New York, NY 10172

AN INTERNATIONAL GUIDE TO CONSULTANTS BY THE THOUSANDS

The *Consultants and Consulting Organizations Directory* provides details on more than 7,000 firms, individuals and organizations active in 135 specialized fields in the U.S. and 50 other countries. Priced at $255, the directory's fifth edition contains 1,385 pages. Entries include name, address, phone number, principals, branch offices, description of services and clients and a listing of areas of specialization. Entries are indexed by specializations, names of principals and geographic location. The 135 areas of specialization range widely through such subjects as advertising, computers, management, personnel, product design, research and development. The publisher also sells, on a subscription basis, directory supplements titled *New Consultants* ($170) as well as a reference guide titled *Who's Who in Consulting* ($135). For further information, write:

Gale Research Co.
Book Tower
Detroit, MI 48226

If you need a consultant to tell you what to do or how to find out, then *you're* the problem.

From: *Further Up the Organization*, Robert Townsend (New York: Alfred A. Knopf, 1984)

RESOURCES FOR MEETINGS, CONVENTIONS, TRADE SHOWS

MEETING-PLANNING SERVICES FROM WESTERN UNION

One Call is Western Union's name for its meeting-planning services, which let you take advantage of the company's communications network. You simply phone the service and provide such basic information as meeting location, number attending (from 50 to 150) and specific requirements. Within five business days One Call delivers a written report to you detailing all necessary information and including firm bids from hotel, airline and ground transportation companies. You then make the bookings. There is a one-time subscription charge of $75 for One Call. There is a $25 charge if you book just one kind of supplier, $15 if you book two, and only $10 if you book all three kinds of suppliers. For literature, write:

Western Union Corp.
1 Lake St.
Upper Saddle River, NJ 07458

MARRIOTT'S NETWORK OF MEETING FACILITIES

Marriott offers specialized facilities and services for large meetings in a network of hotels across the country. Specifically designed for meetings and conventions, the hotels are located in 12 major cities, including Atlanta, Boston, Chicago, Los Angeles, New Orleans and Washington, D.C. For further information, write:

Marriott Corp.
1 Marriott Dr.
Washington, DC 20058

MEETING NEWS
$36/16 issues per year
1515 Broadway
New York, NY 10036

This is a trade magazine of the meeting and convention industry. It is aimed at planners and it is a storehouse of information and a showcase for all the places where business meets and convenes. The lavish advertising, for instance, will give you years of ideas for future sales-meeting sites. Articles by professionals report on techniques for successful meetings. Coverage ranges from product marketing at exhibits to the technology of teleconferencing. (Your management position may qualify you for a free subscription to this controlled-circulation magazine.)

SPECIALISTS IN COMPANY BOOTHS FOR EXHIBITS

Greyhound Exhibitgroup, Inc., designs, builds and manages company booths for conventions and trade shows. Specialists work with clients to plan and construct booths and displays and then the firm handles storage, transportation, set-up, show supervision, dismantling and stor-

age until next use. Booths range from simple designs to elaborate exhibits with audiovisual elements, scale models or special animated effects. Booths can be custom-built for rental or for purchase. Compact portable display systems are also available. The firm has branch operations in Atlanta, Chicago, Cincinnati, Dallas/Fort Worth, Las Vegas, Los Angeles, New York and San Francisco. For literature, write:

Greyhound Exhibitgroup, Inc.
2800 Lively Blvd.
Elk Grove Village, IL 60007

VERSATILE SPECIALISTS IN TRADE SHOW SERVICES

The Freeman Companies offer a full range of services for trade shows, conventions, special

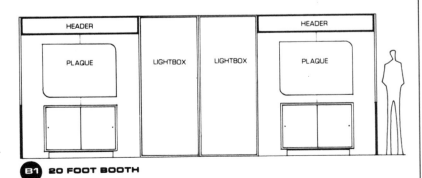

Greyhound Exhibitgroup design for a 20-foot display booth.

B1 **20 FOOT BOOTH**

exhibits and corporate meetings. The organization consists of four companies: Freeman Decorating Co., AVW Audio Visual, Inc., Freeman Design/Display Co. and Sullivan Transfer Co. Coordinated services include design, construction, storage, shipping and assembling of booths and displays. A wide range of audiovisual equipment and services are available. For literature and further information, write:

The Freeman Companies
1300 Wycliff Ave.
Dallas, TX 75207

PORTABLE EXHIBITS
FOR TRADE SHOW DISPLAY

The Folio Co. offers some efficient options in its line of compact and portable exhibit units for use at trade shows and conventions. The Facet model, for instance, is based on 12 Velcro-covered panels that lock together to form an 8-by-10-foot display. Each panel weighs 6 pounds and the whole display fits into two carrying cases. The unit is finished in a combination of two colors, with a wide variety of colors to choose from. Custom services are available. The complete display is priced at $4,298.42

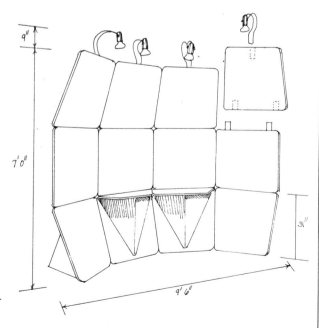

Design and dimensions of the Facet portable exhibit by the Folio Co.

and quantity discounts are offered. For literature and further information, write:

Folio Co.
56 Summer St.
Shrewsbury, MA 01545

PORTABLE DISPLAYS THAT FLY WITH YOU TO TRADE SHOWS

Your display at trade shows and conventions may be more complex and costly than it needs to be. Expo Communications offers a portable alternative to the typical booth. Its Expoframe modular display system provides a variety of options in both tabletop and full-size models. The units combine a metal framework with shelves and panels covered in fabric or vinyl. No tools are needed for assembly and lightweight travel cases are available. Displays range in weight from 17 pounds to 262 pounds. Tabletop prices range from $436.70 to $888 and full-size units vary in price from $827.75 to $2,531.75. For catalog, write:

Expo Communications, Inc.
1206 N. 23rd St.
Wilmington, NC 28402

WORKING WITH SPECIALISTS FOR TRADE SHOW EXHIBITS

Once you establish trade show goals, many firms can assist you in the concept, design and construction of customized exhibits. They'll also help you with graphics, props, animations, photographs, transparencies, sound equipment, projectors, artwork and other details. These firms either sell exhibits for permanent use, rent them for one-time use or lease exhibits for a specified period. Some even install and dismantle booths; set up telephones; provide furniture; consolidate charges for freight, crating, storage, refurbishing and insurance costs; ensure that you meet city building codes; and provide appropriate electrical outlets that match the hall's voltage level. Many also provide assistance in showroom design, mobile exhibiting, private show planning, dealer displays, sales meetings and point-of-purchase displays. Allow these firms anywhere from 60-90 days for construction of your exhibit.

From: *Marketing Problem Solver*, Cochrane Chase and Kenneth L. Barasch (Radnor, PA: Chilton Book Co., 1977)

COMPANY AND EXECUTIVE RELOCATION

HOW TO SELECT A BUSINESS SITE: THE EXECUTIVE'S LOCATION GUIDE
Jon E. Browning
1980/225 pp./$21.95
McGraw-Hill Book Co.
1221 Avenue of the Americas
New York, NY 10020

This handbook is a comprehensive guide for company relocation or expansion to a new site. The author covers planning and organization, assistance from state governments, the selection process and the transfer of personnel. A number of useful checklists are included, covering such factors as energy, construction, labor and transportation requirements. Along with step-by-step directions, the author spells out various pitfalls and problem situations. He also presents specific cost data for employee relocation.

For the dynamic, growth-oriented company . . . it is critical not only to attract the very best people but also to retain them. As a result, the very rural location that offers shelter from high hourly wages, aggressive unions or expensive taxation may also offer little attraction to the highly skilled and highly motivated employees who can find suitable jobs in more stimulating surroundings.

From: *How to Select a Business Site: The Executive's Location Guide*, Jon E. Browning (New York: McGraw-Hill Book Co., 1980)

COMPANY RELOCATION SERVICES BY FANTUS

The Fantus Co. specializes in location consulting, offering a variety of services that include relocation management for both office and plant facilities. The firm prepares studies of potential sites, analyzing such factors as community quality of life and comparative operating costs. Its other consulting services include distribution systems. For literature, write:

Fantus Co., Inc.
75 Main St.
Milburn, NJ 07041

ADVANTAGES OF A CONSULTANT IN A RELOCATION PROGRAM

1. The sporadic nature of the task may not justify supporting an internal function.
2. Maintaining confidentiality may be of utmost importance either to avoid community or employee public relations problems or to keep company officials from being the target of real estate sales efforts.
3. A consultant may be less biased than an internal group.
4. The outside consultant is more likely to make important business issues other than real estate considerations a part of the recommendations.
5. A consultant can interrogate at all levels of the client organization to establish the objectives for relocating or expanding—a task that may be more difficult for an insider.
6. More easily than those within a company, the consultant often can bring together and coordinate the talents of other specialists, as in aerial photography, distribution, etc.

From: *How to Select a Business Site: The Executive's Location Guide* (New York: McGraw-Hill Book Co., 1980)

RELOCATION SERVICES BY MERRILL LYNCH

Merrill Lynch Relocation Management provides a variety of services to facilitate transfer of company executives and employees. Included are sale of home and search for new housing, mortgage finance, consulting on relocation policy and management of group moves. The firm offers a free publication for executives titled *Relocation Management Quarterly,* which reports on such subjects as mortgage finance and tax and legal considerations. Write:

Merrill Lynch Relocation
    Management, Inc.
4 Corporate Park Dr.
White Plains, NY 10604

TRY POWER SUPPLIERS AS INFORMATION SOURCES

Public utility companies can sometimes be valuable sources of information when you are considering moving, expanding or starting operations in an area. The Public Service Electric & Gas Co. of New Jersey, for instance, offers the services of its Area Development Department to companies seeking site-location assistance in the state. Also available from PSE&G is the 38-page illustrated booklet *Brainpower: High Technology in New Jersey,* a review of high-tech industry in the state that also provides an overview of developments in this field. For literature and further information, write:

PSE&G
Box 570
Newark, NJ 07101

RELOCATION SPECIALISTS IN HOME-SALE SERVICES

Providing home-sale assistance to the executives and employees of client companies, Homequity, Inc., offers a wide range of relocation services. The firm offers consultation on corporate relocation policy, and its specialists are available to plan and coordinate the movement of entire company divisions or facilities. Other services include job-search assistance for the employed spouse of a transferee. For literature, write:

Homequity, Inc.
249 Danbury Rd.
Wilton, CT 06897

NATIONAL REAL ESTATE INVESTOR

$42/13 issues per year
6255 Barfield Rd.
Atlanta, GA 30328

This trade magazine covers all aspects of the real estate field, including construction, development, finance, investment and management. In a continuing series, it presents detailed reports on metropolitan areas around the country. Whether you are interested in investment opportunities or in accommodations for your company, this magazine is an inside source of useful information.

DIRECTORY DATA FOR DEALING WITH THE STATES AND TERRITORIES

Directory of State Industrial and Economic Departments (30 pages, $20) provides addresses and phone numbers of the capitols in the 50 states and the territories. The listings include industrial and economic development departments, commerce departments and purchasing agencies. Write:

B. Klein Publications
Box 8503
Coral Springs, FL 33065

A STATISTICAL LOOK AT JOB TRANSFERS

Atlas's 1970 survey showed that in 1969, 60 percent of all corporation executives could expect to be transferred at least once every three years throughout their career—a figure that had decreased to 11 percent by 1981 and remained steady in 1982.

As recently as five years ago, 51 percent of the companies responding to the survey indicated that an unwillingness to accept a transfer involving a move hindered the employee's career. According to this year's survey results, 35 percent of the companies stated their employees can expect a slowdown on the job path by declining to relocate.

From: *Survey of Corporate Moving Practices*, Atlas Van Lines, Inc. (Evansville, IN: Atlas Van Lines, Inc., 1983)

MICHIGAN: INFORMATION AND SERVICES FOR BUSINESS

A major industrial state, Michigan offers several programs for companies interested in locating there. Services include site location, financing assistance and the recruiting and training of labor. The programs are detailed in a comprehensive information kit. Included is the *Directory of Business Resources in Michigan*, a very useful listing of state and federal agencies and publications as well as major business organizations. Write:

Michigan Dept. of Commerce
Box 30225
Lansing, MI 48909

SAMPLING THE SOUTH: WELCOME TO THE CHATTANOOGA AREA

Southern states and cities are among the most active in attracting companies to relocate in their region, and Chattanooga is an instructive example. The city and the tri-state area (Tennessee, Alabama and Georgia) offer a valuable kit of background information. Especially useful is the report *Facts & Statistics*, which presents detailed marketing data for the area as well as information about the work force, transportation, utilities, financial resources, government services and taxes. Also included in the kit are separate reports on such subjects as industrial revenue bonds and industrial training in Tennessee. For the kit and other information, write:

Economic Development Council
Chattanooga Area Chamber of Commerce
1001 Market St.
Chattanooga, TN 37402

IOWA: DATA AND SERVICES AVAILABLE TO EXECUTIVES

Like comparable agencies in other states, the Iowa Development Commission provides information on business opportunities, resources, markets, available labor and transportation, financing, available sites and buildings. Ask for the brochure *Call One*, about the commission's regulatory information service, as well as the brochure *Iowa Chops 70% Off Your Taxes*. Also available are *Statistical Profile of Iowa* and the *Directory of Iowa Manufacturers*. Write:

Marketing Group
Iowa Development Commission
600 E. Court Ave.
Des Moines, IA 50309

PROMOTING INDUSTRY IN NORTH CAROLINA

If your company contemplates a new industrial site, North Carolina would like to help you find it there. The state offers a fully staffed program of industrial location services, including consultation on labor availability, taxes, finances and marketing. A useful resource is the *Directory of North Carolina Manufacturing Firms* ($35), published annually by the Department of Commerce. Another valuable source of economic data is the *Urban Atlas Series* (Urban Institute, University of North Carolina, Charlotte, NC 28223). For literature and further information, write:

North Carolina Dept. of Commerce
Industrial Development Div.
430 N. Salisbury St.
Raleigh, NC 27611

MARYLAND RESOURCES FOR COMPANY MOVES

The Maryland Office of Business and Industrial Development offers comprehensive publications and services to businesses interested in locating or expanding facilities in the state. Information covers socioeconomic data, financing, industrial properties, taxes, foreign trade zones, enterprise zones and business regulations. The agency publishes a useful series of *Opportunity Studies*, which describe locational advantages for selected growth industries.

Studies are available for high-technology industries, medical products and metalworking. For literature and further information, write:

Business and Industrial Development
45 Calvert St.
Annapolis, MD 21401

LOUISIANA: SERVICES FOR BUSINESS DEVELOPMENT

For companies interested in locating in the state, Louisiana offers a variety of services. It provides information and assistance for marketing and site location. Technical and financial assistance is also available. The state also publishes the annual *Directory of Louisiana Manufacturers* ($35), a detailed listing of almost 3,000 companies and their products. The directory is a valuable resource for research as well as for marketing industrial products. For further information, write:

Louisiana Dept. of Commerce
Box 44185
Baton Rouge, LA 70804

BUSINESS PUBLICATIONS WITH A LOCAL FOCUS

The Association of Area Business Publications represents 78 local, state and regional business magazines and tabloids in the U.S. and Canada. The publications are of importance as media for your company's advertising if you are in the business-to-business market. But they are equally important as resources for local information if you are researching product markets or a new plant or job location. For a membership directory, write:

Association of Area
  Business Publications
Box 829
Louisville, KY 40201

NEW ENGLAND BUSINESS
$24/20 issues per year
31 Milk St.
Boston, MA 02109

This magazine reports on business throughout the New England states, with broad coverage of all levels of commerce but with emphasis on medium and large companies. The reporting is thorough, making this magazine a sound resource for researching the region.

CALIFORNIA BUSINESS
$15/12 issues per year
6420 Wilshire Blvd.
Los Angeles, CA 90048

If you need to track the progress of business in California, here is a monthly that will serve you well. The magazine's coverage is broad and its style is polished. Feature articles focus on leading companies and executives as well as on varied aspects of business in the state. Special sections are devoted to articles about investments in the region as well as reports on real estate in California.

THE EXECUTIVE

$18/12 issues per year
3740 Campus Dr.
Newport Beach, CA 92660

This monthly gives you a window on the California business community. Each of its four local editions focuses on a specific part of the state (Orange County, Los Angeles, San Francisco, San Diego). The magazine highlights area business leaders in profile articles and provides regional economic reporting. Whether you are based in the state or have interests in it from afar, *The Executive* provides a way to keep tabs on California.

LOCAL BUSINESS JOURNALS FROM CORDOVAN PUBLISHING

Cordovan publishes weekly tabloids in 12 major cities in the U.S. The papers cover a city and its surrounding region, focusing on local business news and leading companies and executives. Such publications can provide a variety of valuable information for relocation, marketing and investment. The papers are published in the cities listed below. For further information, write to company headquarters.

Atlanta	Phoenix
Dallas/Fort Worth	Pittsburgh
Denver	San Diego
Houston	San Francisco
Los Angeles	Seattle
Miami	Washington

Cordovan Publishing Co.
5314 Bingle Rd.
Houston, TX 77092

RESOURCES FOR ADVERTISING AND PUBLIC RELATIONS

ADVICE FOR TOP EXECUTIVES ABOUT ADVERTISING PROGRAMS

American Business Press, Inc., an association of publishers, provides a useful resource for executives who need basic know-how about advertising. While its focus is on business-to-business advertising, the 32-page booklet *Top Management's Role in Directing, Budgeting and Evaluating Advertising Programs* is a helpful introduction to dealing with consumer advertising as well. The booklet briefly covers direct mail, public relations and trade shows as well as advertising. Write:

American Business Press, Inc.
205 E. 42nd St.
New York, NY 10017

TED BATES & CO.: A LOOK INSIDE THE WORKINGS OF AN AD AGENCY

One of the largest of the giant advertising agencies, Ted Bates & Co. offers a broad range of services in its worldwide operations. For a look inside these operations, the firm offers a 62-page booklet titled *This Is Ted Bates*, a review by Oscar Shisgall of its services on the occasion of its 40th anniversary. The booklet is a useful introduction to the workings of advertising, particularly in the descriptions of several of the firm's major ad campaigns. For a copy, write:

Ted Bates & Co., Inc.
1515 Broadway
New York, NY 10036

Fire the whole advertising department and your old agency. Then go get the best new agency you can. And concentrate your efforts on making it fun for them to create candid, effective advertising for you. Unless you've just done this, the odds favor that you have a bunch of bright people working at cross purposes to produce—at best—mediocre ads.

From: *Further Up the Organization*, Robert Townsend (New York: Alfred A. Knopf, 1984)

Every advertisement should be thought of as a contribution to the brand image.

Take whiskey. Why do some people choose Jack Daniel's while others choose Grand Dad or Taylor? Have they tried all three and compared the taste? Don't make me laugh. The reality is that these three brands have different *images* which appeal to different kinds of people. It isn't the whiskey they choose, it's the image. The brand image is 90 percent of what the distiller has to sell.

From: *Ogilvy on Advertising*, David Ogilvy (New York: Crown Publishers, Inc., 1983)

19 OF THE GIANTS AMONG AD AGENCIES

The services of an advertising agency are usually essential to the success of marketing operations. You may find the services your company needs with one of the hundreds of smaller local agencies or you may need to use one of the giants. Listed below are 19 of the largest agencies in the country, all of them well-known names in mass marketing.

N. W. Ayer, Inc.
1345 Avenue of the Americas
New York, NY 10105

BBDO International, Inc.
383 Madison Ave.
New York, NY 10017

Ted Bates & Co., Inc.
1515 Broadway
New York, NY 10036

Benton & Bowles, Inc.
909 3rd Ave.
New York, NY 10022

Bozell & Jacobs, Inc.
1 Dag Hammarskjold Plaza
New York, NY 10017

Leo Burnett Co., Inc.
Prudential Plaza
Chicago, IL 60601

Dancer Fitzgerald Sample, Inc.
405 Lexington Ave.
New York, NY 10174

D'Arcy-MacManus & Masius
360 Madison Ave.
New York, NY 10017

Doyle Dane Bernbach
437 Madison Ave.
New York, NY 10022

William Esty Co., Inc.
100 E. 42nd St.
New York, NY 10017

Foote Cone & Belding
401 N. Michigan Ave.
Chicago, IL 60611

Kenyon & Eckhardt, Inc.
200 Park Ave.
New York, NY 10166

McCann-Erickson Worldwide
485 Lexington Ave.
New York, NY 10017

Marsteller, Inc.
866 3rd Ave.
New York, NY 10022

Needham Harper & Steers, Inc.
909 3rd Ave.
New York, NY 10022

Ogilvy & Mather, Inc.
2 E. 48th St.
New York, NY 10017

Contrary to the belief of those who regard the words "public relations" and "publicity" as synonymous, they are not the same. *Publicity* is free advertising that a company obtains by sending out prepared information about its activities to a newspaper, magazine or television or radio station for reporting. It is a part of the total public relations effort, but true public relations gives direction to the entire image-building concept.

From: *The Businessman's Guide to Advertising & Sales Promotion*, Herschell Gordon Lewis (New York: McGraw-Hill Book Co., 1974)

J. Walter Thompson Co.
466 Lexington Ave.
New York, NY 10017

Wells Rich Greene, Inc.
767 5th Ave.
New York, NY 10153

Young & Rubicam, Inc.
285 Madison Ave.
New York, NY 10017

ADVERTISING AGE
$104/104 issues per year
740 Rush St.
Chicago, IL 60611

This trade newspaper will keep you well informed about the latest trends in advertising as well as the marketing campaigns of your competitors. The publication covers both print and broadcasting media and it reports on personnel shifts and new-product introductions. There is also regular coverage of legislation and regulations affecting national and international marketing.

PUBLIC RELATIONS: DIRECTORIES OF PR FIRMS AND EXECUTIVES

Updated annually, *O'Dwyer's Directory of Public Relations Firms* lists more than a thousand PR companies as well as thousands of individual PR counselors. The directory carries almost 300 pages of information and is priced at $60. Listings describe services and include numbers of employees and names of clients. Client organizations are cross-indexed for easy access and the PR firms are indexed both geographically and by specializations. The 50 largest PR firms are ranked by net fee income. The

It takes a big idea to attract the attention of consumers and get them to buy your product. Unless your advertising contains a big idea, it will pass like a ship in the night.

I doubt if more than one campaign in a hundred contains a big idea. I am supposed to be one of the more fertile inventors of big ideas, but in my long career as a copywriter I have not had more than 20, if that. Big ideas come from the unconscious. This is true in art, in science and in advertising. But your unconscious has to be *well informed*, or your idea will be irrelevant. Stuff your conscious mind with information, then unhook your rational thought process. You can help this process by going for a long walk, or taking a hot bath, or drinking half a pint of claret. Suddenly, if the telephone line from your unconscious is open, a big idea wells up within you.

From: *Ogilvy on Advertising*, David Ogilvy (New York: Crown Publishers, Inc. 1983)

A total marketing program is necessary for the ultimate sale of a product or service. Advertising, while very important for certain products such as cosmetics, over-the-counter drugs and others, is only one of the tools used to make the marketing system function. Too often, it appears, we give advertising too much or too little credit for what it can accomplish in the overall sale of a product.

From: *Essentials of Advertising Strategy*, Don E. Schultz (Chicago: Crain Books, 1981)

publisher also markets *O'Dwyer's Directory of Corporate Communications* ($70) as well as *O'Dwyer's Directory of Public Relations Executives* ($70). For brochures, write:

J. R. O'Dwyer Co., Inc.
271 Madison Ave.
New York, NY 10016

HOW TO PROMOTE YOUR OWN BUSINESS

Gary Blake and Robert W. Bly
1983/241 pp./$10.95
New American Library
1633 Broadway
New York, NY 10019

This how-to guidebook is written for the entrepreneur promoting a small business. But it is an equally valuable resource for the executive of the giant corporation who is a newcomer to the theory and practice of promotion of all kinds. The authors talk about media relations and publicity, about advertising, marketing and trade shows. They also present a detailed primer on the writing of press releases and advertising copy as well as on the design, production and printing of such material.

NINE LEADING FIRMS IN PUBLIC RELATIONS

Effective public relations can promote your company as well as its products or services.

Your own success grows in the process. The scale of the job that needs to be done will influence the kind of PR capability you want. An in-house staff may be required or you may turn to an outside agency. Public relations services are widely available, from firms that range from one-person operations to large companies. The nine firms listed below are among the largest in the country. Your inquiry letter will bring detailed information about the services they offer.

Ayer Public Relations Service
1345 Avenue of the Americas
New York, NY 10105

Bozell & Jacobs Public Relations
1 Dag Hammarskjold Plaza
New York, NY 10017

Carl Byoir & Associates
380 Madison Ave.
New York, NY 10017

Doremus & Co.
120 Broadway
New York, NY 10271

Daniel J. Edelman, Inc.
221 N. LaSalle St.
Chicago, IL 60601

Usually the invitation to a news conference is extended by phone. This procedure serves two purposes. It establishes a sense of immediacy and it enables the caller to ask for a commitment—will the medium be on hand or won't it? Too aggressive an approach can turn off a potential attendee; too timid an approach can cause an editor to decide the event lacks importance.

From: *How to Handle Your Own Public Relations,* H. Gordon Lewis (Chicago: Nelson-Hall, Inc., 1977)

Hill & Knowlton
633 3rd Ave.
New York, NY 10017

Manning, Selvage & Lee
99 Park Ave.
New York, NY 10016

Ogilvy & Mather Public Relations
2 E. 48th St.
New York, NY 10017

Ruder Finn & Rotman
110 E. 59th St.
New York, NY 10022

HOW TO HANDLE YOUR OWN PUBLIC RELATIONS

H. Gordon Lewis
1976/251 pp./$19.95
Nelson-Hall, Inc.
111 N. Canal St.
Chicago, IL 60606

Whether you handle it yourself or hire a professional to do the job, good public relations for you or your company will be at its best when you understand the process. While this

TRACKING SALES VOLUME TO SPOT PROBLEM PRODUCTS

While the true profitability of a product is sometimes difficult to gauge with accuracy, most companies are able to pinpoint sales in units or dollars for even the least significant items in the product or service lines. When an upward slope of orders or billings for any product changes to a plateau or to a decline, it is not long before everyone involved becomes aware of it.

A discovery that sales volume is below target is, of course, a common occurrence. The issue to be determined is whether this is a blip of no consequence, or the start of continuing slippage. If it cannot be explained away entirely by shifting business conditions, it generally calls for common

remedies, e.g., beefing up the selling or promotion effort. It is the more serious situation—calling for more drastic action—that naturally generates still more concern.

Marshaling the evidence on these issues is usually a task for marketing management; and among the first questions to be asked is whether the product category as a whole is experiencing sluggish sales, or whether the firm's own product is out of line. Several marketing heads allege that sales managers often have a congenital leaning to over-optimism. And so they themselves take pains to insist on rigorous analyses of longer term prospects for products whose sales are lagging.

From: *Business Strategies for Problem Products,* David S. Hopkins (New York: The Conference Board, Inc., 1981)

11 TIPS FOR STAGING NEWS CONFERENCES

1. Start within 10 minutes of the announced time.
2. Don't make long, flowery speeches.
3. Have press kits on hand to distribute to all media representatives, with extras for those who don't attend but might run a story.
4. Have adequate seats but not too many. Have a stack of extra folding chairs in an adjoining room.
5. Have something visual on hand—large photographic blowups, model units, charts or maps, or a display.
6. If the press kit contains a specific announcement, repeat it; then from careful notes ad-lib additional commentary.
7. Have extra people on hand in case attendance is thin.
8. Avoid mugging for the cameras, either still or motion picture.
9. Allow questions and answer them candidly.
10. Have at least one person primed to ask the first question if none comes spontaneously.
11. Anticipate a total length of 20 to 30 minutes.

From: *How to Handle Your Own Public Relations,* H. Gordon Lewis (Chicago: Nelson-Hall, Inc., 1977)

book focuses on the needs of small businesses, it is an excellent introduction for executives of even the largest companies. The author provides a solid grounding in all the basics, from writing press releases to staging newsworthy activities for media attention. A collection of specific public relations projects for various business situations offers a useful source of ideas.

WHEN THE COMPANY IMAGE NEEDS A NEW LOOK

The corporation is seen in many aspects, but its most obvious appearances are in the company

Logos and corporate symbols are the work of William Sklaroff Design Associates. (Samples from the firm's introductory brochure.)

logo, its packaging design, the look of its advertising, its presence in trade shows and exhibitions. The professionals who specialize in these aspects of corporate identity are legion. One of many good examples is the industrial design firm of William Sklaroff Design Associates. If you are contemplating your company image, review this firm's information kit. Write:

William Sklaroff Design Associates
124 Sibley Ave.
Ardmore, PA 19003

SPECIALISTS IN NAMING COMPANIES AND PRODUCTS

NameLab, Inc., is a consulting firm devoted exclusively to devising names for companies

---

HOW TO LINK ADVERTISING WITH PRODUCT DISTRIBUTION

Advertising should be coordinated with product availability. Don't advertise a product until you are physically able to meet the demand that will be created. Have enough product in inventory. Premature promotion causes prospects to become excited, then highly disappointed with your non-delivery. They may even buy your competitor's product.

Long before the advertising campaign begins, presell your proposed advertising to your salesmen, distributors, agents, jobbers and others involved with product distribution. Understanding the advertising campaign and its timing will aid them in coordinating distribution at each level.

From: *Marketing Problem Solver*, Cochrane Chase and Kenneth L. Barasch (Radnor, PA: Chilton Book Co., 1977)

---

and products. The firm's linguists and researchers use a sophisticated system as well as computers to produce candidates. A free brochure describes the system and the firm's services. Also ask for the brochure *Everything You Need to Know About Trademarks*. Write:

NameLab, Inc.
711 Marina Blvd.
San Francisco, CA 94123

FOUR PROMOTION IDEAS THAT PUSH PRODUCT SALES

1. If you want people to read your advertising, offer them an incentive. One of the best attention-getters is a sweepstakes, a technique that gets people emotionally involved in the advertising and builds readership.
2. If you want to increase redemption of a coupon or an offer, add a sweepstakes to the promotion. You'll get a higher rate of return on your coupon.
3. If you want to get more action at the retail level, offer a coupon and promote it to the trade. We've found that retailers are more likely to buy more of the product, build their inventories and give off-shelf displays if a coupon is part of the promotion than through any of the other techniques available.
4. If you want to build response to a couponing program at the retail level, add a trade contest. That usually builds sales volume higher than just a consumer promotion alone.

From: *Sales Promotion Essentials*, Don E. Schultz and William A. Robinson (Chicago: Crain Books, 1982)

SECTION 3

Electronic Tools

RESOURCES FOR COMPUTER LITERACY

HOW A COMPUTER SYSTEM WORKS
John A. Brown and Robert S. Workman
1975, 1979/224 pp./$5.95
Arco Publishing, Inc.
219 Park Ave. S.
New York, NY 10003

The authors present a basic introduction to the workings of mainframe and minicomputer sys-tems. The book is a useful resource for the ex-ecutive who must be familiar with the capa-bilities of such systems and the equipment that is involved. Included are chapters on input/output devices as well as various types of terminals. Also covered are such subjects as time-sharing and computer networks. (If order-ing by mail, add $1 for postage and handling.)

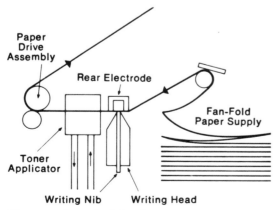

The operating principle of a matrix printer (from How a Computer System Works).

BUSINESS COMPUTER SYSTEMS
$35/12 issues per year
221 Columbus Ave.
Boston, MA 02116

While this magazine deals with equipment as large as mainframes, much of the emphasis is on microcomputers rather than large-scale sys-tems. The style is not heavily technical and the approach is instructional. The broad perspec-tive of the magazine makes it a useful resource for the executive who wants to keep informed about the whole technology. (Your manage-ment position may qualify you for a free subscription to this controlled-circulation mag-azine.)

THE EXECUTIVE'S HANDBOOK TO MINICOMPUTERS

Robert Allen Bonelli
1978/173 pp./$16
Petrocelli Books, Inc.
1101 State Rd.
Princeton, NJ 08540

While the desktop microcomputer has become a personal tool for the executive, minicomputer systems continue to be the workhorses of large-scale applications in business and industry. As with the giant mainframe computers, however, few executives are familiar with minicomputers. This book offers a useful introduction to minicomputer systems. The author explains the technology and presents a guide for selecting and applying these systems. He details examples of five basic minicomputer systems and shows how their hardware and software are applied to specific tasks.

COMPUTER HANDBOOK FOR SENIOR MANAGEMENT

Douglas B. Hoyt
1978/212 pp./$18.95
Macmillan Publishing Co.
866 3rd Ave.
New York, NY 10022

This book offers valuable guidance for executives administering computer operations for the first time. With a minimum of technical data, the book deals with such aspects as executive

---

AUDIO RESPONSE AND COMPUTER POSSIBILITIES

With an audio response system, any touch-tone telephone can be a computer terminal. When a dial-up connection is made with the computer, data can be entered or information requested by means of the touch-tone keyboard. The computer responds immediately by acknowledging receipt of data or by giving the inquirer requested information in audible words over the telephone receiver.

Computer-stored data must be converted (translated) into intelligible words. The controlling program directs the computer to search among words previously recorded by voice and to select words that correspond to the data requested. These audible words are returned to the inquirer through his telephone receiver. Audio response increases the reach of a communication network, to the extent of available telephone lines, over all geographic areas.

From: *How a Computer System Works*, John A. Brown and Robert S. Workman (New York: Arco Publishing, Inc., 1979)

---

responsibilities and the delegation of authority to technicians. Detailed directions cover such areas as financial controls, training programs, use of consultants and negotiating contracts for equipment and services. A variety of charts and graphs illustrate the text.

PLANNING FOR COMPUTER SYSTEMS

Bringing in a computer system can work wonders, but the process has a potential for costly mistakes. If you need to do some homework in this area, Isaacs Associates, Inc., offers the guidance of *Do It Right the First Time*, a manual that outlines the questions and answers an executive needs to know. Prepared by management consultants who specialize in computer systems and priced at $15, the guide deals with evaluating such factors as costs and return on investment as well as step-by-step planning. Write:

Isaacs Associates, Inc.
33 N. LaSalle St.
Chicago, IL 60602

TAKING THE MEASURE OF A MINICOMPUTER

While the capabilities of the microcomputer continue to develop, there is a startling difference in scale when you consider the dimensions of the minicomputer. Wang Laboratories, for instance, markets its VS 100 minicomputer systems to serve up to 128 workstation terminals simultaneously. The VS

100 has a main memory of up to 8 million characters, with disk storage of up to 10 billion characters. For literature and further information, write:

Wang Laboratories, Inc.
1 Industrial Ave.
Lowell, MA 01851

LARGE-SCALE COMPUTER SERVICES FROM CSC

Large-scale computer systems, whether mainframe or minicomputer, can drain giant amounts of a company's capital. An alternative is to buy services from a firm such as Computer Sciences Corp. Among its many services, CSC

The Wang VS 100 minicomputer systems are designed to serve up to 128 workstation terminals simultaneously.

operates the worldwide Infonet remote computing service, with users in more than 60 countries linked into its centralized host computers. Terminals in your company's offices are connected in a network running on CSC computers. A very wide range of data processing and communications functions are available, including electronic mail, data base management, financial management and economic forecasting. For literature and further information, write:

Computer Sciences Corp.
2100 E. Grand Ave.
El Segundo, CA 90245

The use of micro-based tools is like riding a bicycle: easy, even second nature, once you know how, but the learning of it wasn't effortless. There is more enthusiasm than accuracy in much of the advertising and proselytizing which claims that it is.

From: *Mastering Micros*, Hannah I. Blank (Princeton, NJ: Petrocelli Books, Inc., 1983)

you. For literature and further information, write:

Burroughs Corp.
Burroughs Pl.
Detroit, MI 48232

BURROUGHS: MICROCOMPUTER TAKES ON MINICOMPUTER WORK

The microcomputer is growing into its future, having rapidly progressed from home to business status. At Burroughs, the desktop computer is the basis for the B-20 systems, which are designed for applications requiring the power and flexibility of a minicomputer without its higher costs. The modular B-20 systems offer up to 640K of internal memory and mass-storage capacities of millions of characters. The desktop workstations can stand alone or be connected in networks. The B-20 systems could be your first or next step in taking full advantage of what the computer can do for

COMPUTERS AND DATA PROCESSING
Ray Strackbein and
   Dorothy Bowlby Strackbein
1983/94 pp./$5.95
Arco Publishing, Inc.
219 Park Ave. S.
New York, NY 10003

If you are entirely new to computers or if you are a confused beginner, this book could provide the orientation you need. The authors take you through the subject step by step, building understanding by stages. The book covers all the basic functions, applications, equipment and terminology. (If ordering by mail, add $1 for postage and handling.)

MANAGING THE COSTS OF COMPUTER TECHNOLOGY

The rapid rate of technical changes in computer operations makes application of financial controls more difficult. When a financial or other manager begins to grasp the know-how needed to get the computer under financial control, a new array of hardware or software may be brought in with its new terminology and complexities and change the environment in which data processing is being done. For example, equipment with "multiprocessing" capabilities uses computer hardware on multiple jobs simultaneously, which changes the basis for charging users for the computer time they use.

Important data processing decisions are made by different groups: (1) computer managers usually influence decisions most on new hardware and new software systems, and (2) the users of computer services may influence decisions most on whether to extend or abandon the types of services they have been supplied. This shared responsibility creates an opportunity for "passing the buck," and makes it more important and more difficult to identify accountability properly. This divided responsibility also creates a need to see beyond conflicting viewpoints so that decisions are in the economic best interests of the total organization.

From: *Computer Handbook for Senior Management*, Douglas B. Hoyt (New York: Macmillan Information, 1978)

CHECKLIST GUIDE FOR ASSESSING DATA PROCESSING SAFEGUARDS

Phillip G. Elam
1983/64 pp./$5
Pilot Books
103 Cooper St.
Babylon, NY 11702

This handbook poses hundreds of specific questions for evaluating safeguards for data processing. The considerations covered range from fire hazards to air-conditioning requirements. Separate sections deal with personnel, security and disaster-planning factors. (If ordering by mail, add $1 for postage and handling.)

COMPUTER NEGOTIATIONS REPORT

$265/12 issues per year
1513 E. Livingston St.
Orlando, FL 32803

This newsletter deals with contracts and lawyers and the complexities of providing data processing facilities for a company. The language is nontechnical and it is a sound resource for executives who need background in this area.

COMPUTERIZED BANKING FOR THE CORPORATION

The era of corporate banking by computer has arrived and Citibank is one of the leaders in the new technology. The booklet *Electronic Banking: An Executive's Guide* is a review of the firm's electronic banking services for both domestic and international customers. Its 24 pages also serve as a primer for the nonfinancial executive keeping informed on financial technology. Write:

Citibank
Electronic Banking and
    Cash Management Div.
399 Park Ave.
New York, NY 10043

IMPACT: OFFICE AUTOMATION
$45/12 issues per year
2360 Maryland Rd.
Willow Grove, PA 19090

This monthly newsletter from the Administrative Management Society offers 16 pages of information and guidelines for office operations. It focuses on technology, reporting on new products and systems and providing direction for their efficient use. The newsletter stresses developing trends and features a section that reviews noteworthy articles appearing in other publications. (Subscription is $30 for society members.)

COMPUTERS AND QUESTIONS ABOUT VISUAL DISPLAY UNITS

The growing use of desktop computers, word processors and other equipment using visual display units has been accompanied by questions about comfort and safety. The Computer and Business Equipment Manufacturers Assn. (CBEMA) offers the following literature on the subject. *The Installation and Use of Visual Display Units* (50¢) points out potential problems and solutions. *How to Use Your Visual Display Unit Comfortably* (50¢) focuses on the operator's perspective. *VDU Fact Sheets* ($1) summarize current research on health, safety and comfort. Write:

CBEMA Publications
311 1st St., N.W.
Washington, DC 20001

PERSONAL COMPUTERS FOR THE EXECUTIVE OFFICE

IBM PC: THE PERSONAL COMPUTER THAT SETS THE PACE FOR THE FIELD

In a field so relatively new and still so filled with innovation that standards have not yet been fixed, the IBM Personal Computer has become the model for much of the development in the industry. Software developers, for instance, target the IBM PC for their programs. The variety of software for the PC is extensive and competing computer manufacturers often design a compatibility into their units that makes possible the use of the PC software. Selling for about $3,000 and upward, the basic PC has a 64K internal user memory, expandable up to 640K (that is, 640 kilobytes or characters, sometimes written 640KB). It comes with a choice of one or two diskette drives for a storage capacity of up to 720K, and it also has five expansion slots for system expansion.

BUYING YOUR FIRST PERSONAL COMPUTER

Consider carefully the programs and accessories that are available for the machine you want to buy. The wider the base of hardware and software, the greater the value of your computer. If you have a specific application in mind, look into software very deeply. Find the best programs for your application and buy the computer that they run on.

Use all the information resources at your disposal for your research. Join the computer club in your area. Ask for demonstrations at computer stores. Buy some books and magazines. Their cost is trivial compared with the computer's, but they'll pay off handsomely.

If you know someone who's already using a computer in your intended application, make the simple choice: buy the same computer your friend has. He can guide you past the difficult parts, and when something breaks down, you can swap components back and forth to find the defective one.

Whatever you spend on hardware, expect to spend about the same amount on software in the first year. And whatever you set aside for software, expect to spend more.

From: *The Computer Dictionary*, John Prenis (Philadelphia: Running Press, 1983)

A pacesetter in the development of computer technology, the IBM Personal Computer sells for about $3,000.

An enhanced or "extended" form of the PC is the PC XT, priced at upward of $5,000. The PC XT has a 128K memory, expandable up to 640K. For storage memory, it is equipped with one hard-disk drive that provides more than 10 million characters (10 megabytes, sometimes written 10M, or 10MB), plus one diskette drive with 360K capacity. It has eight expansion slots as well as a built-in adapter for linking the computer with other units. The basic PC and the PC XT have been further developed in more advanced systems. The PC-3270 (under $6,000), for instance, can run elaborate graphics software as well as multiple displays, or "windows," on its monitor. The PC XT-370 (about $9,000) offers desktop use in conjunction with a mainframe computer, and the IBM 9002 (under $7,000) is a desktop system designed for up to four users running multiple tasks simultaneously. When you seek IBM literature, ask for a copy of *The Guide*, a very useful catalog in magazine format that covers both hardware and software. For literature and dealer information, write:

IBM Corp.
Box 1328
Boca Raton, FL 33432

APPLE: PERSONAL COMPUTERS WITH WIDE VERSATILITY

One of the largest of the computer manufacturers, Apple offers a range of choices of hardware and an extensive selection of software. The model IIe has a 64K internal memory and a storage-memory capacity that is expandable with up to six floppy-disk drives. It is priced under $1,500. The model III is a high-power unit available with either 128K or 256K of internal memory and priced starting at about $3,000. It is expandable with up to three floppy-disk drives as well as a mass-storage hard-disk drive with a capacity of 5 million characters. Introduced with the Lisa model computer, the "mouse" is one of the newer developments in the Apple line. It is a command device with which the user controls a pointer on the screen to handle operations. For literature and further information, write:

Apple Computer, Inc.
20525 Mariani Ave.
Cupertino, CA 95014

Radio Shack TRS-80 model 4 personal computer with two-disk-drive system has 368K of storage capacity and sells for $1,999.

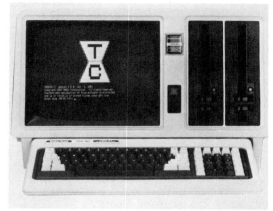

The TRS-80 model 16B, with two disk drives, sells for $5,798.

RADIO SHACK COMPUTERS: SYSTEMS FOR MANY USES

Radio Shack's TRS-80 line of personal computers offers a broad range of models as well as such peripherals as printers and a wide variety of software programs. The model 4 is a basic desktop unit. With a cassette system and 16K of memory, it sells for $999, while a single-disk-drive system with 184K is $1,699 and a two-disk-drive system with 368K of storage capacity is $1,999. The model 4P is a compact transportable version of the model 4. With 64K of memory, two disk drives and 184K of storage capacity, the model 4P weighs only 26 pounds and sells for $1,799. Offering higher operating speeds and larger memory capacity, the model 16B has a multi-user operating system designed to serve up to three people simultaneously. A single-disk-drive version sells for $4,999 and a two-disk-drive system is $5,798. Both versions have 256K of internal memory, and each disk drive provides 1.25 million characters of storage. The TRS-80 model 2000 computers are high-performance units designed to run software programs based on the MS-DOS system. In a version with two floppy-

The TRS-80 model 2000 computer runs software programs based on the MS-DOS system.

disk drives, the model 2000 sells for $2,750, while a second version with one floppy and one hard disk sells for $4,250. For literature, write:

Radio Shack
1 Tandy Center
Fort Worth, TX 76102

Features of the NEC Advanced Personal Computer include a dual floppy-disk storage capacity of up to 2 million characters.

PORTABLE COMPUTERS FROM RADIO SHACK

Radio Shack offers a selection of ultra-small computer units. The TRS-80 model PC-3, for instance, is a pocket-size unit that combines calculator functions with the programmed problem-solving of a computer. The programs function in such areas as advanced math, statistics and finance. The computer sells for $99.95. It is combined with a printer-recorder unit that is priced at $119.95. The TRS-80 model 100 is a book-size unit that weighs only 4 pounds. It is designed for travel and convenience and is priced at $799. Using built-in software, the computer functions as appointment calendar, phone directory, address book and word processor. For literature, write:

Radio Shack
1 Tandy Center
Fort Worth, TX 76102

DESKTOP COMPUTER LINE FROM NEC

The Advanced Personal Computer line from NEC offers a wide choice of capacities and features. The basic system has 128K of internal memory along with a single floppy-disk drive with 1 million characters of storage memory. The basic system is priced at under $3,000. Enhancement options include monochrome or color graphics as well as a hard-disk drive with 10 million characters of storage memory. For literature and dealer information, write:

NEC Information Systems, Inc.
5 Militia Dr.
Lexington, MA 02173

PERSONAL COMPUTERS FROM DIGITAL EQUIPMENT

Well-known for its VAX high-speed, high-capacity minicomputers for larger applications, the Digital Equipment Corp.'s personal computers offer several choices for desktop use. The Rainbow 100 model, for instance, features an operating system designed to handle a wide variety of software programs. Priced at $3,495, the computer has 64K of internal memory and

TRS-80 pocket computer combined with its printer-recorder unit.

The Professional 350 personal computer from Digital Equipment is priced at $4,995.

800K of storage memory with dual floppy disks. A hard-disk memory storage of 5 million characters is optional. The more sophisticated Professional 350 model is priced at $4,995. It has 256K of internal memory, along with 800K of storage memory as well as the optional hard-disk memory. For literature and further information, write:

Digital Equipment Corp.
146 Main St.
Maynard, MA 01754

Digital Equipment's Rainbow 100 personal computer is priced at $3,495.

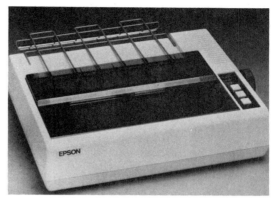

Epson RX-80 dot-matrix 80-column printer sells for a suggested retail price of $499.

PERSONAL COMPUTERS FROM EPSON FOR DESKTOP AND BRIEFCASE

Epson America, Inc., markets both a desktop personal computer and a notebook-size machine. The QX-10 personal computer, including monitor and disk drive, retails for under $3,000. The machine's main memory has a range of 64 to 256K. Two floppy disks each have a capacity of 380K. The machine features a keyboard with plain-English command keys and it runs the firm's own VALDOCS software system (with option for CP/M capability). The firm's notebook-size HX-20 portable computer is battery-powered and will fit in a briefcase. With built-in word processing software and a microcassette storage system, the

unit retails for $795. Memory is 16K of RAM (expandable to 32K) and 32K of ROM (expandable to 64K). The unit includes a built-in microprinter and has a graphics capacity. Epson also markets a line of dot-matrix printers. For literature and dealer information, write:

Epson America, Inc.
3415 Kashiwa St.
Torrance, CA 90505

Epson QX-10 personal computer includes disk drive and is priced at under $3,000.

THE RIGHT QUESTIONS FOR COMPUTER BEGINNERS

The problem for people who have not yet tackled computer technology is that they don't know what questions to ask. When they talk to someone who is knowledgeable they literally don't speak the same language. A businessman whose office now consists of typewriters, adding machines and copy machines can be intimidated by a first meeting with a computer salesperson. People already immersed in computerese have difficulty beginning from square one when they talk with potential customers. The basic question—What do you want a computer to do?—might leave most people wondering, What *can* a computer do for me?

From: *Before You Buy a Computer,* Dona Z. Meilach (New York: Crown Publishers, Inc., 1983)

The Hewlett-Packard HP 150 personal computer features compact design. It is priced at $3,995 (photo courtesy of Hewlett-Packard Co.).

The Compaq personal computer weighs 28 pounds and is suitcase size for portability.

HEWLETT-PACKARD: DATA PROCESSORS FROM VERY SMALL TO VERY LARGE

Hewlett-Packard markets a wide range of data processing equipment. Its personal computer is the HP 150, but the firm also sells large business computers as well as the book-size portable HP-75C (and even smaller programmable pocket calculators.) The HP 150 personal computer has 256K of memory (expandable to 640K), and, with monitor and built-in dual disk drive, the unit is priced at $3,995. It features HP Touch, by which the user gives directions to the computer by touching the display screen. The HP 150 can be linked to the HP 3000 business computer as well as to IBM mainframes. For literature and dealer information, write:

Hewlett-Packard Co.
Box 10301
Palo Alto, CA 94303

COMPAQ: PERSONAL COMPUTING THAT YOU CAN TAKE WITH YOU

The Compaq personal computer offers both portability and power. The 28-pound unit has 128K of memory (expandable to 512K). A single disk drive provides 320K of storage (a second drive is optional). Priced at about $3,000, the computer is compatible with IBM Personal Computer software and hardware. A more powerful version of the unit is available in the Compaq Plus model, priced at about $5,000. The portable is 20 inches wide, 8½ inches high and 16 inches deep, which makes it suitcase size for traveling. For brochures and dealer information, write:

Compaq Computer Corp.
20333 FM 149
Houston, TX 77070

FURNITURE FOR YOU AND YOUR COMPUTER

Prudential Business Furniture is a wholesale supplier. The firm's catalog is a convenient way to shop for furniture ideas. It features a variety of stands and carts to accommodate the personal computer, for instance. The firm also markets executive desks and chairs as well as

The Toshiba T100 portable computer fits into its own attaché case.

such equipment as fireproof safes and files. For catalog, write:

Prudential Business Furniture
219 E. 42nd St.
New York, NY 10017

COMPUTERS AND WORD PROCESSORS FROM TOSHIBA

Toshiba offers a range of personal computer models, including the T300, a 16-bit desktop unit that sells for under $4,000 with dual floppy-disk drives and a color display. The unit has 192K of internal memory, and each of the

Toshiba's model T300 computer with color display sells for under $4,000.

disk drives has 640K memory. The display features tilt and swivel for ease of viewing. The firm's model T100 desktop computers include a portable configuration that fits into its own attaché case. It is priced at under $2,000 and has a liquid-crystal display 40 characters wide and 8 lines deep. The unit's internal memory is 64K. Toshiba also offers the EW-100 word processing systems that feature dual floppy-disk drives. A single disk will store up to 460 pages of text or other data. The units are priced at upward of $5,000. For literature, write:

Toshiba America, Inc.
2441 Michelle Dr.
Tustin, CA 92680

MULTI-USER COMPUTER SYSTEMS FROM ALTOS

Altos specializes in multi-user desktop computer systems, offering a wide choice of hardware and software. The firm's model 586, for instance, will support up to five terminals. The unit has 512K of internal memory along with

Altos model 586 multi-user computer will support up to five terminals and is priced at $7,990.

Model C-300 terminal for use with Cado ATS computer systems.

floppy- and hard-disk drives for a storage memory capacity of more than 12 million characters. The computer is priced at $7,990. For literature and dealer information, write:

Altos Computer Systems
2641 Orchard Pkwy.
San Jose, CA 95134

MULTI-USER COMPUTER SYSTEMS FROM CADO

The options in computer systems continue to grow. If you have contemplated a minicomputer for your company, you also need to consider the cost advantages of a microprocessor-based system. The Cado Systems Corp. markets two such system. The Tiger ATS 32 and the Tiger ATS 64 support up to 32 and 64 terminals respectively. The firm markets a wide selection of software programs for the systems. For literature and dealer information, write:

Cado Systems Corp.
2771 Toledo St.
Torrance, CA 90510

LIST

$24.95/12 issues per year
3381 Ocean Dr.
Vero Beach, FL 32963

Devoted to the business uses of personal computers, this monthly covers hardware topics, but it focuses on software. Reviews of software programs are detailed and include interviews with program users. A monthly feature of the magazine is the Software Locator, a directory of programs on the market. In special presentations in the January and July issues, the Locator section lists approximately 4,000 software programs.

SPREAD SHEET SOFTWARE FOR YOUR COMPUTER

One of the best-known names in software, Microsoft markets a variety of program packages.

Multiplan spread sheet software by Microsoft is priced at $250 (photo courtesy of Microsoft Corp.).

Sales statistics as they appear on a computing screen running Multiplan spread sheet software (photo courtesy of Microsoft Corp.).

Included in the firm's line is Multiplan, a popular example of the electronic work sheet or spread sheet. Designed for use on the IBM and Apple computers, this software program handles such complex projects as forecasts, financial plans and budget consolidation. The program is priced at $250. For literature and dealer information, write:

Microsoft Corp.
10700 Northup Way
Bellevue, WA 98004

USING A CONSULTANT WHEN BUYING A COMPUTER

Computer consultants charge from $10 to $50 per hour. (The average seems to be about $20.) Ten hours with a first-rate consultant might set you back $500, but a good consultant will save you far more than that.

A consultant can, for example, establish the actual computing needs of your business; suggest machines and programs that will fill those needs and recommend the best places to buy. After the equipment is purchased, the consultant can take care of installation and do the training.

I do not recommend, however, giving a consultant carte blanche in your business. The selection and installation of a personal computer is far too important to trust to an "outsider" no matter how expert. Become involved in every step of the process or assign the task to someone trusted *within* your organization.

From: *The Personal Computer in Business Book*, Peter A. McWilliams (Los Angeles: Prelude Press, 1983)

RUNNING YOUR COMPUTER ON INTEGRATED SOFTWARE

A package that combines several functions, Incredible JACK is a popular example of integrated software. The package combines word processing, data base management, spread sheet analysis as well as the sorting and printing of mailing labels. The software runs on the Apple II computers and is priced at $179. A supplementary program called JACKreport ($99) adds a report-generating capability. Another version of this software, called Jack2 and priced at $495, runs on the IBM PC and the IBM XT computers. For literature and dealer information, write:

Business Solutions, Inc.
60 E. Main St.
Kings Park, NY 11754

The WordStar word-processing software program by MicroPro has companion software programs for such functions as spelling correction and indexing.

MICROPRO: SOFTWARE OPTIONS FOR YOUR PERSONAL COMPUTER

MicroPro markets a variety of software programs for the major personal computer models, but its best-known program is WordStar, a word-processing program. Priced at $495, the program offers a variety of features for producing error-free memos, letters, reports. Companion software includes indexing and spelling correction. The firm's line of software includes InfoStar ($495), a data base management system, and CalcStar ($195), an electronic spread sheet. For literature, write:

MicroPro International Corp.
33 San Pablo Ave.
San Rafael, CA 94903

DATA BASE SOFTWARE FROM ASHTON-TATE

Producer of dBase II, one of the most popular data base software programs, Ashton-Tate also publishes a selection of books about personal computers. Among the firm's books are *Every-*

man's Database Primer by Robert A. Byers ($19.95) and *dBase II for the First-Time User* by Alan Freedman ($19.95). For literature and further information, write:

Ashton-Tate
10150 W. Jefferson Blvd.
Culver City, CA 90230

DATA BASE SOFTWARE FOR YOUR COMPUTER

Software Publishing Corp. markets PFS:FILE, one of the best-known software programs for data base management. The program runs on the IBM, Apple and other personal computers. Other programs in the PFS line provide word processing, graphics and reports. The programs sell for between $125 and $175, depending on the computer system. The firm offers useful booklets detailing the software and their uses. For literature, write:

Software Publishing Corp.
1901 Landings Dr.
Mountain View, CA 94043

SOFTWARE VARIETY FROM PEACHTREE

Among the better known software programs from Peachtree are the PeachText word-processing programs and the PeachCalc electronic spread sheet. The firm also markets the Personal Calendar and the Project Management programs as well as accounting and graphics software packages. A very useful resource from Peachtree is its publication *Peachware Quarterly* (4 issues for $9 annual subscription, or $3 for a single issue). This magazine presents articles about software applications and it incorporates the firm's product catalog. Write:

Peachtree Software, Inc.
3445 Peachtree Rd., N.E.
Atlanta, GA 30326

SHOPPING BY MAIL FOR HARDWARE, SOFTWARE

Part of the fascination of personal computing is the mass of hardware and software now on the market. A convenient way to shop this market is in the mail-order catalogs of suppliers. Alpha Byte Computer Products offers a wide variety of items ranging from applications software to modems and monitors. Write for the firm's "Hot Sheet" listing:

Alpha Byte Computer Products
31304 Via Colinas
Westlake Village, CA 91362

MAIL-ORDER COMPUTER SHOPPING

Conroy-Lapoint sends out a monthly listing of its hardware and software offerings. The list is

---

FIRST FIND THE PROGRAM, THEN BUY THE COMPUTER

If more often than not, you like the way a computer processes words or numbers, what you like is the program, not the computer. Buying a computer because of a good program is like buying a car because you like the countryside in which you took a test drive.

Ask the salesperson the name of the program running on the computer. Ask if the program will run on any other computer. (Some programs can, some can't.) If it can, then ask him to run the same program on other computers.

An adage in computer buying is, "Find the program first, then buy the computer that runs the program best."

From: *The Personal Computer in Business Book*, Peter A. McWilliams (Los Angeles: Prelude Press, 1983)

---

long and varied, but it shows an emphasis on software for the Apple and IBM personal computers. Prices are marked down substantially in many cases. Write:

Conroy-Lapoint
Box 23068
Portland, OR 97223

COMPUTERWORLD

$44/62 issues per year
375 Cochituate Rd.
Framingham, MA 01701

This tabloid newspaper reports on all aspects of computer technology, ranging from mainframes down to minis and microcomputers. If your interest does not go beyond limited use of your personal computer, this publication is not for you. But if you want to keep up with what is going on, these editorial and advertising pages will serve you well.

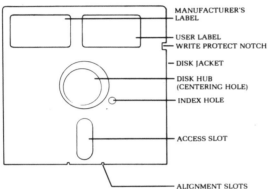

The elements of a floppy-disk jacket (from Before You Buy a Computer).

BEFORE YOU BUY A COMPUTER
Dona Z. Meilach
1983/210 pp./$8.95
Crown Publishers, Inc.
1 Park Ave.
New York, NY 10016

The author provides a thorough introduction to all the basics of computers. She explains the underlying technology in clear detail, focusing on personal computers but giving the reader a broad view of the field. She uses a step-by-step approach, with guidance for the reader who wants to research beyond the material in the book. The text is illustrated extensively with photos and drawings.

PC WORLD
$24/12 issues per year
555 De Haro St.
San Francisco, CA 94107

This monthly magazine is for all those users of the IBM Personal Computer as well as all those other personal computers on the market that are compatible with IBM PC software. This adds up to a lot of readers and the number is growing constantly. They are well served by this magazine, which zeros in on both product and how-to information. The advertising offers an enormous variety of hardware and software.

PORTABLE COMPUTER
$16.97/12 issues per year
500 Howard St.
San Francisco, CA 94105

If you are shopping for a computer that is small enough to travel around with you, here is a magazine that is devoted exclusively to the portables. It reports on the newest hardware and reviews software, and its articles tell how to get the most out of this expanding technology.

POPULAR COMPUTING
$15/12 issues per year
70 Main St.
Peterborough, NH 03458

This magazine is one that you can grow with. If you are a beginner with the personal computer,

this monthly can challenge and guide you in the learning process. As you advance, you will be able to get more and more out of its pages. There is an emphasis on instruction. The articles deftly explain the way through complex subjects, whether reviewing new hardware and software or reporting on developing technology. Issues commonly run over 200 pages and they are thick with product advertising.

INFOWORLD
$31/51 issues per year
1060 Marsh Rd.
Menlo Park, CA 94025

This weekly magazine will keep you current in both the technology and the culture of the personal computer. It may, in fact, bring you more information than you need or want if you are new to the computer. The magazine reports on new hardware and reviews the latest in software. Throughout, the emphasis is on how-to information and practical applications.

INFORMATION MANAGEMENT
$10/12 issues per year
101 Crossways Park W.
Woodbury, NY 11797

Published for professionals in the field of data management, this magazine provides a monthly update on developments in computer applications and office automation. Typical articles are relatively short and do not pursue technical detail. Subject variety offers the executive a wide sampling of the field. (Your management position may qualify you for a free subscription to this controlled-circulation magazine.)

LEARNING COMPUTER SKILLS

**COMPUTER INSTRUCTION
ON VIDEOTAPE CASSETTE**

Kennen Publishing offers videotape instruction for mastering your personal computer. Each program tape is between 2 and 2½ hours long and is organized in 10 lessons. Combined with use of the computer, the lessons require ap-proximately 4 to 6 hours of study. Priced at $69.50 each, the programs are available for such computers as the IBM PC and the IBM PC XT as well as the Apple II, Apple IIe and Apple III. For literature, write:

Kennen Publishing
150 Shoreline Hwy., Bldg. E
Mill Valley, CA 94941

Kennen Publishing's videotape programs provide instruction in the use of major personal computers.

USING YOUR COMPUTER TO LEARN YOUR COMPUTER

Another major firm specializing in computer learning programs, Cdex Corp. bases its system on diskettes which you run in your computer. There are programs on how to use the IBM and Apple personal computers as well as on the use of a wide variety of popular software. The programs are priced at $69.95 and under. For catalog and other literature, write:

Cdex Corp.
5050 El Camino Real
Los Altos, CA 94022

WORKSHOP COURSES FOR COMPUTER TRAINING

Personal Computer Learning Centers offer workshop courses in major cities for training in the use of such software programs as VisiCalc and Lotus 1-2-3. Classes are restricted to 6 to 10 students, with two instructors per class. Courses range in length from two to six hours and in cost from $150 to $350. Corporate rates are available when three or more executives from the same company take a course, and the courses can be presented on company premises. For literature and further information, write:

Personal Computer Learning
   Centers of America, Inc.
1820 Jefferson Pl., N.W.
Washington, DC 20036

THE ELECTRONIC SPREAD SHEET AND WHAT IT CAN DO FOR YOU

Work sheet (spread sheet) software enables you to manipulate and recalculate rows and columns of numbers and see instantly the results of recalculation. You may change the value of a variable or the definition of the relationship among various variables, and as soon as you do so the entire work sheet is recalculated before your eyes. If you want to add an item, or shift the position of a column or row, or duplicate a formula of relationships, or increase each new occurrence on a line by some percentage—to name a few capabilities—you can do so with an absolute minimum of effort and surprisingly quickly.

From: *Mastering Micros*, Hannah I. Blank (Princeton, NJ: Petrocelli Books, Inc., 1983)

MASTERING YOUR COMPUTER WITH SOFTWARE SIMULATIONS

American Training International markets a variety of software packages that simulate popular business software programs now on the market. You run the simulation on your desktop computer and it takes you step by step through the program. For literature and further information, write:

American Training International
12638 Beatrice St.
Manhattan Beach, CA 90066

SOFTWARE EXPERTISE FROM SOFTWAREBANC

If your use of the desktop computer takes you into advanced areas, a firm like SoftwareBanc could be a very helpful guide. The company combines software sales with software education and it is well known for its seminars on dBase II, Lotus 1-2-3 and UNIX. Presented by Adam B. Green, the seminars are conducted in major cities, last five days and cost $200 per

day. The firm also markets a videotape instruction package on the use of dBase II ($295). For literature and further information, write:

SoftwareBanc, Inc.
661 Massachusetts Ave.
Arlington, MA 02174

NEXIS: LARGE-SCALE INFORMATION RETRIEVAL

For executives with extensive information needs, the NEXIS data bases provide full-text access to a long list of newspapers, magazines, wire services and newsletters. Among these data bases, for example, are *The New York Times, Business Week,* the Associated Press and Reuters. Access is via a NEXIS terminal and display (with hard-copy printer as an option). There is a monthly subscription charge ($50) plus scaled use charges (beginning at $90 per hour for the first five hours of monthly use). For complete information on data bases and charges, write:

Mead Data Central
Box 1830
Dayton, OH 45401

DIALOG: INFORMATION RETRIEVAL FROM MORE THAN 170 DATA BASES

Using your personal computer or other terminal unit, DIALOG can link you over telephone

DIALOG catalog lists more than 170 data bases (*reprinted courtesy of DIALOG Information Services, Inc.*).

lines with more than 170 different data bases. With no registration fee, you are charged for actual time you are connected to a data base, rates varying for the different data bases. The service is accessible for 22 hours every working day plus weekend hours. The range of subject material is broad, including science and technology, economics and business, and current affairs. Write for a data base catalog and informational material:

DIALOG Information Services, Inc.
3460 Hillview Ave.
Palo Alto, CA 94304

THE SOURCE: DATA BASE ACCESS WITH YOUR PERSONAL COMPUTER

The Source is an example of the growing number of data base services. It is accessed over telephone lines with your personal computer, desktop terminal or communicating word processor. You pay a $100 registration fee and then hourly charges for the time you are actually connected to The Source. The daytime rate in the continental U.S. is $20.75 per hour, while the nighttime rate is $7.75 per hour. Data base services of interest to executives include abstracts from the business press, updated reports on the securities markets, economic and financial forecasting and national and international news. The Source can also be used as a medium for electronic mail and computer conferences. For information, write:

Source Telecomputing Corp.
1616 Anderson Rd.
McLean, VA 22102

Start-up kit for The Source can be purchased at retail outlets by paying the $100 registration fee.

SERVICES AND PRODUCTS FROM CONTROL DATA CENTERS

Control Data Business Centers, Inc., a subsidiary of the Control Data Corp., specializes in service and product support for companies with up to 500 employees. With more than 50 centers across the country, the system offers financial services, computer-based training and seminars, data processing, computer hardware and software. Financial services include equipment financing and leasing as well as asset-based lending. Training and seminar programs cover such areas as sales, computer literacy and business planning and strategy. Check your telephone directory for a center near you, or write:

Control Data Business Centers, Inc.
300 St. Paul Pl.
Baltimore, MD 21202

COMPUTER TRAINING WITH AUDIO CASSETTES

FlipTrack Learning Systems offers a line of learning kits for use with personal computers. The kits consist of audio cassettes and lesson manuals. There are kits for learning how to use both specific computer models and specific software programs. *How to Operate the IBM Personal Computer* ($57) comes with three cassettes, while *How to Operate the Apple III* ($110) includes four cassettes and a demonstra-

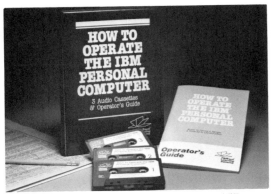

FlipTrack learning kit for the IBM PC is $57.

Learning kit for the Apple III by FlipTrack includes four cassettes and a diskette and is priced at $110.

FlipTrack learning kit for Lotus 1-2-3 software is priced at $75.

Learning kit by FlipTrack for use with VisiCalc software includes four audio cassettes.

tion diskette. There are kits for learning how to use such software programs as Lotus 1-2-3 ($75) and VisiCalc ($75). Designed for basic instruction, the cassettes talk the user step by step through the learning process. For literature, write:

FlipTrack Learning Systems
999 Main
Glen Ellyn, IL 60137

COMPUTER TRAINING WITH VIDEO CASSETTES

Micro Learning Concepts markets videotape training programs for newcomers to computers. Its program *Introduction to Personal Computers* ($99.95) consists of a videotape cassette and a *Quick Reference Guide* text. Similar programs are available for training in the use of

VisiCalc and other software. For literature, write:

Micro Learning Concepts, Inc.
380 Lexington Ave., Suite 1208
New York, NY 10017

SMALL COMPUTER BOOK CLUB: GETTING THE PICK OF THE FIELD

The number of books on personal computers continues to grow. The Small Computer Book Club offers one way to ease the selection process. The club's selections range from books on specific machines to a wide variety of books on hardware and software and their uses. For information, write:

The Small Computer Book Club
Front and Brown Sts.
Riverside, NJ 08370

COMPUTERS: A COMPREHENSIVE GUIDE

Cris Popenoe
1983/56 pp./$2
Yes! Bookshop
1035 31st St., N.W.
Washington, DC 20007

This directory of books about computers lists and describes several hundred titles. There are, for instance, more than 20 books about the IBM Personal Computer alone. The publisher

also sells these books by mail order, this directory serving as its catalog.

THE PERSONAL COMPUTER BOOK

Peter A. McWilliams
1982/300 pp./$9.95
Ballantine Books
400 Hahn Rd.
Westminster, MD 21157

If you are new to computers and especially if they make you uneasy, this might be the perfect book for you to start out with. The author eases you into the subject with an understanding manner and a lively sense of humor. In both his text and the captioned antique drawings, he turns the learning process into fun. The book is a very useful introduction to the basics, covering how the personal computer works and the various uses it can be put to. Along with advice about selecting a computer, the author presents a buying guide to major units on the market. (If ordering by mail, add $1 for postage and handling.)

THE PERSONAL COMPUTER IN BUSINESS BOOK

Peter A. McWilliams
1983/287 pp./$9.95
Ballantine Books
400 Hahn Rd.
Westminster, MD 21157

If you are a beginner with the personal computer and you wonder what one could do for

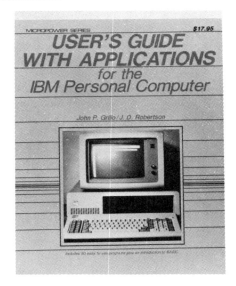

you in your office, this book could serve you well. The author's cheerful sense of humor makes this basic introduction seem like fun and his buying-guide sections will take much of the mystery out of the software and hardware on the market. Separate chapters cover such aspects as spread sheeting, graphics, accounting, word processing, electronic mail, data bases and networking. (If ordering by mail, add $1 for postage and handling.)

SCIENTIFIC AMERICAN
$24/12 issues per year
415 Madison Ave.
New York, NY 10017

This monthly is a valuable resource of information about the science that underlies our technology. Articles report on research in all areas of science, including such high-technology fields as space and genetic engineering as well as data processing and automation.

USER'S GUIDE WITH APPLICATIONS FOR THE IBM PERSONAL COMPUTER
John P. Grillo and J. D. Robertson
1983/257 pp./$17.95
Wm. C. Brown Publishers
2460 Kerper Blvd.
Dubuque, IA 52001

An example of the rapidly growing number of how-to books for the personal computer, this

manual will guide you through your first work with your IBM PC and then take you into more advanced aspects of programming. After an introduction to the basics, there is step-by-step instruction all along the way. The publisher also markets a diskette ($39.95) containing the programs in the *User's Guide*, as well as a selection of other how-to guides and diskettes for the personal computer.

ELECTRONIC LIFE: HOW TO THINK ABOUT COMPUTERS
Michael Crichton
1983/209 pp./$12.95
Alfred A. Knopf
201 E. 50th St.
New York, NY 10022

If you are a newcomer, this introduction to computers and their use will guide you smoothly through the many questions that confront you. The author, who is better known for his novels, clearly understands the state of mind of the newcomer and he is able to offer both information and reassurance. The book is organized as a series of topics in alphabetical order. The author makes the complex quite understandable and he offers practical advice in such areas as buying your first computer and software. He also takes you through the basics of operating and programming a computer.

THE COMPUTER AGE
Michael L. Dertouzos
   and Joel Moses, Editors
1979/491 pp./$9.95
MIT Press
28 Carleton St.
Cambridge, MA 02142

This book is a collection of articles by 20 authorities on technology and computer science. The writers visualize the role that the computer will play over the next 20 years and the changes it will bring in society. The articles range widely in their specific subject matter, providing a valuable resource for assessing future computer technology.

THE FIFTH GENERATION: ARTIFICIAL INTELLIGENCE AND JAPAN'S COMPUTER CHALLENGE TO THE WORLD
Edward A. Feigenbaum and
   Pamela McCorduck
1983/275 pp./$15.95
Addison-Wesley Publishing Co.
Jacob Way
Reading, MA 01867

This book offers a fascinating look into the future of computer technology, a fifth generation of computers in which artificial intelligence will come into its own. At the same time, the authors provide a detailed view of how Japan's industrial policy works. The Japanese have launched a program to develop the fifth-generation technology, and the authors report both on their progress and on the lack of response in the U.S. to this challenge.

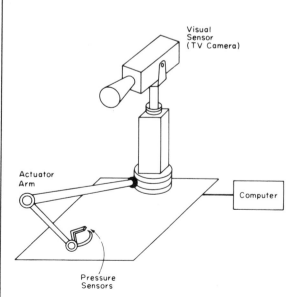

◀ *Components of a general-purpose programmable robot (from* The Computer Age*).*

ELECTRONIC NEWS FROM DOW JONES

The Dow Jones News/Retrieval service links your desktop computer by phone to a wide selection of data bases that provide business, economic, investment and general news and information. Included are *The Wall Street Journal, Barron's* and the Dow Jones News Service. There are company profiles as well as company earnings forecasts. Current market quotes include stocks, bonds, mutual funds, Treasury issues, options. There is even an electronic shopping service. Subscription fees and usage rates vary in three different plans. For further information, write:

Dow Jones News/Retrieval
Box 300
Princeton, NJ 08540

IT GUARDS YOUR COMPUTER AND SCREENS YOUR PHONE CALLS

The IMM Corp. specializes in security devices for computer systems. Its MicroSentry is an automated and self-contained unit that connects with your phone line to protect your personal computer from access by an unauthorized caller dialing through your modem. The unit operates with 16 three-digit code numbers to permit authorized access only. The codes can also be used to limit access to your phone line and screen calls as they come in.

The unit is priced at $695. For literature and further information, write:

IMM Corp.
100 N. 20th St.
Philadelphia, PA 19103

COMPUTER AGE EDP WEEKLY

$120/52 issues per year
7620 Little River Tpke.
Annandale, VA 22003

Prepared for executives within the industry, this newsletter reports weekly on developments in the computer field. It offers executives outside the industry an information source for tracking this key technology as well as assessing investment opportunities.

THE WORD PROCESSING BOOK

Peter A. McWilliams
1982/319 pp./$9.95
Ballantine Books
400 Hahn Rd.
Westminster, MD 21157

At first sight, this might seem a book more appropriate for your secretary. However, if you are learning the basics of personal computers and word processing, this book will give you a solid introduction to both. The author presents his material with a bright sense of humor in text and illustrations and he is thorough in his coverage of the major software and hardware on the market. (If ordering by mail, add $1 for postage and handling.)

WORD PROCESSING SIMPLIFIED AND SELF-TAUGHT

Jane Christensen
1983/121 pp./$4.95
Arco Publishing, Inc.
219 Park Ave. S.
New York, NY 10003

This handbook explains how word processing systems work and the results they can produce. Various types of systems are described with directions for their operation. The author explains such functions as editing, formatting and file management as well as the hardware and software that are involved. Photos illustrate the text throughout. (If ordering by mail, add $1 for postage and handling.)

HOW THE TYPEWRITER BECOMES A WORD PROCESSOR

Here is a simple way to introduce word processing in your office. The Systel II links up with your secretary's electronic typewriter to transform it into a component of a word processing system. Priced at under $3,000, the unit is compatible with most typewriters, including the IBM, Royal and Remington Rand. The system provides the capabilities of word processing, and the typewriter still works as a typewriter when it is needed. For literature and dealer information, write:

Systel Computers, Inc.
399 W. Trimble Rd.
San Jose, CA 95131

IBM: ELECTRONICS THAT MAKE THE OFFICE RUN SMOOTHLY

IBM markets a variety of equipment that can help make the executive suite hum with efficiency. Among the firm's copying machines,

IBM model 102 tabletop copying machine produces letter-size plain-paper copies at the rate of 12 copies a minute.

for instance, is the model 102, a tabletop unit that produces letter-size plain-paper copies at the rate of 12 copies a minute. IBM's Displaywriter word-processing equipment offers a wide choice of components and options. Unlike systems that use a computer with word processing software, the Displaywriter is dedicated exclusively to word processing and is designed for maximum efficiency. For literature and dealer information, write:

IBM Corp.
900 King St.
Rye Brook, NY 10573

IBM Displaywriter word-processing equipment is available in a wide choice of components and options.

TELECOMMUNICATIONS

TELECOMMUNICATIONS FROM WESTERN UNION

Western Union offers a variety of telecommunications services that can link your office with others around the world. The EasyLink and Teletex services permit you to link your electronic equipment into a vast network of possibilities. Your desktop or larger computer, a word processor or even an electronic typewriter can hook you up with other subscribers to the services for printout electronic mail. You are also linked into the Telex system. Together, these services bring you into a network of more than 1.5 million terminals. With EasyLink you can set up a company network connecting your various locations as well as your customers and suppliers. You can also send out Mailgrams, telegrams and cablegrams. A further move into telecommunications would be the installation of the Telex system itself, requiring the use of a teletypewriter terminal. Telex offers speed and economy in communications as well as providing access to information sources. For literature and further information, write:

Western Union Corp.
1 Lake St.
Upper Saddle River, NJ 07458

TELECOMMUNICATIONS WORLDWIDE WITH GTE

Along with such telephone services as Sprint long distance, the General Telephone and Electronics Corp. markets a wide variety of services with its Telenet data-communications network. Linked with your computer, this network provides access to data base information, computer applications and electronic mail communications. The Telenet annual directory details these computer-based services. For literature and further information, write:

General Telephone and Electronics Corp.
1 Stamford Forum
Stamford, CT 06904

TELEPHONY
$45/52 issues per year
55 E. Jackson Blvd.
Chicago, IL 60604

This weekly is a journal for the communications industry. It is highly technical in some aspects, but it is also a useful source of information about the expanding field of telecommunications. The news columns as well as the articles and the advertising provide access to the latest in technology and applications.

The 3M model EMT 9140 facsimile transceiver handles documents up to 8½ by 14 inches.

LONG-DISTANCE SERVICES AND TELEPHONE EQUIPMENT

Below are listed six major suppliers of long-distance and other telecommunications services. An asterisk indicates those suppliers that also market telephone equipment:

* AT&T Communications
  670 White Plains Rd.
  Scarsdale, NY 10583
  (Toll free: 800-222-0400)

* GTE Sprint
  Box 974
  Burlingame, CA 94010
  (Toll free: 800-521-4949)

* ITT Longer Distance
  100 Plaza Dr.
  Secaucus, NJ 07096
  (Toll free: 800-526-3000)

  MCI Telecommunications Corp.
  110 King St.
  Rye Brook, NY 10573
  (Toll free: 800-624-2222)

* SBS Skyline
  1 State St. Plaza
  New York, NY 10004
  (Toll free: 800-852-5000)

* Western Union Long-Distance Services
  1 Lake St.
  Upper Saddle River, NJ 07458
  (Toll free: 800-562-0240)

TELECOMMUNICATIONS
$36/12 issues per year
610 Washington St.
Dedham, MA 02026

Rapidly expanding technology is transforming the field of telecommunications. New equipment and applications are bringing widespread changes in the ways that companies communicate. Computer systems are networked internationally via satellite. Top management consults together in live video teleconference sessions transmitted over long-distance lines. This magazine for professionals can keep you up to date on new developments as they happen. (Your management position may qualify you for a free subscription to this controlled-circulation magazine.)

TELECOMMUNICATIONS PRODUCTS FROM 3M

One of several communications products of 3M, the model EMT 9140 facsimile transceiver is a desktop message terminal that sends and receives copies via standard telephone lines. Broadly compatible with other units, this facsimile machine handles documents up to 8½ by 14 inches. For Telex transmissions, 3M offers the Whisper Writer Package 83, which combines a teleprinter module and a keyboard module. The keyboard's memory permits off-line preparation of more than 10 minutes of corrected messages for transmission. An elec-

The Whisper Writer Package 83 Telex terminal has a keyboard memory for off-line preparation of more than 10 minutes of corrected messages for transmission.

tronic-mail system, the Whisper Exchange, is a service marketed by 3M to provide a firm's company-wide communications. Available in rental programs starting at $1,500 per month, the network consists of Whisper Writer teleprinters and other terminals linked over telephone lines. For literature and further information, write:

3M Business Communication
  Products Division
Box 33600
St. Paul, MN 55133

THE BUSINESS OF MANAGING THE FIRM'S PHONE BILL

CP National's Software & Systems Division specializes in the hardware and software for automated management of telecommunications usage. Software systems are designed both for individual locations and for networks, and the systems are combined with hardware to collect and process data from remote locations. An information kit on cost control and reduction is available. Write:

CP National
Software & Systems Division
242 Old New Brunswick Rd.
Piscataway, NJ 08854

HIGH-SPEED FACSIMILE TRANSMISSION FROM SANYO

The Sanyo model 935 facsimile unit features high-speed operation for reduced phone-transmission costs. Offering broad compatibility with other machines, the compact desktop unit transmits copies of documents, photographs, drawings. For literature and dealer information, write:

Sanyo Business Systems Corp.
51 Joseph St.
Moonachie, NJ 07074

COPIERS, FACSIMILE UNITS FROM PITNEY BOWES

Specialists in the technology of paper flow, Pitney Bowes markets two compact tabletop copying machines. The model 3800 is a plain-paper

The Pitney Bowes model 3800 desktop copier can deliver 20 letter-size copies per minute.

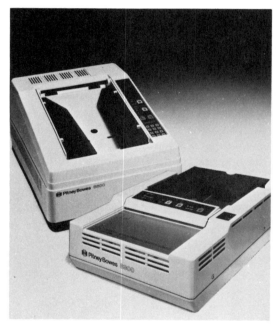

These Pitney Bowes facsimile units are the model 8600 at the left and the 8300 at the right.

copier that can deliver 20 letter-size copies per minute. Paper feed is via dual cassettes that hold 250 sheets each, and the unit has reduction and enlargement features. The firm's second copier is the model 9600, a larger machine with a capacity of 30 copies per minute. The firm also markets two desktop facsimile units, the models 8300 and 8600. Both units feature automatic functions. The 8600, a larger machine, offers broader compatibility with other transceivers. The company offers a free booklet on paper-handling efficiency, covering its equipment for copying, collating and other functions as well as its postage-metering units. For literature and further information, write:

Pitney Bowes
Walter H. Wheeler, Jr. Dr.
Stamford, CT 06926

TELECONFERENCING

VIDEO TELECONFERENCING NETWORK AT MARRIOTT HOTELS

Marriott markets teleconferencing services in a network of its hotels across the country. Each of the network hotels has a permanently installed dish antenna for receiving video transmission nationwide via communications satellite. The hotels are located at such cities as Chicago, Dallas, Atlanta, Boston, Los Angeles and Washington, D.C. Several of the hotels are located at or near a major airport. The network eases access to a conference program broadcast from one location to audiences at hotels around the country. For further information, write:

Marriott Corp.
1 Marriott Dr.
Washington, DC 20058

HILTON HOTELS AND AT&T TEAM FOR TELECONFERENCING

Hilton Hotels offer video teleconferencing at more than 30 facilities across the country in a network of AT&T transmission. The service is available in both one-way and two-way video and audio communications and it is designed for use in both small and large meetings. For literature and further information, write:

Hilton Hotels Corp.
9880 Wilshire Blvd.
Beverly Hills, CA 90210

HOLIDAY INNS: GRAND-SCALE VIDEO TELECONFERENCING

With more than 1,000 locations available for audiences, Holiday Inns offer video teleconferencing on a grand scale. The chain uses HI-NET, its own system, to transmit via satellite to its locations across the country. An illustrated booklet details all the services offered in the teleconferencing system. For literature and further information, write:

Holiday Inns, Inc.
3742 Lamar Ave.
Memphis, TN 38195

TELECONFERENCING WITH WESTERN UNION

If you have not held your first teleconference yet, you might want to talk with Western

Union about its VideoConferencing service. Broadcasting via space satellite, the service beams your live television meeting program to any one or more audience meetings around the country. Each audience group receives the program on a large screen up to 30 by 40 feet in size. An audio-response capability is also available so that members of the audience can talk with the meeting speakers. The service is designed for product introductions, sales and stockholder meetings, seminars, employee-relations programs. Western Union provides complete service that includes the production of the meeting program either in a rented studio or at your company. For illustrated brochure and further information, write:

Western Union Corp.
1 Lake St.
Upper Saddle River, NJ 07458

TELECONFERENCING OVERSEAS WITH AT&T

The AT&T Video Teleconferencing service provides live television broadcasting via satellite, with interaction in both directions, between conferees at both ends of the transmission. For example, you and your executive committee might confer with the top executives of your subsidiary in London. At both ends of the conference there is a capability for presenting charts, graphs and other visual displays. The cost for a one-hour video teleconference is approximately $3,000 between New York and London. For further information, write:

AT&T Communications
195 Broadway
New York, NY 10007

TELECONFERENCING TECHNOLOGY FROM NEC

Telecommunications and the traditional business meeting have come together, and meetings will now never be quite the same. Teleconferencing brings people together via audio, video and facsimile transmissions, and NEC America, Inc., is one of the leaders in the new technology. Along with system planning, the firm markets electronic equipment for telephone transmissions, video cameras and projectors, as well as other components involved in teleconferencing. For details of this technology, write for the booklet *Teleconference System*.

NEC America, Inc.
532 Broad Hollow Rd.
Melville, NY 11747

VIDEO: WHAT CAN IT DO FOR YOU AND YOUR COMPANY?

The JVC Company of America specializes in professional video equipment, some of which is well adapted for use by company personnel for employee communications, training, sales and

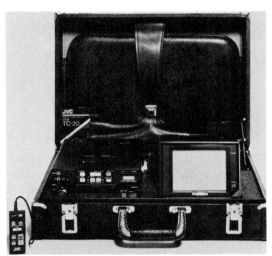

The THR-63U portable video system combines a compact video player with a 5-inch television monitor, both of which fit into an attaché case (photo courtesy of JVC Company of America).

other applications. As an introduction for the executive, the firm offers its booklet *What Does My Company Have to Do to Get Started in Video Communications?* The booklet answers basic questions and describes some of the equipment that the firm markets, among which are videocassette cameras, recorders, players and monitors. The THR-63U portable video system, for instance, combines a compact video player unit with a 5-inch television monitor, both of which fit into an attaché case. Priced at $1,650, the unit's typical use would be to show a video program to a prospective customer or client. Write:

JVC Company of America
41 Slater Dr.
Elmwood Park, NJ 07407

KEEPING IN TOUCH: CAR PHONE, POCKET PAGER

If you seek ways to increase your productivity, consider using a car telephone or a remote paging unit to keep in closer touch with your work. The latest technology in car phones is cellular transmission, for which Motorola markets the DYNA TAC mobile radiotelephone. An optional speaker allows the driver to leave the unit's handset cradled, and its automated features include storage of up to 30 frequently dialed numbers. Motorola also markets a line of radio pagers. The smallest unit in the line is

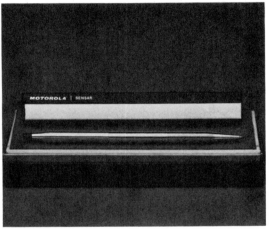

Motorola's miniaturized Sensar radio pager is shown next to a ballpoint pen.

The Motorola DYNA TAC mobile radiotelephone for your car.

the Sensar, which weighs just over an ounce and will fit in your pocket next to your pen. The battery-operated pager can signal two distinct call-page messages. Write:

Motorola, Inc.
1301 E. Algonquin Rd.
Schaumburg, IL 60196

MOBILE PHONE SERVICE FROM WESTERN UNION

Western Union offers a complete service program for operation of a cellular mobile phone in your car. The program is based on local centers for the installation and servicing of the telephone units. The units are designed for ease of operation and include such features as automated redialing. For literature, write:

Western Union Corp.
1 Lake St.
Upper Saddle River, NJ 07458

SECTION 4

The Executive Management Library

MANAGEMENT STRATEGIES

TOP MANAGEMENT STRATEGY
Benjamin B. Tregoe
    and John W. Zimmerman
1980/128 pp./$5.95
Simon and Schuster
1230 Avenue of the Americas
New York, NY 10020

The practical conclusions of this study of management strategy are based on a distinction between strategy and long-range planning. Strategy, the authors stress, defines what the company is to become, providing a framework within which plans are projected and necessary changes can be made. The authors show how the unique characteristics of a company must be identified in order to determine the specific strategy that will work for that company, enabling it to survive change and continue to grow.

*STRATEGY AND THE RISKS OF
SURVIVING WITHOUT IT*

In a sense, organizations are like living organisms. They must adapt to survive. Some organizations have been able to adapt by focusing primarily on present operations. These organizations face the future by continually improving operating effectiveness. They are action-prone and go for the operational fix: capital expenditure expansion or delays, hiring limitations, tighter inventory control, increasing or reducing staff services, price changes, more efficient delivery systems, and the like. While information about the future is important for these organizations, it is used mainly to set limits on the expansion of current operations.

But the operations palliative, if taken alone, is dangerous medicine for treating a crisis or change which could threaten the survival of the business. If an organization is headed in the wrong direction, the last thing it needs is to get there more efficiently. And if an organization is headed in the right direction, it surely does not need to have that direction unwittingly changed by operational action taken in a strategic void.

From: *Top Management Strategy*, Benjamin B. Tregoe and John W. Zimmerman (New York: Simon and Schuster, 1980)

> Every organization has a momentum or direction. It is headed somewhere. Top managers who do not consciously set strategy risk having their organization's momentum or direction developed implicitly, haphazardly or by others inside or outside the organization.
>
> From: *Top Management Strategy*, Benjamin B. Tregoe and John W. Zimmerman (New York: Simon and Schuster, 1980)

DECISION MAKING AT THE TOP
Gordon Donaldson and Jay W. Lorsch
1983/208 pp./$16.95
Basic Books, Inc.
10 E. 53rd St.
New York, NY 10022

This book studies the decision-making process among the top executives of 12 anonymous companies, each a major corporation in its industry. The authors, both Harvard professors, led their research team in an extensive interview program that produced some of the most striking material in the book. The authors conclude that long-term growth, rather than short-term financial results, is the guiding factor for corporate leaders. The book describes examples of major management decisions and details their results. A special section summarizes the belief systems of management at the companies studied.

GAME THEORY: A NONTECHNICAL INTRODUCTION
Morton D. Davis
1970, 1983/252 pp./$8.95
Basic Books, Inc.
10 E. 53rd St.
New York, NY 10022

Using a minimum of mathematics, the author guides the reader into an understanding of the basics of game theory, showing how it works to clarify the processes of decision making. The author spells out the many implications of game theory as it applies to such areas as business, economics and politics, with an emphasis on its application to understanding basic human behavior. Included are sample problems with which the reader can build actual experience with game theory.

DECISION MAKING FOR LEADERS
Thomas L. Saaty
1982/291 pp./$24.95
Lifetime Learning Publications
10 Davis Dr.
Belmont, CA 94002

The author presents his Analytical Hierarchy Process, a decision-making process that is designed to combine intuitive elements with a basis of logic. The book develops the workings of the process with detailed and practical examples. Applications of the process include predicting likely outcomes, selecting alternatives, setting priorities and conducting cost vs. benefit comparisons. In a special section, programs derived from the author's process are offered for use in computers and programmable calculators.

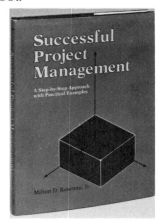

SUCCESSFUL PROJECT MANAGEMENT
Milton D. Rosenau, Jr.
1981/266 pp./$27
Lifetime Learning Publications
10 Davis Dr.
Belmont, CA 94002

The author presents a basic introduction that is designed for the executive facing a first assignment as a project manager. The book uses a step-by-step approach, with an emphasis on practical examples and case studies. Each chapter develops a stage in the management process, building conceptual understanding of working principles. Included are chapters on aspects of planning, organizing project teams, control tools and reviews.

THE RISE AND FALL OF CORPORATE NEW VENTURE DIVISIONS
Norman D. Fast
1977/219 pp./$39.95
University Microfilms International
300 N. Zeeb Rd.
Ann Arbor, MI 48106

The author studies the widespread development of new venture divisions in American corporations in the 1960s. He traces the progress of several of these divisions, in particular those at Du Pont, Ralston Purina and the Standard Chemical Co. This research indicates ways in which such ventures can be made more productive.

◀ *The relationship between original project plans and the need for subsequent replanning (from Successful Project Management).*

PRACTICAL MANAGEMENT SKILLS FOR ENGINEERS AND SCIENTISTS
William C. Giegold
1982/430 pp./$26
Lifetime Learning Publications
10 Davis Dr.
Belmont, CA 94002

Written for technical and scientific personnel taking on management responsibilities, this broad introduction to fundamental skills and methods offers a useful review resource to executives. The author deals with such elements as leadership, delegation and organizational politics as well as such management functions as planning. Both concepts and skills are emphasized, with extensive use of case histories for illustration.

Among all the theories and models proposed to define management functions, the *classical model* is the most complete. Attributed to Henri Fayol, a French industrialist, the classical model has been with us since the first third of this century. Fayol divided management into five task areas: planning, organizing, coordinating, commanding and controlling.

From: *Practical Management Skills for Engineers and Scientists,* William C. Giegold (Belmont, CA: Lifetime Learning Publications, 1982)

THE PRODUCTIVITY PRESCRIPTION: THE MANAGER'S GUIDE TO IMPROVING PRODUCTIVITY AND PROFITS
David Bain
1982/308 pp./$21.95
McGraw-Hill Book Co.
1221 Avenue of the Americas
New York, NY 10020

Written by a management consultant, this guide presents systematic remedies for improvement in the areas of production, service, quality and profit. The author focuses on employee motivation, productivity and quality measurement and organizational goal-setting.

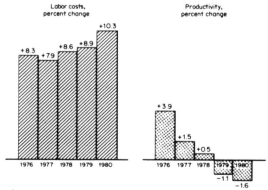

Changes in labor costs compared with changes in productivity in the U.S. from 1976 through 1980 (from The Productivity Prescription: The Manager's Guide to Improving Productivity and Profits).

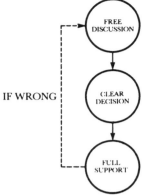

The ideal decision-making process (from High Output Management).

The book's prescriptions are detailed and accompanied by illustrations and examples, including four in-depth case studies. Emphasizing incentives and involvement in decision making, the author spells out the employee role in productivity.

THE BARNARD CONCEPT OF THE EXECUTIVE ROLE

The executive functions serve to maintain a system of cooperative effort. They are impersonal. The functions are not, as so frequently stated, to manage a group of persons. I do not think a correct understanding of executive work can be had if this narrower, convenient, but strictly speaking erroneous, conception obtains. It is not even quite correct to say that the executive functions are to manage the system of cooperative efforts. As a whole it is managed by itself, not by the executive organization, which is a part of it. The functions with which we are concerned are like those of the nervous system, including the brain, in relation to the rest of the body. It exists to maintain the bodily system by directing those actions which are necessary more effectively to adjust to the environment, but it can hardly be said to manage the body, a large part of whose functions are independent of it and [are functions] upon which it in turn depends.

From: *The Functions of the Executive*, Chester I. Barnard (Cambridge, MA: Harvard University Press, 1982)

HIGH OUTPUT MANAGEMENT
Andrew S. Grove
1983/235 pp./$16.95
Random House
201 E. 50th St.
New York, NY 10022

President and a founder of the Intel Corp., the author uses his experience as an executive to define and describe the ideas, principles and techniques that he believes yield high productivity. He focuses his presentation for middle managers and applies the principles and discipline of manufacturing to spell out his approach. The result is practical advice, illustrated with specific examples.

CLEARINGHOUSE FOR PRODUCTIVITY

The Commerce Productivity Center at the U.S. Dept. of Commerce serves as a clearinghouse for information on how to improve productivity, quality and competitiveness in U.S. business and industry. The center has access to the department's research facilities and can provide articles, publications, reference and referral services, bibliographies and reading lists. Research topics include productivity measurement and programs, quality improvement and

Japanese management techniques. For further information, write:

Commerce Productivity Center
U.S. Dept. of Commerce
Rm. 7413
Washington, DC 20230

MANUFACTURING PRODUCTIVITY FRONTIERS
$100/12 issues per year
10 W. 35th St.
Chicago, IL 60616

This monthly publication comes from the Manufacturing Productivity Center at the Illi-

nois Institute of Technology. While it is aimed at a readership of technical professionals, you do not at all have to be an engineer to make use of the material presented here. In articles, reports and reviews, you can learn the latest about such subjects as robotics, computer applications and manufacturing systems.

PRODUCTIVITY
$126/12 issues per year
Box 16722
Stamford, CT 06905

This monthly newsletter reports on productivity improvement in industry as well as in white-collar and service operations. The newsletter presents both original reporting and reprint material.

June 1983
Vol. 7, No. 6

Manufacturing Productivity
FRONTIERS

THE U.S. NEWS WASHINGTON LETTER
$39/52 issues per year
2300 N St., N.W.
Washington, DC 20037

This four-page weekly report is concise and packed with news from Washington. It offers the executive an efficient source of information from the capital.

> As a middle manager, of any sort, you are in effect a chief executive of an organization yourself. Don't wait for the principles and the practices you find appealing or valid to be imposed from the top. As a *micro* CEO, you can improve your own and your group's performance and productivity, whether or not the rest of the company follows suit.
>
> From: *High Output Management*, Andrew S. Grove (New York: Random House, 1983)

MANAGING

$39/12 issues per year
757 3rd Ave.
New York, NY 10017

Targeted for the management of small-to-medium companies, this newsletter is a useful resource for the executive who wants to keep in touch with the entrepreneur's perspective. Each issue devotes a special two-page section to guidance for the entrepreneur.

RESEARCH INSTITUTE RECOMMENDATIONS

$48/52 issues per year
589 5th Ave.
New York, NY 10017

This newsletter offers a weekly update on economic conditions and business activity, with emphasis on political and governmental aspects. A publication of the Research Institute of America, the newsletter offers recommendations in such areas as personal and business tax savings.

CHASE ECONOMETRICS LETTER

$144/12 issues per year
10076 Boca Entrada Blvd.
Boca Raton, FL 33433

This monthly newsletter reports on economic statistics and trends. Recent and current economic developments are highlighted and detailed. The newsletter reports on governmental regulation and activity affecting the economy. Various sectors of the economy are featured from issue to issue.

AUTOMATION: RESOURCES FOR LEARNING HOW IT WORKS

If you contemplate automation of manufacturing operations or if you simply want to know more about the process, the Bodine Corp. offers useful information on the subject. Specialists in assembly machines, the firm has published two booklets: *Bodine's Assembly Primer*, and *The Anatomy of a Money-Making Assembly System*. Write:

Bodine Corp.
317 Mountain Grove St.
Bridgeport, CT 06605

> The major difference between the most and least successful executives lies precisely in the latters' lack of awareness. The hallmark of this difference is that the successful executive is critical of his own performance; the unsuccessful, of the performance of others.
>
> From: *The Exceptional Executive*, Harry Levinson (New York: New American Library, 1971)

Many give lip service, but few delegate authority *in important matters*. And that means all they delegate is dog work. A real leader does as much dog work for his people as he can: he can do it, or see a way to do without it, ten times as fast. And he delegates as many important matters as he can because that creates a climate in which people grow.

From: *Further Up the Organization*, Robert Townsend (New York: Alfred A. Knopf, 1984)

ROBOTICS UPDATE

$67/12 issues per year
10076 Boca Entrada Blvd.
Boca Raton, FL 33433

If you follow developments in high technology and automation, this newsletter will keep you posted on breakthroughs, patents, new applications and trends in the field of robotics. Coverage includes case histories of robotic applications. A monthly calendar lists seminars, conferences and expositions.

TECHNOLOGY ILLUSTRATED

$18/12 issues per year
38 Commercial Wharf
Boston, MA 02110

A magazine for the general reader, this monthly spotlights technology, particularly in

new consumer products. It offers a convenient way to keep track of what is coming into the marketplace. The reading is easy and it is extensively illustrated with color photography.

TECHNOLOGY UPDATE

$150/52 issues per year
11001 Cedar Ave.
Cleveland, OH 44106

This newsletter presents brief summaries from newspapers, magazines and other sources to provide a weekly review of developments in technology. Categories covered include health and medicine, chemicals, energy, materials, engineering, computers and robotics. Reprints of the complete text of summarized material can be ordered from the publisher.

The successful businessman is the one who can, in an appreciable percentage of instances, correctly foresee developments, promptly take advantage of emerging opportunities and effectively forestall problems. No businessman can have a perfect batting average, but it is the man with the highest prediction-and-prevention record who reaches the top most quickly and remains there most securely.

From: *How to Be a Successful Executive*, J. Paul Getty (New York: Playboy, 1981)

HIGH TECHNOLOGY

$21/12 times per year
38 Commercial Wharf
Boston, MA 02110

This monthly magazine reports on new developments in all areas of technology, from medical research to consumer products. Included are industrial materials and processes as well as coverage of such fields as aerospace. The articles include assessment of the business implications for new developments.

The problem in America is that our fascination with the tools of management obscures our apparent ignorance of the art. Our tools are biased toward measurement and analysis. We can measure the costs. But with these tools alone we can't really elaborate on the value of a turned-on Maytag or Caterpillar work force churning out quality products or a Frito-Lay salesperson going that extra mile for the ordinary customer.

From: *In Search of Excellence: Lessons from America's Best-Run Companies*, Thomas J. Peters and Robert H. Waterman, Jr. (New York: Harper & Row, 1982)

CORPORATE ORGANIZATION STRUCTURES: MANUFACTURING
Allen R. Janger
1973/96 pp./$25
The Conference Board, Inc.
845 3rd Ave.
New York, NY 10022

Bound in a large-format portfolio, this collection presents organization charts from more than 70 of the largest manufacturing companies in the U.S. The author examines the basic variations among the examples and identifies common patterns of organization. The charts themselves offer a useful resource for study and comparison.

CORPORATE ORGANIZATION STRUCTURES: SERVICE COMPANIES
Allen R. Janger
1977/103 pp./$30
The Conference Board, Inc.
845 3rd Ave.
New York, NY 10022

This collection of organization charts from 60 service companies shows a wide variety of organizational approaches in the several fields covered. Included are examples from transportation, communications, construction and retail companies as well as utilities. A large format makes even the most detailed charts fully readable.

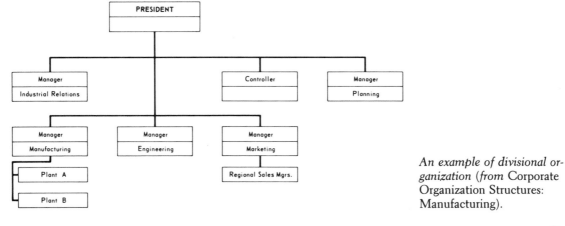

An example of divisional organization (from Corporate Organization Structures: Manufacturing).

STRATEGIC CHOICES AND HOW THEY ARE MADE

Usually it is argued that strategic choice is and should be an entirely rational matter: Managers weigh the economic factors in a decision and make a logical choice. From this perspective major changes in strategy are effected easily and rationally, in one fell swoop. But once again we have found a very different picture. Major shifts in strategy do not occur suddenly or rapidly. On the contrary, the process of strategic change is basically an incremental one, and each step is relatively small. Thus it takes many years for the management of a company to achieve major strategic changes. Moreover, strategic decisions are not the product of simple economic logic alone. Because these decisions often depend on forecasts of future events, they involve considerable uncertainty and ambiguity. To analyze these complexities top managers draw upon their experience and judgment—judgment that has been shaped by the shared beliefs passed on to them by their predecessors. Thus to some extent, their decisions always reflect nonrational considerations, because they have been filtered through their belief systems.

From: *Decision Making at the Top*, Gordon Donaldson and Jay W. Lorsch (New York: Basic Books, 1983)

EXECUTIVE SKILLS: A MANAGEMENT BY OBJECTIVES APPROACH

George Odiorne, Heinz Weihrich and Jack Mendleson
1980/319 pp./$14.95
Wm. C. Brown Publishers
2460 Kerper Blvd.
Dubuque, IA 52001

Covering all aspects of Management by Objectives (MBO), this book is a collection of 25 articles by the authors and other contributors, including Peter F. Drucker. The articles provide a broad overview as well as very specific examination of MBO methods. Included are articles about the evolution of the approach as well as on such subjects as strategic planning and the setting of objectives. Case-study material is used to illustrate the articles.

HARVARD BUSINESS REVIEW

$30/6 issues per year
Soldiers Field, Teele Hall
Boston, MA 02163

This bimonthly review shares the high standing of its sponsor, the Harvard Graduate School of Business Administration. The magazine studies the workings of management in all its aspects. Some of its articles take a theoretical approach, but for the most part the emphasis is on expanding the practical knowledge and skills of the executive. It is a publication that can challenge your thinking and supply a steady source of ideas and direction for your work.

THE INCOMPLEAT BOARD
Robert Kirk Mueller
1981/283 pp./$29.95
Lexington Books
125 Spring St.
Lexington, MA 02173

The author, who has been chairman of the board of Arthur D. Little, Inc., as well as a board member of several other companies, theorizes about the nature and function of the board of directors. He maintains that the board is inherently "incomplete," in the sense of an open system. By contrast, he calls the management of a corporation a closed system. Thus, the board must be both open to innovation and flexible rather than structured. The author includes detailed guidelines for assessing board member performance.

THE STRUCTURE OF THE CORPORATION: A LEGAL ANALYSIS
Melvin A. Eisenberg
1976/333 pp./$9.95
Little, Brown & Co.
34 Beacon St.
Boston, MA 02106

Although it is written by an attorney for attorneys, this book provides a very useful reference

THE LIFE CYCLE OF THE BOARD OF DIRECTORS

Strangely, there is a paradox in the nature of success in this thinking shop or corporate boardroom. The board matures and develops certain norms, patterns and rhythms. It also acquires a history and identity. Importance of individual founding members of the board and its psychological leaders diminishes, in time, in explaining organizational outcomes. The board shifts from a personal to an impersonal metaphor. The outcomes are characterized by a closed-board system with a life of its own rather than by the formative, open, more individualistic system that existed before the institutionalization stage becomes firm.

As this governance process unfolds, however, the composition of success changes. New norms, beliefs, values and structural components become incorporated within the framework of existing patterns of the newly created closed system. Such is possible only if the board system opens its boundaries and allows new energy, information and thinking to penetrate. Conversely, the board can easily remain an unresponsive closed system if the incumbent directors are not sympathetic to change and insist on perpetuating the status quo.

From: *The Incompleat Board*, Robert Kirk Mueller (Lexington, MA: Lexington Books, 1981)

Number of Shareholders	Approximate Number of Corporations
1-10	1,630,000
11-99	70,000
100-499	26,500*
500-1499	5,000
1500-2999	1,700
3000-10,000	1,200
Over 10,000	600

*This figure combines corporations with 100-299 shareholders (24,000) and corporations with 300-499 shareholders (2,500).

Approximate distribution of corporations by number of shareholders as of 1970 (from The Structure of the Corporation: A Legal Analysis*).*

resource on the legal aspects of corporate organization. The footnotes are dense with citations, but the text is quite clear and easy to read. The book is comprehensive, dealing with aspects that range from the legal role of shareholders to the legal requirements for the board of directors. Included is coverage of structural changes such as mergers and acquisitions.

JOURNAL OF BUSINESS STRATEGY
$56/4 issues per year
210 South St.
Boston, MA 02111

This journal deals with strategic planning in the large corporation. Its contributors are leading executives, business school professors and professional consultants. Typical articles present case-history material, with emphasis on the perspective of the CEO.

RESOURCES FOR CORPORATE PLANNING

The North American Society for Corporate Planning, an association with more than 4,000 members, publishes various material of use to planners. Its *Planning Resource Guide* ($10) is an index to articles that have appeared in its journal, *Planning Review*, as well as to taped

presentations from its annual conferences. For information on membership and publications, write:

North American Society
   for Corporate Planning, Inc.
300 Arcade Sq.
Dayton, OH 45402

PLANNING UPDATE
$150/52 issues per year
11001 Cedar Ave.
Cleveland, OH 44106

Presenting a broad review of information related to corporate planning, this newsletter summarizes material from newspapers, magazines and other sources. Categories covered include strategic and operational planning as well as research and development. Reprints of the complete text of summarized material can be ordered from the publisher.

CHANGEMENT
Peter H. Burgher, Editor
1979/277 pp./$18.95
Lexington Books
125 Spring St.
Lexington, MA 02173

This collection of 29 articles examines change and the management of change. Written by authors in the fields of management and psychology, the articles vary widely in their point of view and subject material. The opening selec-

The final act of business judgment is of course intuitive. Perhaps there are formal ways of improving the logic of business strategy, or policy making. But the big work behind business judgment is in finding and acknowledging the facts and circumstances concerning technology, the market and the like in their continuously changing forms.

From: *My Years with General Motors*, Alfred P. Sloan, Jr. (Garden City, NY: Anchor Books, 1972)

tions are concerned with identifying and understanding change, both in its many forms and in its many effects. Further articles deal with initiating change and controlling its impact.

IMPLEMENTING STRATEGY
Lawrence G. Hrebiniak
   and William F. Joyce
1984/252 pp./$6.95
Macmillan Publishing Co.
866 3rd Ave.
New York, NY 10022

The authors examine the process of strategy implementation, tracing the interrelationships of planning, organizational-design and human-resource decisions. The book focuses on such direct relationships as that between strategy formulation and subsequent implementation decisions and specific structural changes in the organization.

Types of strategy implementation (from Implementing Strategy).▶

PLANNING REVIEW
$50/6 issues per year
300 Arcade Sq.
Dayton, OH 45402

Published by the North American Society for Corporate Planning, this journal covers all aspects of planning. Articles focus both on planning itself and on such directly related subjects as economics and finance. Case studies deal with specific company experiences. Of particular interest are the advertisements for computer software for planners.

Implementation Horizon

	Long	Short
Large	Sequential intervention	Complex intervention
Small	Evolutionary interventions	Managerial interventions
	Long	Short

Strategic Problem Size

EXECUTIVE SKILLS

THE CHANGING WORLD OF THE EXECUTIVE
Peter F. Drucker
1982/271 pp./$17.95
Times Books
3 Park Ave.
New York, NY 10016

Largely a selection of his columns in *The Wall Street Journal*, these short articles present the author's views on the challenges that face the executive. The author ranges over a variety of subjects, but his basic focus is on changing circumstances. He covers such subjects as computer technology, foreign management methods, reindustrialization and production sharing with foreign manufacturers. Some of this material dates to the mid-1970s, but all of it remains pertinent and often reflects how clearly the author perceives the direction of new developments. This broad sampling of Drucker's ideas and point of view provides an ideal introduction for anyone unfamiliar with his books on management.

THE FULLY EFFECTIVE EXECUTIVE
Gerald Kushel
1983/184 pp./$15
Contemporary Books, Inc.
180 N. Michigan Ave.
Chicago, IL 60601

A management consultant, the author specializes in executive-effectiveness studies. His book offers guidance aimed at self-development for professional and personal success. He builds his approach to a great extent upon his survey of more than 500 executives, from which he has drawn a small core of "fully effective" examples. The book uses both self-tests and brief case studies to develop its presentation.

Achieving high-level success requires the support and the cooperation of others. And gaining this support and cooperation of others requires leadership ability. Success and the ability to lead others—that is, getting them to do things they wouldn't do if they were not led—go hand-in-hand.

From: *The Magic of Thinking Big*, David J. Schwartz (New York: Cornerstone Library, 1982)

One thing we can be sure of when an appointment does not turn out as well as expected is that the executive who made the decision and who selected and appointed the person made the wrong decision or—equally often—made the decision the wrong way. To blame the failed promotion on the promoted person—as is usually done—is no more rational than to blame a capital investment that has gone sour on the money that was put in.

From: *The Changing World of the Executive*, Peter F. Drucker (New York: Times Books, 1982)

HOW TO GET PEOPLE TO DO THINGS
Robert Conklin
1979/214 pp./$11.95
Contemporary Books, Inc.
180 N. Michigan Ave.
Chicago, IL 60601

The author writes about human relationships and how they are affected by attitude and motivation. He offers guidance to the reader for transforming negative attitudes to positive to improve relationships with others. The book's emphasis is on a practical understanding of human behavior, and the author illustrates his advice with examples both from business situations and from everyday experience.

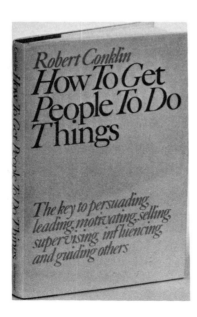

FREDERICK W. TAYLOR AND THE RISE OF SCIENTIFIC MANAGEMENT
Daniel Nelson
1980/259 pp./$19.50
University of Wisconsin Press
114 N. Murray St.
Madison, WI 53715

This biography of one of the better-known names from turn-of-the-century business history provides a helpful background in modern management methods. Taylor, who is associated with the use of time studies, was a proponent of "scientific management." His ideas influenced changes in industry and became part of the development of today's management practices.

MANAGEMENT BY MULTIPLE OBJECTIVES
Sang M. Lee
1981/225 pp./$20
Petrocelli Books, Inc.
1101 State Rd.
Princeton, NJ 08540

Extending the management-by-objectives approach, the author shows how integrating management systems and technologies can achieve

Objective: Increase sales by 5% during the coming year
Date: 3/5

Plan Activities	President	VP-Sales	VP-Marketing	VP-Production	VP-Finance	VP-Personnel	VP-Research & Design	Mgr-Management Science	Mgr-Reg. Sales	Mgr-Computer Operations
1. Increase advertising budget by 10%	G	O S	D	D				N	N	
2. Develop a new sales training program		O S	G	N		S			C	
3. Develop a new bonus system for sales personnel	A	O	G	C	S	N	N	C N	C N	C N
4. Increase sales force by 2%		G	N			S			O	

Responsibility Code
G = General
O = Operating
S = Specific
C = Consultative
N = Notification
A = Approval

This responsibility-analysis chart identifies the roles of members of a task force (from Management by Multiple Objectives).

multiple and often conflicting organizational objectives. Thus the concept of MBO becomes MBMO, which, the author believes, provides the concepts and approaches for multiple-objective decision making.

EXECUTIVE

Harry Levinson
1968, 1981/370 pp./$7.95
Harvard University Press
79 Garden St.
Cambridge, MA 02138

A guide to understanding the psychological and social aspects of the executive's role, this book is about human behavior—both individual and organizational. A basic premise is that to be effective the executive must understand his or her own behavior and motivation as well as that of subordinates. The author examines the dynamics of power and leadership and he presents 14 case studies to illustrate the human interactions that are involved. In a separate chapter, the author focuses on the executive as teacher, emphasizing the importance of the mentor role in the organization. A valuable resource, this book has become a classic in its field.

THE FUNCTIONS OF THE EXECUTIVE

Chester I. Barnard
1938, 1982/334 pp./$6.95
Harvard University Press
79 Garden St.
Cambridge, MA 02138

Recognized as a classic, this book is the work of a man who spent most of his career as an executive with AT&T. The author develops a theory of organization in which he examines the cooperative processes that the executive must manage. The book is theoretical in approach, dealing with such concepts as the nature of leadership, authority and responsibility. This resource provides perspectives on some of the most basic ideas about management theory and practice.

Innovation is chancy. But surely there is a reason, other than luck, why some managements, a Procter & Gamble or a 3-M, for instance, have done consistently so much better in product development and product introduction than most others. One reason is that all the businesses with a high batting average systematically appraise their innovation performance against expectations. Then one can improve. And then, above all, one can know what one is good at. Most businesses manage innovation by promise. The competent innovators manage by results.

From: *The Changing World of the Executive*, Peter F. Drucker (New York: Times Books, 1982)

BALANCING THE CONFLICTS OF MULTIPLE OBJECTIVES

Management will be vitally concerned with the analysis of multiple objectives, not only with their formulation but with priorities and trade-offs. There exists an ever increasing pressure in the simultaneous satisfaction of government regulations, economic optimization and other organizational goals. Materials shortage (e.g., energy) and increasing costs are forcing managers to be more concerned with economic optimization (minimizing operational costs). Yet, government regulations to cope with the same basic problem have forced organizations to be further removed from economic optimization. We will see more direct conflict between the organization's economic survival and other objectives that are related to social responsibilities of the organization.

Managers will be held increasingly more accountable with regard to the legitimacy of their objectives, priorities and conflict resolution among objectives. Thus, we will see greater application of systematic approaches in dealing with multiple goals and their trade-offs. Computer-based interactive approaches will be more widely used in objective formulation and priority setting.

From: *Management by Multiple Objectives*, Sang M. Lee (Princeton, NJ: Petrocelli Books, Inc., 1981)

MANAGEMENT WITHOUT TEARS
James O. McDonald
1981/149 pp./$8.95
Crain Books
740 Rush St.
Chicago, IL 60611

This very practical guide deals with everyday situations that face all levels of management. The author's advice ranges widely, but most of his counsel has to do with human relations. This material is presented in brief commentaries on such topics as handling gripers, interviewing job seekers, controlling work load, preparing for meetings.

EXECUTIVE LEADERSHIP
Albert Ellis
1972, 1978/190 pp./$5.95
Institute for Rational Living, Inc.
45 E. 65th St.
New York, NY 10021

A psychotherapist, the author offers advice for reducing the stress and increasing the effectiveness and satisfaction of the work of the executive. The book deals with such aspects as self-discipline, decisiveness, concentration and relations with others. The author also focuses on handling emotional upsets, hostility and depression.

WOMANING: OVERCOMING MALE DOMINANCE OF EXECUTIVE ROW
Dean B. Peskin
1982/317 pp./$17.95
Ashley Books, Inc.
30 Main St.
Port Washington, NY 11050

This guide for women in management offers a man's perspective on the insights and tactics that the individual woman must have in order to make a successful career. A management consultant, the author examines male-female behavioral relationships and indicates ways in which women are able to gain power. The author focuses on practical advice, including

HOW TOUGH PLUS FAIR EQUALS EFFECTIVE STYLE

Remember that "tough" can mean something other than harsh. It can apply to the boss who is stern, even very demanding, but fair. And the fact is that no one outside of a family business will go beyond the first few levels of authority without that kind of toughness. It means being implacable in your demand for excellence, in setting and attaining goals, while adamantly refusing to brook the slightest lapse from honest effort.

Nothing in that definition argues harshness. There is no necessity even in the most resolute and demanding kind of toughness for doomsday threats, nastiness or fear, nothing to occasion that breeder of emotional sabotage, resentment. Your tough-minded demand that everyone in your group strive for the best possible performance and results, should be coupled with a sharp concern and respect for their dignity, human failings and human feelings.

From: *The Art of Being a Boss*, Robert J. Schoenberg (New York: New American Library, 1980)

careful counsel about pitfalls and how to deal with them.

UNDERSTANDING PERSONALITY AND MOTIVES OF WOMEN MANAGERS
Harish C. Tewari
1978/149 pp./$39.95
University Microfilms International
300 N. Zeeb Rd.
Ann Arbor, MI 48106

This book reports on a study of 61 women managers to determine their achievement, affiliation and power motives. Detailed in its results, the report is a valuable resource. One major conclusion of the report is that women managers are significantly different from women in general in their need for achievement and power.

MANAGEMENT MEMO FROM HAY ASSOCIATES

Called the *Management Memo*, this small but useful publication comes from the management-consulting firm of Hay Associates—with their compliments. Each memo studies an individual subject (such as CEO succession, or compensation policy). The subjects are presented concisely, with clear analysis and specific recommendations. Write:

Hay Associates
229 S. 18th St.
Philadelphia, PA 19103

THE LEVINSON LETTER
$98/24 issues per year
Box 95
Cambridge, MA 02138

Focusing on the psychological aspects of management, this newsletter offers commentary and counsel on such subjects as leadership, executive stress and the management of change. Case histories study conflict situations, and special sections explore major issues that confront the executive. The newsletter takes its name from its author, clinical psychologist Dr. Harry Levinson.

I have long made it a policy to observe how the men an executive hires and promotes prove out, for this offers a usually reliable insight into the quality of the executive himself. If he consistently hires good men and if he is able to recognize and reward the most deserving among his subordinates, this is an indication of his own sound judgment and ability. If, on the other hand, a manager has a record of picking losers, I'm inclined to doubt his qualifications for the job he holds.

From: *How to Be a Successful Executive*, J. Paul Getty (New York: Playboy, 1981)

MY YEARS WITH GENERAL MOTORS
Alfred P. Sloan, Jr.
1963/541 pp./$7.95
Doubleday & Co.
245 Park Ave.
New York, NY 10017

This book is as much a history of the automobile industry as it is an account of the author's half century at General Motors. In both respects, it is a valuable resource, detailing the evolution of the giant industrial corporation in our economy as well as the development of the executive function. The author, who was CEO at General Motors for 23 years, devotes much of his attention to tracing the organization of the corporation's top management. The book offers a perspective on management concepts that can be seen developing over the years to become today's accepted principles.

HOW TO BE A SUCCESSFUL EXECUTIVE
J. Paul Getty
1971/192 pp./$2.50
Berkley Publishing Group
200 Madison Ave.
New York, NY 10016

The author speaks with the authority of his own enormous business success and his advice makes fascinating reading. Getty rambles at times, but he has much to tell, both from his own personal experiences and from those of other executives. This book does not present a formal program for success. Instead, it relies heavily on anecdotes to make its points.

SKILLS FOR SUCCESS
Adele M. Scheele
1979/248 pp./$9.95
William Morrow & Co.
105 Madison Ave.
New York, NY 10016

The author, a career counselor, guides the reader through the strategies that produce success. She emphasizes self-awareness and the development of interpersonal relationships, and she defines specific career-building skills. Offering guidance for both men and women, the author shows how attitudes figure in career success.

BOARDROOM REPORTS
$49/24 issues per year
Boardroom Building
Millburn, NJ 07041

Emphasizing practical management strategies, this publication draws much of its material

from other newsletters. The reporting is concise and ranges over all aspects of business management. Coverage spotlights material that offers personal guidance to the executive.

PERSONAL REPORT FOR THE EXECUTIVE

$36/26 issues per year
589 5th Ave.
New York, NY 10017

Published by the Research Institute of America, this newsletter offers commentary and advice in matters of interpersonal relationships. It deals with conflict situations as well as a variety of aspects of executive leadership.

EXECUTIVE PRODUCTIVITY

$72/12 issues per year
10076 Boca Entrada Blvd.
Boca Raton, FL 33433

This monthly newsletter focuses on executive skills and efficiency. It reports on all aspects of executive responsibility, with emphasis on developing practical techniques in such areas as time management.

BASIC TECHNIQUES THAT NEUTRALIZE RESISTANCE

By far the most valuable utensils in neutralizing resistance are asking questions and listening. This takes patience.

It's difficult to sit back, listening with interest while resistance is being expressed. Most people feel the urge to debate. Most feel they have to "set the other person right" with the facts, "get some sense" into the head of the one resisting.

Think back, for a moment, to why people resist. Many times it is only a process of asking for more time to make a decision. The individual is saying, "Slow down. Let me think about it. You're asking me to change or spend my money or do something I hadn't considered before, and I can't go through that as quickly as you're asking me to." So stalls are used. Asking questions and patiently listening will provide the breathing time necessary to eliminate the resistance.

From: *How to Get People to Do Things*, Robert Conklin (Chicago: Contemporary Books, Inc., 1979)

AMA: COMPREHENSIVE SERVICES FOR EXECUTIVES IN ALL FIELDS

The largest membership organization for professional managers, the American Management Associations offers a wide variety of services to members in its 12 divisions. The divisions cover all aspects of management, ranging from general management through finance, manufacturing, marketing, packaging, human resources. Membership includes such services as the monthly magazine *Management Review*, the research facilities of the Management Information and Library Service and a broad program of training courses. There are also periodic reports and surveys for members, and the AMA is also a major publisher of professional books. Books are available by individual purchase or through the AMA Book Club. Training programs are provided for all levels of management, including CEO's and top-management teams. Annual membership is based on three classifications: individual ($110), com-

Growth and progress are related, for there is no resting place for an enterprise in a competitive economy. Obstacles, conflicts, new problems in various shapes and new horizons arise to stir the imagination and continue the progress of industry. Success, however, may bring self-satisfaction. In that event, the urge for competitive survival, the strongest of all economic incentives, is dulled. The spirit of venture is lost in the inertia of the mind against change.

From: *My Years with General Motors*, Alfred P. Sloan, Jr. (Garden City, NY: Anchor Books, 1972)

pany ($585) and a third category ($325) for organizations with fewer than 250 employees and/or $25 million or less in annual income or budget. For brochures and further information, write:

American Management Associations
135 W. 50th St.
New York, NY 10020

HARVARD'S STOREHOUSE OF MANAGEMENT EXPERTISE

The Harvard Business Review Reprint Series offers access to collections of the magazine's articles from over the years. Related articles are bound in paperback covers, with an average of 15 articles in each book. There are 120 books in the series, organized in eight categories: general management, organizational behavior, marketing, finance, managerial economics, international management, planning and control, and production and operations. (A data base of articles from the magazine is also available: write to HBR/Online, John Wiley & Sons, 605 3rd Ave., New York, NY 10158.) For a descriptive catalog of the Reprint Series ($5) or a free catalog of reprint listings, write:

HBR Reprint Series
Soldiers Field
Boston, MA 02163

FORMATIVE YEARS IN BUSINESS: A LONG-TERM AT&T STUDY OF MANAGERIAL LIVES

Douglas W. Bray, Richard J. Campbell and Donald L. Grant
1974, 1979/236 pp./$17.50
Krieger Publishing Co.
Box 9542
Melbourne, FL 32901

This book reports on the Management Progress Study at AT&T, which traced the development of 274 management recruits over a period of several years. The study seeks to identify the causes and effects of success and failure in a management career. The researchers focus on such aspects as personal qualities and lifestyles, making the book a valuable resource for executives seeking new perspectives on their careers.

GAME-PLAYING FOR MANAGEMENT SKILLS

Didactic Systems, Inc., specializes in management-training services and materials. Of particular interest are the firm's simulation programs, in which small groups of executives act out management situations. Called Simulation/Games, they deal with such aspects as management by objectives, time management, planning and marketing. The company also offers consulting and workshop services. For catalog, write:

Didactic Systems, Inc.
Box 457
Cranford, NJ 07016

TACTICS

FUNDAMENTALS OF APPLIED INDUSTRIAL MANAGEMENT
Joseph Glasser
1962, 1975/627 pp./$20
Branden Press
21 Station St.
Boston, MA 02147

Particularly for the executive unfamiliar with factory operations, this text provides a sound and comprehensive introduction to the basics of industrial management. The author traces

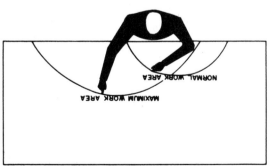

The normal work area in relation to the maximum work area (from Fundamentals of Applied Industrial Management).

the development of current management methods and examines the organization of the manufacturing company down to the foreman level. Chapters on production cover research and development, as well as manufacturing facilities, machinery and equipment. The author deals with work measurement and simplification, and several chapters are devoted to the various aspects of industrial relations.

THE GLACIER PROJECT: CONCEPTS AND CRITIQUES
Jerry L. Gray, Editor
1976/452 pp./$27.50
Crane, Russak & Co.
3 E. 44th St.
New York, NY 10017

This collection of articles provides several viewpoints on organization and management theories that have grown out of research in England. The Glacier Project takes its name from the Glacier Metals Co. and the research program that has studied the psychological and sociological forces that affected the structuring and management of the factory. Included in the research are theories of work measurement, pay systems and levels of management.

MANAGEMENT-SIMULATION GAMES FOR SHARPENING EXECUTIVE SKILLS

Simtek, Inc., markets a wide selection of computerized management-simulation games. Transmitted over telephone lines to your computer terminal, such a game pits small teams of executives against one another in working out a management scenario. The scenarios deal with management situations from a variety of industries. Cost is based on a fee of $60 per team member. For further information, write for the firm's directory ($6.45):

Simtek, Inc.
Box 109
Cambridge, MA 02139

PUTT'S LAW AND THE SUCCESSFUL TECHNOCRAT
Archibald Putt
1981/165 pp./$9.25
Exposition Press, Inc.
Box 2120
Smithtown, NY 11787

This satire of the maneuverings in the management of technology follows in the tradition of

POWER AND KNOWLEDGE, THE CRUCIAL COMBINATION

Top management deals primarily with ill-structured problems. Hence, knowledge and its analysis are vital commodities at the top of an organization. When in high office, executives are keenly aware of the value of knowledge, critically analyzed and properly interpreted. Working with one's hands and feet at the top of an organization is neither feasible nor appropriate.

Power, however, is not the same as knowledge, and attaining high position does not anoint an individual with superior foresight or with exceptional insight into causes and consequences. Higher managers have wider access to information, but this is not knowledge of the future or of the responses of others.

When a higher manager has power but lacks knowledge, he can endanger his organization. Therefore, a higher manager must regularly update his knowledge so that he can question the assumptions of his advisors. He must search beyond the obviously favorable consequences of their recommendations to the wider, long-range effects. Thus the manager must continually reeducate himself, regardless of his power, so he can understand and evaluate the concepts his advisors use.

Top managers are usually willing to support education of middle managers. On the other hand, they often appear less willing to open themselves to new knowledge, especially when they believe they have found satisfactory solutions to current problems. They become adept at managing the current stability, but unless they reach out and stretch themselves with new knowledge, their management of change falters.

From: *Information, Organization and Power: Effective Management in the Knowledge Society*, Dale E. Zand (New York: McGraw-Hill Book Co. 1981)

the Peter Principle and Parkinson's Law. Hiding behind an assumed name, the author is said to be a well-known scientist and engineer. He offers advice that can guide the reader in the search for successful executive style.

DON'T DEAL YOURSELF OUT OF THE GAME

One of the problems encountered by middle managers is that their thinking is frequently pirated by their superiors without due credit being given to the creator of the thoughts. A tactic to counter this theft is to *keep a key*. Keys come in many forms. One report writer quoted some important figures from a market study that was cited in a footnote. Guess who knew where the market study was to be found? Thus, the report's true author became known to top management. Make others come to you for the key, don't give it away.

One naive assistant not only wrote his boss's reports, but also gave him all of the supporting documents, even the work sheets. He had nothing to show for his efforts. There was no reason for the boss ever to consult him again on the matter.

A variation of the keep-a-key tactic entails making other people deal directly with you, rather than with someone else. An assistant was asked by his boss to survey the other vice-presidents about a matter. He could have asked them to reply to his boss, but he didn't. Instead, he asked that he be told their feelings.

Don't deal yourself out of the game.

From: *Handbook of Management Tactics*, Richard Buskirk (New York: Hawthorn Books, 1976)

DISCIPLINE OR DISASTER: MANAGEMENT'S ONLY CHOICE
Paul M. Magoon and John B. Richards
1966, 1977/159 pp./$8.95
Exposition Press, Inc.
Box 2120
Smithtown, NY 11787

This handbook of labor relations presents guidelines for managing industrial workers. It is directed to supervisory personnel in a factory setting, but it provides a useful resource for the executive distant from the shop floor. Both labor-relations specialists, the authors relate their approach to the emotional and job-security needs of workers. The book deals with labor contracts, arbitration and the practicalities of industrial discipline.

HANDBOOK OF MANAGEMENT TACTICS
Richard Buskirk
1976/242 pp./$5.95
E. P. Dutton
2 Park Ave.
New York, NY 10016

This book is a collection of hundreds of examples of initiatives, deceptions, bluffs, ploys, maneuverings, evasions and power plays that are basic to the behavior patterns of aggressive competition. Discounting any ethical judgment, the author presents this material in the form of miniature case studies. The material is well dramatized and very readable. Separate sections deal with the tactics of business operations, personal relationships and negotiations.

THE NEW EXECUTIVE WOMAN
Marcille Gray Williams
1977/242 pp./$3.50
New American Library
1633 Broadway
New York, NY 10019

Writing from her own experiences as well as from interviews with more than 20 other successful women executives, the author presents

Another cluster of characteristics successful people share is an openness, an openmindedness, an approachability, a willingness to believe in the possible, a seemingly incongruous naivete, an unselfconsciousness and a sense of humor. They are aware that circumstances change but that circumstances, however good or bad, are only circumstances. How they will deal with the circumstances, not the circumstances themselves, is what is important and they are confident they will be able to handle whatever changes occur. The strength of their personal relationships derives not from toughness but from flexibility.

From: *How to Make Things Go Your Way*, Ralph Charell (New York: Cornerstone Library, 1981)

advice that is both realistic and enlightened with insight. The book is directed to women executives, but it is a resource from which men in management could learn much about their women colleagues. Focusing on practical guidance for career success, the author quotes extensively from the women executives she interviewed. Pitfalls are identified and there are chapters on business etiquette, travel and wardrobe.

CORPORATE ETIQUETTE
Milla Alihan
1970/175 pp./$3.50
New American Library
1633 Broadway
New York, NY 10019

This handbook on proper manners in the business world begins with basic etiquette and expands into all aspects of interpersonal behavior on the executive level. An industrial psychologist and consultant, the author shows how executive effectiveness and success depend on such elements as courtesy, diplomacy, charm, tact, discretion. Using detailed examples and focusing on such considerations as rank, she guides the reader through board meetings and

business letters as well as business lunches and travel on the company plane.

THE EXCEPTIONAL EXECUTIVE
Harry Levinson
1968/336 pp./$2.95
New American Library
1633 Broadway
New York, NY 10019

A classic in management literature, this book is a study of the psychological elements in the executive role. The author points to self-awareness as a major essential quality for success in executive leadership and shows how this aspect of personality works in the executive's behalf. Among the many concepts developed here is that of the executive as teacher within the organization.

INFORMATION, ORGANIZATION AND POWER: EFFECTIVE MANAGEMENT IN THE KNOWLEDGE SOCIETY
Dale E. Zand
1981/209 pp./$16.50
McGraw-Hill Book Co.
1221 Avenue of the Americas
New York, NY 10020

The author examines the interplay between managerial behavior and the corporation's use

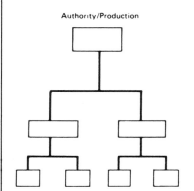

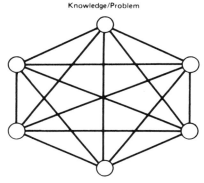

Two basic types· of small-group organization (from Information, Organization and Power: Effective Management in the Knowledge Society).

of knowledge. As the acquiring and processing of knowledge becomes more and more the focus of the corporation, it effects organization and the decision-making process. The author traces the response of management and offers practical guidance for the executive.

THE MANAGEMENT TACTICIAN
Edward C. Schleh
1974/190 pp./$21.95
McGraw-Hill Book Co.
1221 Avenue of the Americas
New York, NY 10020

This handbook of management tactics concentrates on solving basic operational problems. A management consultant, the author focuses on such aspects as decentralization, accountability and incentives. Along with an emphasis on morale and productivity, he shows how to eliminate conflict among managers. Included is guidance on the use of computer technology.

THE ART OF GETTING YOUR OWN SWEET WAY
Philip B. Crosby
1981/230 pp./$17.95
McGraw-Hill Book Co.
1221 Avenue of the Americas
New York, NY 10020

The author offers guidance for dealing successfully with others both in business and in personal life. He presents a systematic format for what he terms situation management and situation prevention. His premises are based on patterns of human behavior and he uses very realistic case histories to demonstrate how his approach works. The book is both down-to-earth and specific, a useful resource for ideas about management style.

MANAGING TIME AND MANAGING MEETINGS

**THE TIME TRAP: HOW TO
GET MORE DONE IN LESS TIME**
R. Alec Mackenzie
1972, 1975/195 pp./$3.95
McGraw-Hill Book Co.
1221 Avenue of the Americas
New York, NY 10020

A management consultant who specializes in time management, the author gives practical coaching for dealing with procrastination, interruptions, decision making and delegation. Included are chapters on self-appraisal, time planning, blocking interruptions and working more efficiently with your secretary. The author makes extensive use of examples of actual time-management problems and their solutions.

**SHOOTING THE EXECUTIVE
RAPIDS: THE FIRST
CRUCIAL YEAR
OF A NEW ASSIGNMENT**
John D. Arnold
1981/268 pp./$21.95
McGraw-Hill Book Co.
1221 Avenue of the Americas
New York, NY 10020

This book offers detailed guidance for the executive in a new assignment, whether it be with a new employer or in another part of his or her company. The author draws on his experience as a management consultant for realistic case-study illustrations of a variety of situations. He deals with such factors as the resistance of insiders and he spells out strategies that yield success.

When asked to identify their major time wasters, managers will invariably list external causes first, such as the telephone, meetings, visitors, paperwork and delays. After time-management problems and principles have been discussed, a new source is invariably identified—the man within, generating such time wasters as lack of delegation, fire fighting, lack of plans and priorities, the open-door policy and procrastination.

From: *The Time Trap*, R. Alec Mackenzie (New York: McGraw-Hill Book Co., 1975)

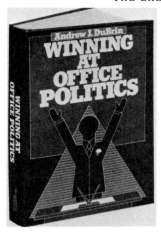

WINNING AT OFFICE POLITICS
Andrew J. DuBrin
1978/287 pp./$14.95
Van Nostrand Reinhold Co.
135 W. 50th St.
New York, NY 10020

The author examines the maneuvering for advantage which goes on at all levels in an organization. He sorts out hundreds of variations and shows the patterns they follow. The book's emphasis is on understanding the political process in order to use it effectively and avoid its pitfalls. The author focuses on basic strategies for cultivating peers and inferiors as well as superiors and he details the power-building strategies that advance a career.

A DIFFERENT KIND
OF DIRECTORY ASSISTANCE

The Directory of Directories lists almost 7,000 entries that detail directories, lists and guides of all kinds from the U.S. and nearly 80 foreign countries. Priced at $100, the directory's second edition has 1,003 pages. It is organized into 16 sections for categories ranging from general business directories to entries for specific industries and lines of business. Included are directories of manufacturers, importers and exporters from around the world, as well as sec-

tions with such categories as law, government, science and engineering. Entries include such data as publisher addresses and phone numbers as well as directory contents and prices. Directories are indexed both by title and by subject. For further information, write:

Gale Research Co.
Book Tower
Detroit, MI 48226

FORBES
$39/26 issues per year
60 5th Ave.
New York, NY 10011

Every two weeks, *Forbes* updates its long-running commentary on what is happening in the

world of business. Coverage is broad and reporting is detailed. Success stories study the how and why of the achievements of companies and their executives. The magazine closely follows developments in investments and finance. Each issue presents the Forbes Index, which tracks economic activity, and the Forbes/Wilshire 5000 Review, which charts performance and prospects in the equity markets.

INC.

$24/12 issues per year
38 Commercial Wharf
Boston, MA 02110

Inc. magazine is about the management of small and medium-size companies, but the success stories it reports offer instructive lessons with much wider applications. Typical articles spotlight the entrepreneur who builds a company to spectacular success. The reporting is detailed. The types of companies covered range widely and often include high-tech enterprises.

TIME MANAGEMENT AND DEALING WITH VISITORS

When a staff member asks whether he may drop in for a few minutes, answer by asking the urgency of the matter. If it is not an emergency, then ask, "Can it wait 10 minutes? I'll drop by." A Dutch managing director in Holland listed these advantages of such a procedure: (1) It avoids an interruption and allows you to finish the matter at hand before seeing the subordinate. (2) By preventing his coming to sit down by your desk, you do not lose control of your own office. (3) By going to his office, you maintain control of the situation because you can leave at any time. (4) You are nearer the problem—the files, the blueprint, whatever the question involves. (5) You pay him a compliment by going to him.

If a visitor does not announce his purpose, do not invite him into your office, where you lose control. Go to see him in the outer office or in the lobby. Give him a friendly handshake and a warm inquiry, "Can I help you?" to determine the reason for the call immediately. Meeting the visitor outside your office makes it much easier to limit the duration of the call.

From: *The Time Trap*, R. Alec Mackenzie (New York: McGraw-Hill Book Co., 1975)

SOURCE

$60/12 issues per year
10076 Boca Entrada Blvd.
Boca Raton, FL 33433

This monthly newsletter reports on sources of business information. Included are government agencies, consulting groups, business organizations and publishers. Print as well as data base sources are covered.

JOHN NAISBITT'S TREND LETTER

$87/26 issues per year
1211 Connecticut Ave., N.W.
Washington, DC 20036

This newsletter reports on social, political and economic matters and relates them to developing trends. Its concept and approach are directly related to author John Naisbitt's successful book *Megatrends*. His consulting firm, The Naisbitt Group, Inc., also publishes a quarterly *Trend Report*. The quarterly is published in a national edition ($1,250 per year) and four regional editions ($875 per year each).

THE NAISBITT GROUP, INC.: TRACKING TRENDS THAT CAN CHANGE THE FUTURE

Author John Naisbitt's consulting firm offers clients its research expertise in studying social, political and economic trends and how they relate to management decisions. Naisbitt's book *Megatrends* as well as his *Trend Letter* and *Trend Report* all use a common methodology to trace developing changes. Anticipating such changes with appropriate corporate strategy is the objective of the consulting services. Write:

The Naisbitt Group, Inc.
1211 Connecticut Ave., N.W.
Washington, DC 20036

THE HOLT EXECUTIVE ADVISORY

$48/24 issues per year
290 Post Rd. W.
Westport, CT 06880

This newsletter provides a twice-monthly update on the economy and business activity as well as news of government and politics. The emphasis is on interpretive background information.

The idea that everyone wins in a successful negotiation is not being presented here solely on ethical grounds. In actuality it is considered simply good business. It is a matter of securing long-range objectives instead of short-term advantages. Negotiated solutions are likely to be longer-lasting when each party has gained and has a stake in maintaining the conclusion.

From: *The Fundamentals of Negotiating*, Gerard I. Nierenberg (New York: E. P. Dutton, 1973)

The meeting is the communications switchboard of every organization. It stands at the center of almost all company decisions. More than 75 percent of executive time is spent around the meeting room table. That's a lot of time out of a working life. But no one has found an alternative to the meeting and no one is likely to.

From: *How to Win the Meeting*, Frank Snell (New York: Hawthorn Books, 1979)

MANAGEMENT STRATEGIES FOR WOMEN
Ann McKay Thompson
  and Marcia Donnan Wood
1980/267 pp./$6.25
Simon and Schuster
1230 Avenue of the Americas
New York, NY 10020

Drawing on their own experience as executives, the authors present practical guidance for women in management. This is a book of coaching, some of it on an elementary level, but all of it valuable. The authors use such devices as self-tests to draw the reader into a process of attitude adjustment and they maintain a sense of humor throughout the book. They are entirely forthright in dealing with the problems and challenges that face the woman executive today. For the male reader, these pages could offer a positive perspective on his relationships with women colleagues.

IDEAS FOR SMOOTHER MANAGEMENT

The Effective Executive offers guidance for improving management skills. Its articles concentrate on human factors and the techniques of good communications. Included are articles about such personal interests as health and finances. This twice-monthly publication is sold in quantity subscriptions only (for instance,

five to nine copies are priced at 92¢ each per issue). For a sample issue, write:

Dartnell Corp.
4660 Ravenswood Ave.
Chicago, IL 60640

ENTREPRENEUR
$24.50/12 issues per year
2311 Pontius Ave.
Los Angeles, CA 90064

This is a magazine of ideas for starting small businesses. The emphasis is on entrepreneurship. There are insights here for the executive who seeks a perspective on this aspect of management.

THE NEW OFFICE ETIQUETTE
George Mazzei
1983/255 pp./$13.95
Poseidon Press
1230 Avenue of the Americas
New York, NY 10020

The ground rules for graceful interaction in the business world have changed somewhat in recent years, but the requirements of basic good manners remain largely unaltered. The author spells out the changes and presents savvy advice for working with them. He deals with a wide variety of common situations that range

THE NEEDS THEORY OF NEGOTIATING

Needs and their satisfaction are the common denominator in negotiation. If people had no unsatisfied needs, they would never negotiate. Negotiation presupposes that *both* the negotiator and his opposer want something; otherwise they would turn a deaf ear to each other's demands and there would be no bargaining. This is true even if the need is merely to maintain the status quo. It requires two parties, motivated by needs, to start a negotiation. Individuals dickering over the purchase and sale of a piece of real estate, a labor union and management bargaining for a new contract, or the directors of two corporations discussing the terms of a proposed merger—are all seeking to gratify needs.

From: *The Fundamentals of Negotiating,* Gerard I. Nierenberg (New York: E. P. Dutton, 1973)

from telephone manners to the etiquette of the business lunch. Throughout the book he fully takes into account the shifting relationship between men and women in the corporation today.

EXECU-TIME
$65/24 issues per year
Box 631
Lake Forest, IL 60045

Devoted to time-management techniques, this newsletter concentrates on practical help for the executive. It deals with such aspects as delegating responsibilities, working with priorities and running meetings. It also offers tips on controlling time-consuming distractions.

TECHNIQUES FOR TIME MANAGEMENT

Offering consulting and training services, Alec Mackenzie & Associates specializes in time management. Its seminar program for executives aims for a savings of two hours per day,

for instance. The firm also markets time-management products. Time Tactics ($74) is an annual diary and planning system based on the Mackenzie approach. Author Mackenzie's successful book *The Time Trap* is the subject of a presentation about time management on film or videotape ($550). The book is also the basis for a software program called *Time Management.* Priced at $295, the software will run on the IBM PC as well as the Apple II, IIe and III personal computers. Write:

Alec Mackenzie & Associates, Inc.
Box 130
Greenwich, NY 12834

THE ART OF NEGOTIATING
Gerard I. Nierenberg
1968, 1981/192 pp./$5.95
Simon and Schuster
1230 Avenue of the Americas
New York, NY 10020

The process of coming to agreement involves us in negotiation continuously and on many levels. Skill comes with experience. The author suggests, however, that this art can be mastered by systematic study. He analyzes the process and identifies its basic elements, illustrating their interaction with detailed examples. He demonstrates the specifics of negotiating technique, basing his approach on the premise that success requires an understanding of the individual needs of the negotiators.

FUNDAMENTALS OF NEGOTIATING
Gerard I. Nierenberg
1968, 1971, 1973/306 pp./$6.50
E. P. Dutton
2 Park Ave.
New York, NY 10016

Combining two earlier books by the author in a revised version, this volume is a thorough introduction to the principles and techniques of negotiation. The author analyzes the process on the basis of the needs of the participants and traces the behavioral elements involved. He examines specific techniques and applies them in such circumstances as buying and selling, corporate negotiations and labor relations. The author uses anecdotes and realistic examples to make this valuable resource lively reading.

DEVELOPING YOUR NEGOTIATION SKILLS

The Institute for Negotiation Research conducts training seminars around the country. The programs are designed to develop the skills and strategies needed for the transaction of business and personal life. Seminars vary in length and structure. The fee for a typical two-day seminar is $525. The programs are directed by Dr. Chester L. Karrass, author of *The Negotiating Game* and *Give & Take*. The institute also markets a variety of study materials,

READING YOUR OPPONENT FOR NEGOTIATING SUCCESS

Besides listening to your opponent in an attempt to learn his desires and needs, you must also closely observe his gestures. For example, in a friendly conference, if one member suddenly sits back and folds his arms with some abruptness, you would know at once that trouble had arrived. Gestures are tremendously important. They convey many shades of meaning, and have their psychological undertones and overtones. Therefore, observe the gestures of your opposer carefully and continuously to gain a clue to his thinking.

We are using the term "gesture" in the broadest possible sense. It includes much more than simple body motions. Tension can be shown by any number of signs such as blushing, contraction of the facial muscles, fidgeting, undue preoccupation, strained laughter or giggling, or even just staring in silence. Actually these are nonverbal means of communication. Dr. Sandor Feldman analyzes over fifty different gestures and other nonverbal expressions. These include bodily movement, posture, facial expression and mannerisms of all kinds.

In any negotiation you are, of course, talking with your opposer. At the same time you are looking at him and seeing him. Psychologists make a distinction between *looking* and *seeing*. When we examine our outside world, we *look*. It is a form of spying and is objective. But when we *see*, we take in, we absorb, we comprehend the general impression subjectively.

From: *The Art of Negotiating*, Gerard I. Nierenberg (New York: Cornerstone Library, 1981)

THE PART MINUTES PLAY IN EFFECTIVE MEETINGS

Once the meeting is over, the chairman must nail down exactly what happened by sending out minutes that summarize the discussion that occurred, the decision made and the actions to be taken. And it's very important that attendees get the minutes quickly, before they forget what happened. The minutes should also be as clear and as specific as possible, telling the reader what is to be done, who is to do it and when. All this may seem like too much trouble, but if the meeting was worth calling in the first place, the work needed to produce the minutes is a small additional investment (an activity with high leverage) to ensure that the full benefit is obtained from what was done.

From: *High Output Management*, Andrew S. Grove (New York: Random House, 1983)

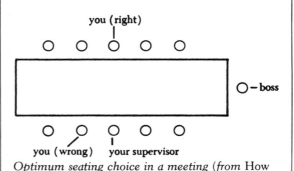

Optimum seating choice in a meeting (from How to Win the Meeting).

including a program of 11 one-hour audio cassettes ($285). For brochures, write:

Institute for Negotiation Research, Inc.
1625 Stanford St.
Santa Monica, CA 90404

THE SCIENCE OF BUSINESS NEGOTIATION
Philip Sperber
1979/79 pp./$10
Pilot Books
103 Cooper St.
Babylon, NY 11702

The author, who is an attorney and specializes in negotiation, presents a handbook on basic theory and techniques. He examines preparations that include selection of time and place and he identifies mistakes commonly made in the initial session. In a separate section, the author focuses on 50 basic considerations in the negotiating process. (If ordering by mail, add $1 for postage and handling.)

HOW TO WIN THE MEETING
Frank Snell
1979/163 pp./$4.95
E. P. Dutton
2 Park Ave.
New York, NY 10016

The author offers coaching in techniques and tactics for making your mark and winning your way as a meeting participant. His advice emphasizes the practical over the theoretical. Included are chapters on taking the most advantageous seat, maintaining concentration, sizing up the other meeting participants and presenting material persuasively.

SOLVING PROBLEMS IN MEETINGS
James D. Jorgensen with Ivan H.
 Scheier and Timothy F. Fautsko
1981/99 pp./$16.95
Nelson-Hall, Inc.
111 N. Canal St.
Chicago, IL 60606

This book is a useful resource for analyzing and developing your skills both as a meeting leader and as a participant. The authors examine the nature of meetings, defining why some fail and why some succeed in producing constructive results. Along with its systematic approach to meetings, the book provides a variety of adaptable ideas on the subject.

MAKING MEETINGS MORE PRODUCTIVE
Myron Gordon, Ph.D.
1981/178 pp./$12.95
Sterling Publishing Co.
2 Park Ave.
New York, NY 10016

This guide for meeting leaders develops techniques for managing the diverse personalities in a group. The author, a psychologist, uses case histories to show how a leader can smooth communication and foster teamwork by meeting participants. Emphasis is on leadership style and the importance of agenda.

MEETINGS AND THEIR EFFECT ON PRODUCTIVITY

If your meetings are more than window dressing or hot air, they are critical to the health of your group or organization. This is the only time that members of a group actually see themselves as a group—when everyone is sitting in the same room working together. These group experiences directly affect how individuals feel about their group, how committed they are to decisions and how well they work as a team and individually. And many meetings generate a ripple effect. A meeting of fifteen people can affect how 300 people work—or don't work—for the rest of the day or week or even permanently.

From: *How to Make Meetings Work*, Michael Doyle and David Straus (New York: Jove Publications, 1982)

HOW TO MAKE MEETINGS WORK
Michael Doyle and David Straus
1976/301 pp./$3.50
Berkley Publishing Group
200 Madison Ave.
New York, NY 10016

If you are looking for ways to make your meetings produce better results, this book is a useful starting point. The authors have developed what they call the interaction method. It makes use of two neutral participants in a meeting: a "facilitator," who acts as director and moderator, and a "recorder," who notes the statements of the meeting members. Instead of running the meeting, the executive in charge becomes an active participant. This concept emphasizes an open exchange of ideas, and the authors describe the practical elements of the process in detail. Even though this method might not provide the format you are looking for, you will find a storehouse of material here to stimulate your thinking about meetings.

ACCOUNTING AND OTHER SPECIALIZED AREAS

ACCOUNTING FOR NON-ACCOUNTANTS
John N. Myer
1947, 1979/249 pp./$14.95
E. P. Dutton
2 Park Ave.
New York, NY 10016

This college-level text could be used as a reference or it could be your self-study resource. The book covers all the basics, with separate sections on partnerships and corporations as well as on merchandising and manufacturing businesses. The book is thoroughly illustrated and its chapters are followed by questions and problem exercises.

THE EXECUTIVE'S ACCOUNTING PRIMER
Robert L. Dixon
1971, 1982/395 pp./$32.50
McGraw-Hill Book Co.
1221 Avenue of the Americas
New York, NY 10020

A very useful resource either for reference or for self-study, this book is designed to provide a working familiarity with accounting. Along with presenting the basics of accounting language and methods, the book offers the essentials for analyzing financial data and statements for decision making. The author's style is nontechnical and he provides test problems with each chapter and in a supplementary section.

COST ACCOUNTING CONCEPTS FOR NON-FINANCIAL EXECUTIVES AND MANAGERS
Joseph Peter Simini
1976/162 pp./$3.95
McGraw-Hill Book Co.
1221 Avenue of the Americas
New York, NY 10020

Requiring no accounting training, this book is directed to the executive who needs a basic understanding of cost-accounting concepts. The book offers the executive a means of better communication with the accountant as a source of data for planning and decision making. The author uses nontechnical language and takes the reader through all the basics, including labor and raw-materials costs as well as

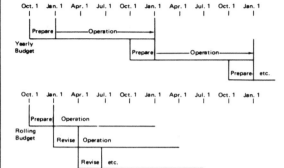

Timetables of a yearly budget compared with a rolling budget (from Cost Accounting Concepts for Non-Financial Executives and Managers).

accounting for overhead and budgets. Also covered are cost principles applied to sales and administrative expenses.

UNDERSTANDING FINANCIAL STATEMENTS
John N. Myer
1964, 1968/206 pp./$2.50
New American Library
1633 Broadway
New York, NY 10019

This handbook shows how to read and interpret various financial statements without an accountant's training. The author explains the accounting process and the meaning of such financial documents as the income statement, balance sheet and statement of retained earnings. Using examples from various types of businesses, the book provides a means for assessing the condition of a business as well as making managerial decisions.

ECONOMICS DECIPHERED
Maurice Levi
1981/306 pp./$6.95
Basic Books, Inc.
10 E. 53rd St.
New York, NY 10022

If economics is not part of your expertise, this book could be your guide to the field. The author, an economist, uses a question-and-answer format to present all the basics of the subject. The writing style makes for easy reading and the material is organized with a logic that makes the book a useful crash course in economics.

UNDERSTANDING THE ECONOMY: FOR PEOPLE WHO CAN'T STAND ECONOMICS
Alfred L. Malabre, Jr.
1975/184 pp./$3.50
New American Library
1633 Broadway
New York, NY 10019

If you are intent on remedying a lack of savvy about the economy, this book could be your starting point. A business journalist, the author succeeds in making his subject material easy and interesting to read. The book deals with all the basics and might be the perfect place to start building your expertise.

RUNNING PRESS GLOSSARY OF ACCOUNTING LANGUAGE
Robert T. March
1978/78 pp./$2.95
Running Press
125 S. 22nd St.
Philadelphia, PA 19103

Accounting language turns up repeatedly in many business situations, and this small handbook can resolve the questions that result. The author defines more than 600 of the most common terms in accounting language, in some cases providing detailed explanations. The easy-to-read text makes this a useful resource. (If ordering by mail, add 75¢ for postage and handling.)

BUSINESS MATH BASICS
Robert E. Swindle
1983/323 pp./$18.95
Wadsworth, Inc.
10 Davis Dr.
Belmont, CA 94002

If math represents a gap that you must close, a textbook such as this could be the right resource for you. This volume opens with a review of elementary math and then proceeds to such areas as marketing, banking and accounting. The instructional material is clearly presented, with extensive illustration.

CASH FLOW PROBLEM SOLVER
Bryan E. Milling
1981/293 pp./$32.95
Chilton Book Co.
Chilton Way
Radnor, PA 19809

Cash flow is a vital consideration for any business, regardless of scale. Designed for medium-size and smaller companies, this book offers step-by-step guidance for managing cash flow. At the same time, for the nonfinancial executive in a larger company, this book offers an excellent introduction to the workings of the cash-flow process as well as its common problems and practical solutions.

RUNNING PRESS GLOSSARY OF BANKING LANGUAGE
Laila Batz
1977/85 pp./$2.95
Running Press
125 S. 22nd St.
Philadelphia, PA 19103

The author presents more than 600 of the most common terms in banking language. In many instances, she goes beyond a simple definition of the term to give a basic explanation of the banking function that is involved. The definitions and explanations are nontechnical and common abbreviations are included. (If ordering by mail, add 75¢ for postage and handling.)

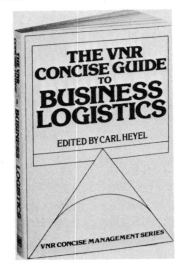

SIMPLIFIED ACCOUNTING FOR NON-ACCOUNTANTS
Rick Stephan Hayes and C. Richard Baker
1980/291 pp./$3.50
Berkley Publishing Group
200 Madison Ave.
New York, NY 10016

Offering a basic introduction to the subject, this book could be your remedy for a lack of background in accounting. The authors have scaled their material to the operations of a smaller business, but all the essential elements of accounting are presented here, and in simple terms that accommodate the newcomer. The text is extensively illustrated.

TRAINING
$36/12 issues per year
731 Hennepin Ave.
Minneapolis, MN 55403

This monthly for specialists in personnel and company training programs will keep you up to date on the latest trends in this area. Included are articles on training at executive levels as well as on management methods. Especially useful is the advertising, which presents products and services that range from computer-based learning programs to seminar training opportunities.

THE VNR CONCISE GUIDE TO BUSINESS LOGISTICS
Carl Heyel, Editor
1979/134 pp./$7.95
Van Nostrand Reinhold Co.
135 W. 50th St.
New York, NY 10020

Designed as an overview to serve executives not directly involved with business logistics, this book covers the basics of transportation, warehousing, materials handling, supply scheduling and related operations. The book is a collection of individual articles written by specialists. Also included are articles on purchasing, vendor rating and inventory management.

INTERVIEWING FOR THE DECISIONMAKER
Lawrence R. O'Leary
1976/127 pp./$18.95
Nelson-Hall, Inc.
111 N. Canal St.
Chicago, IL 60606

Making the right choices in hiring and promoting the people who work for you will have much to do with the progress of your career. Effective interviewing is a key factor. An industrial psychologist and management consultant, the author provides a thorough introduction to the interviewing process. He examines the behavioral elements involved and presents practical guidelines both for the interview itself and for the evaluation of findings.

THE EXECUTIVE PROGRAM: PROFESSIONAL BOOKS FOR MANAGERS

The Executive Program is a book club that covers a broad range of subject areas of interest to the executive. Book selections cover management ideas and techniques, executive skills, career planning, personal finance and such specialized fields as accounting and finance. Write:

The Executive Program
Front and Brown Sts.
Riverside, NJ 08370

FORTUNE BOOK CLUB: SELECTIONS FOR WIDELY VARIED READING

The Fortune Book Club offers members a wide range of reading. Selections include books on management methods and executive skills as well as on such other subjects as personal finance and investments. Operated by the Book-of-the-Month Club, this club's selections also offer books of more general interest, including some fiction. Write:

Fortune Book Club
485 Lexington Ave.
New York, NY 10017

AMA BOOK CLUB: VOLUMES OF PROFESSIONAL EXPERTISE

A major publisher of professional books, the American Management Associations offer both their own titles and those of other publishers in the AMA Book Club program. The books that are offered deal with management methods as well as executive skills and technical areas. Selection is made from a monthly bulletin, and free dividend books are included in the program. For further information, write:

AMA Book Club
135 W. 50th St.
New York, NY 10020

A VERY SMALL MAGAZINE ABOUT MANAGING PEOPLE

Bits & Pieces, a booklet-size magazine for executives, is a most unusual publication. It concentrates on common-sense thinking about management, and its material is often in the form of humor and quotes from noted personalities. It is really a very, very small monthly serving of food for thought for the executive. It is, in fact, so small that it is sold in quantity (two to four copies sell for 99¢ each). Write for a sample copy ($1.25):

Economics Press, Inc.
12 Daniel Rd.
Fairfield, NJ 07006

THE ART OF MANAGING MANAGERS

Neil R. Sweeney
1981/147 pp./$13.95
Addison-Wesley Publishing Co.
Jacob Way
Reading, MA 01867

Focusing on the needs of the middle manager, this book details 17 skills that the author counts as critical and unique for that area of responsibility. Among the skills covered are long-term scheduling, evaluating work groups and spotting problems from numbers and reports. The author's perspective is on the role of the middle manager as director and leader of first-line managers.

RESEARCH RESOURCE ON OFFICE OPERATIONS

The Administrative Management Society, with a membership of middle and upper managers, publishes a variety of research materials of interest to executives. In particular, the society annually surveys middle-management compensation and office-worker salaries around the country. For information on membership and publications, write:

Administrative Management Society
2360 Maryland Rd.
Willow Grove, PA 19090

DEVELOPING MANAGERIAL INFORMATION SYSTEMS

Andrew M. McCosh, Mawdudur
  Rahman and Michael J. Earl
1981/387 pp./$34.95
Halsted Press
605 3rd Ave.
New York, NY 10158

The authors offer this study of the many aspects of management information systems (MIS) both for specialists in this field and for executive users of the systems. The book deals

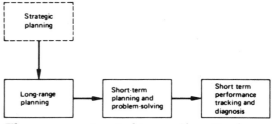

The management control process (from Developing Managerial Information Systems).

with MIS designed for operational planning and control, management planning and control as well as strategic planning. The authors spell out the role of computer technology and examine systems options that do not use the computer.

OFFICE ADMINISTRATION AND AUTOMATION
$19/12 issues per year
51 Madison Ave.
New York, NY 10010

This monthly update on the modern office keeps track of developments that range from new computer technology to new approaches in personnel management. The magazine emphasizes the practical and covers a wide range of topics that include systems planning, training and office design.

SUPERVISION
$23.50/12 issues per year
424 N. 3rd St.
Burlington, IA 52601

This monthly magazine is for the supervisor in the factory. But, in fact, it can provide the executive with a practical perspective on industrial relations. The emphasis is on the nuts and bolts of the production process and the people who make it work. The magazine could be a useful resource for pursuing such objectives as increased productivity.

MANAGEMENT WORLD
$18/12 issues per year
2360 Maryland Rd.
Willow Grove, PA 19090

A publication of the Administrative Management Society, this monthly's focus is on efficient business operations. It covers such areas as office automation, employee motivation, the working environment, training and productivity. The magazine's perspective is that of middle management, making the publication a useful resource for the top executive who must keep in touch with the needs of the total organization. (Subscription is included in society membership.)

MARKETING, ADVERTISING AND SALES MANAGEMENT

THE MARKETING PLAN
Robert K. Skacel
1976/64 pp./$14.95
Crain Books
740 Rush St.
Chicago, IL 60611

This spiral-bound manual gives step-by-step directions for preparing a marketing plan. The format of the manual sets a model for the organization of the plan, and the author identifies needed data and gives specific guidance for each section. The plan is designed to provide a

working framework and schedule for the marketing process.

MARKETING PROBLEM SOLVER
Cochrane Chase and Kenneth L. Barasch
1973, 1977/446 pp./$34.95
Chilton Book Co.
Chilton Way
Radnor, PA 19809

This nuts-and-bolts how-to manual is a very useful resource, especially to an executive new

AMONG THE PITFALLS OF MARKET RESEARCH

Nor can market research predict how retailers will react to a product. Levi Strauss and Company created a high-quality, low-priced men's suit in 1980 and got a very reassuring response from its extensive consumer testing. But when the company began to sell to the trade, it found itself hamstrung by the traditional Levi's association with casual clothing. Retailers envisioned the suit as a competitor to polyester clothing, not a less

expensive alternative to classier attire. The suit, which was already a good buy, had to be reduced still further in price because the retailers felt they had to display it next to other low-priced clothes. They also had doubts about its chances in the marketplace, so not enough were ordered to give the line a fighting chance. Although consumers liked the suit, the retail trade, with its own perception of self-interest, did not.

From: *Life and Death on the Corporate Battlefield*, Paul Solman and Thomas Friedman (New York: Simon and Schuster, 1982)

to any of the areas of marketing. The authors cover marketing, advertising and public relations operations on a step-by-step basis, outlining responsibilities, schedules and means of tracking results. Included are checklists, procedures, fill-in forms and samples. Separate chapters deal with such areas as marketing research and planning, product planning and development, distribution and pricing.

MARKETING NEWS
$24/26 issues per year
250 S. Wacker Dr.
Chicago, IL 60606

A tabloid published every two weeks by the American Marketing Association, this resource can keep you informed about the field and provide stimulation for marketing ideas. Especially useful is the advertising for marketing research agencies and services. (Subscription is $12 for association members.)

PSYCHOLOGICAL PRINCIPLES OF MARKETING AND CONSUMER BEHAVIOR
Steuart Henderson Britt
1978/532 pp./$33.95
Lexington Books
125 Spring St.
Lexington, MA 02173

This book studies the psychology involved when a person is confronted with an advertise-ment or a sales presentation. The book is comprehensive in its examination of the subject, covering all aspects of consumer behavior as it relates to marketing. Research findings are detailed and the author presents numerous examples of familiar advertising for analysis.

MARKETING EXPERTISE FROM THE PROFESSIONALS

The American Marketing Association provides access to a wide variety of published material by practitioners and educators in the field. The association publishes the *Journal of Marketing* ($30/4 issues per year) and the *Journal of Marketing Research* ($36/12 issues per year). For information about membership and other publications, write:

American Marketing Association
250 S. Wacker Dr.
Chicago, IL 60606

MARKETING UPDATE
$150/52 issues per year
11001 Cedar Ave.
Cleveland, OH 44106

Providing a weekly overview of the marketing field, this newsletter presents concise summaries from newspapers, magazines and other sources. The coverage ranges from legal decisions and government regulation to developments in such areas as advertising, public rela-

CONTRAST THAT CATCHES THE CONSUMER'S ATTENTION

The Volkswagen "Think Small" advertisements were excellent examples of contrast. A stark white background was contrasted with a small black photograph of a Volkswagen. It also carried a contrast to the audience's expectations in the headline, so different from the typical "Think Big" cliché.

An example of movement as a form of contrast to the environment are billboard signs that change messages or characters as the viewer changes his point of vision. If the viewer is in a car and moving, this message change will happen more rapidly, as a contrast to a static environment.

Moving point-of-purchase displays in supermarkets, such as mobiles, are a noticeable contrast with most of the shelf stock displays in the store; thus the novelty of motion can stimulate attending to a product.

Package shape may be used to create contrast. Pepperidge Farms packages its herb stuffing in a bag, whereas other brands appear in a box. The product may be viewed through see-through cellophane. It also has a much different tactile sensation than the boxes. L'Eggs pantyhose packages are egg-shaped, displayed in multilevel circular trays. They contrast with the rest of the store's angular displays and packages through their unorthodox shape, thus calling for increased consumer attending.

From: *Psychological Principles of Marketing and Consumer Behavior*, Steuart Henderson Britt (Lexington, MA: Lexington Books, 1979)

tions, marketing research and testing, sales management and distribution. Reprints of the complete text of summarized material can be ordered from the publisher.

PREPARING CONTRACT-WINNING PROPOSALS AND FEASIBILITY STUDIES
Tim Whalen
1982/48 pp./$5
Pilot Books
103 Cooper St.
Babylon, NY 11702

The author presents step-by-step guidance for producing proposals and feasibility studies. This manual is a basic introduction to all aspects of the process and includes criteria for proposals for industry as well as government agencies. (If ordering by mail, add $1 for postage and handling.)

SALES & MARKETING MANAGEMENT
$42/16 issues per year
633 3rd Ave.
New York, NY 10017

This trade magazine is a useful resource, providing broad coverage of its field. Subjects include marketing strategies, sales force motivation, product packaging, retailing, advertising and product development. Typical articles present case histories of specific companies. The magazine's reports on marketing trends make it a sound source of new ideas.

MARKETING TIMES
$15/6 issues per year
330 W. 42nd St.
New York, NY 10036

Published by Sales and Marketing Executives International, a professional association, this magazine covers all the basics, including planning, marketing research, recruiting and managing sales personnel.

PREMIUM/INCENTIVE BUSINESS
$33/12 issues per year
1515 Broadway
New York, NY 10036

Premiums and incentives are in use in every level of marketing today. Do you wonder how effectively your company exploits them? Do you keep yourself posted on the latest trends in this area? If you need a dependable supply of background information, here is a trade magazine that will provide it each month. (Your management position may qualify you for a free subscription to this controlled-circulation magazine.)

BUSINESS MARKETING
$20/12 issues per year
740 Rush St.
Chicago, IL 60611

If your company is in the business of selling goods and services to other businesses, here is a trade magazine to keep you posted about the marketing process. Main areas covered are advertising, marketing research and direct-mail promotion. While the advertising is dominated by trade magazines seeking your company's ads, the reporting will keep you up to date on developments and trends.

THE BUSINESSMAN'S GUIDE
TO ADVERTISING
AND SALES PROMOTION
Herschell Gordon Lewis
1974/218 pp./$14.50
McGraw-Hill Book Co.
1221 Avenue of the Americas
New York, NY 10020

This handbook is a very effective introduction to the basics, beginning with a review of the options in advertising media and sales promotion methods. The author examines the elements of copywriting as well as layout, graphics and printing. He also discusses the broadcast media, direct mail, publicity and public relations. Included is guidance on the use of advertising agencies and marketing research as well as advice on costs and budgeting.

OGILVY ON ADVERTISING
David Ogilvy
1983/224 pp./$24.95
Crown Publishers, Inc.
1 Park Ave.
New York, NY 10016

The author spells out his ideas about advertising, using his many years of experience to pinpoint what he believes makes an ad produce results. A founder of the Ogilvy & Mather agency, Ogilvy presents a fascinating repertory of examples of both success and failure. He focuses his commentary on 185 illustrations of print advertisements and television commercials, providing a broad introduction to the field. Included are such areas as corporate advertising and direct-mail marketing. The book is a valuable resource for testing advertising ideas against the thinking of a master of the art.

MARKETING & MEDIA DECISIONS
$40/14 issues per year
1140 Avenue of the Americas
New York, NY 10036

Which media should your company's advertising dollars go into? Do you have the right advertising strategy to begin with? These are the kinds of questions you can ask when you read this magazine. It reports on where and how companies are investing their ad dollars, and why. (Your management position may qualify you for a free subscription to this controlled-circulation magazine.)

TRADESHOW WEEK
$189/48 issues per year
12233 W. Olympic Blvd.
Los Angeles, CA 90064

Although this newsletter is published primarily for those who run and service trade shows, it is a valuable source of information for executives who deal with the marketing area. Each issue, for instance, includes calendars for future trade shows in the U.S. and overseas. Included in the subscription are three directories: *National Tradeshow Services, Major Exhibit Halls* and *Tradeshow 150* (a statistical analysis of the largest trade shows in the U.S.).

A. C. NIELSEN: RESEARCH FOR DECISION MAKING

A name most widely known for its media-research ratings for television, the A. C. Nielsen Co. offers a wide range of research and information services for business and industry. Marketing research is a major area of operations, with services for planning, screening and evaluating individual products and entire marketing programs. Included are programs for test-marketing new products. The firm also offers computer-based information services in such areas as petroleum, high technology and machinery. For literature detailing services, write:

A. C. Nielsen Co.
Nielsen Plaza
Northbrook, IL 60062

ADVERTISING STRATEGY
Larry Percy and John R. Rossiter
1980/301 pp./$32.95
Praeger Publishers
383 Madison Ave.
New York, NY 10017

This study of advertising is based on communication theory and presents the research findings of professionals in this field. The authors examine the mechanisms that produce advertising results, relating psychological elements to theory and practice. The book is a valuable resource for the executive who seeks a deeper background in this subject.

ESSENTIALS OF
ADVERTISING STRATEGY
Don E. Schultz
1981/131 pp./$10.95
Crain Books
740 Rush St.
Chicago, IL 60611

The author presents a basic introduction to the process of selling products and services with advertising. He focuses on creating the right sales message, one with a strategy that persuades the consumer to buy. Along with examining the steps in setting strategy, the author uses examples of actual advertising to show how sales messages are put together.

READINGS IN ADVERTISING
AND MARKETING MANAGEMENT

The Association of National Advertisers publishes a selection of books and reports on advertising and marketing management. These materials are particularly valuable resources for the executive seeking to expand his or her background in these specialized areas. Of special usefulness are several books and reports on client relations with advertising agencies, including a guideline report titled *Selecting an Advertising Agency* ($15). For brochure, write:

Association of National Advertisers, Inc.
155 E. 44th St.
New York, NY 10017

SALES PROMOTION ESSENTIALS
Don E. Schultz
   and William A. Robinson
1982/234 pp./$11.95
Crain Books
740 Rush St.
Chicago, IL 60611

This handbook of sales-promotion techniques is an introduction to all the basics. The authors review various promotion approaches and also show how they can be integrated with advertising for maximum results. Coverage includes the use of coupons, contests, sweepstakes, bonus packs, trading stamps and premiums. The book is well illustrated with photos of promotion materials.

THE MERCHANDISING REPORTER
$90/12 issues per year
1 Landmark Sq.
Stamford, CT 06901

A specialized but expanding aspect of marketing is the licensed use of comic-strip characters, sports figures and other celebrities to merchandise consumer products. This magazine covers legal and business developments in the licensing field as well as such related areas of merchandising as trademark protection. No matter how far removed you might be from the marketing function, a resource such as this publication can keep you in touch with the marketplace.

EARLY WARNING FORECAST
$147/12 issues per year
221 Columbus Ave.
Boston, MA 02116

Aimed at giving the reader the means to make product and market forecasts, this newsletter gives a monthly summary of the outlook for the industrial economy, the summary based on business-cycle and industrial-market indicators. These data are combined with sales and other data from the reader's company to calculate forecasts. Included in the subscription are a forecasting manual, a companion newsletter titled *Calling the Turns* and access to consultation by letter or telephone. The publisher also conducts seminars around the country on this forecasting method.

SALES AND MARKETING EXECUTIVE REPORT
$78/26 issues per year
4660 Ravenswood Ave.
Chicago, IL 60640

This newsletter concentrates on management ideas and methods for marketing and sales. The emphasis is on practical guidance for managing sales personnel, with coverage of such varied aspects as sales promotions and meetings.

EIGHT VOLUMES OF EXECUTIVE KNOW-HOW

The Dartnell Executive Library is a collection of eight handbooks on management subjects. The areas included are office administration, personnel administration, public relations, advertising, sales management, marketing management, sales promotion, and direct mail and mail order. Each volume has more than 1,000 pages. The set of eight is priced at $403, while individual volumes vary at $53.50 or $57.50. The publisher also markets a series of management manuals on such subjects as employee benefits, time management, training programs and budgeting and purchasing. For a catalog, write:

Dartnell Corp.
4660 Ravenswood Ave.
Chicago, IL 60640

SALES MANAGER'S BULLETIN
$96/24 issues per year
24 Rope Ferry Rd.
Waterford, CT 06386

Whether your responsibility includes sales management or you simply want to keep in touch with its theory and practice, this twice-monthly newsletter would serve you well. It deals with the practicalities of directing sales operations as well as with aspects of marketing.

THE AMERICAN SALESMAN
$23/12 issues per year
424 N. 3rd St.
Burlington, IA 52601

Whatever your executive level and function, somewhere along the line you have links with the marketing of goods or services. That pro-

---

SETTING EXPLICIT STANDARDS FOR NEW-PRODUCT PROPOSALS

Managements in companies having explicit standards or criteria for judging the merits of new-product proposals cite the following reasons for doing so:

- Screening criteria help to remind product planners of the company's intended marketing, financial and other goals.
- Screening criteria help to avoid waste by eliminating the possibility of early investment of time on projects that stand virtually no chance of management approval.
- Screening criteria help to chart a logical course for all those charged with responsibility for developing and marketing new products.

Managements recognize that during the early stages of a proposed project, there may be relatively little solid information available about some criteria. This may force some preliminary decisions based on tentative estimates. But, in many cases, proposals are subject to multistage evaluation, and second chances are available for improving or revising earlier estimates.

From: *Evaluating New-Product Proposals*, E. Patrick McGuire (New York: The Conference Board, Inc., 1979)

---

cess is based on person-to-person selling, ultimately, and this magazine could be the resource you need for keeping tuned in to the process. This monthly deals with the many aspects of selling, ranging from training and motivation to basic strategies and specialized techniques.

PROFESSIONAL SELLING
$48/24 issues per year
24 Rope Ferry Rd.
Waterford, CT 06386

The techniques needed for selling goods and services are acquired and polished by firsthand selling experience, but there is also much to be

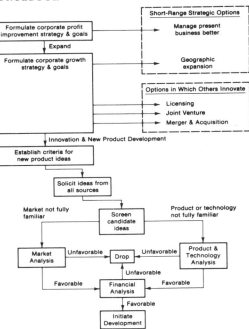

learned secondhand. This newsletter presents twice-monthly guidance for the sales person— as well as valuable insights and ideas for the executive who may be far removed from the selling function.

INNOVATION: MANAGING THE DEVELOPMENT OF PROFITABLE NEW PRODUCTS

Milton D. Rosenau, Jr.
1982/183 pp./$25
Lifetime Learning Publications
10 Davis Dr.
Belmont, CA 94002

The author presents a comprehensive introduction to the process of generating, developing and introducing profitable new products.

Framework for successful new-product development (from Innovation: Managing the Development of Profitable New Products).

He discusses the strategic considerations of product innovation, assessment of market potential, sources and evaluation of ideas, financial analysis and the actual management of product innovation. The author makes extensive use of case histories of both successes and failures, and useful checklists and flow charts are included for use by the reader.

NEW-PRODUCT FORECASTING

Yoram Wind, Vijay Mahaja and
    Richard N. Cardozo, Editors
1981/564 pp./$35.95
Lexington Books
125 Spring St.
Lexington, MA 02173

A reference resource for marketing research, this book reports on 14 of the major new-product forecasting models. The editors have col-

TACTICAL FACTORS AND NEW-PRODUCT DEVELOPMENT

Many firms find that new products do not develop the way they should because management does not recognize the first-level differences. A firm that had been quite successful making and selling large generators developed a line of home standby generators. It was assumed that the marketing department would handle the marketing of the standby generators, the manufacturing department the manufacturing, and the engineering department the engineering. It did not work. Selling to a home is entirely different from selling to a utility. In their large generator business they were used to building in longevity and strength. Home standbys needed neither, and if you built this in, they would be too costly. The engineers who worked on large generators could not get themselves to accept the low quality, as they saw it, that was perfectly acceptable on standby generators. Sales of the home standbys did not take off until they were put under a division manager who had complete control of marketing, manufacturing and engineering and was not bound by past practice. In most cases new products should be placed under a new product manager with complete control until the first-level marketing, manufacturing and engineering problems become clear.

From: *The Management Tactician*, Edward C. Schleh (New York: McGraw-Hill Book Co., 1974)

lected articles from 34 authors both to demonstrate the models in their applications and to provide background on research techniques and data. Included are separate chapters on computer applications and the use of consumer panels.

EVALUATING NEW-PRODUCT PROPOSALS
E. Patrick McGuire
1979/108 pp./$22.50
The Conference Board, Inc.
845 3rd Ave.
New York, NY 10022

Based primarily on practices at 203 manufacturing and service firms, this research report studies methods for evaluating proposals for new products and services. Included are specific criteria as well as various sample checklists for evaluating proposals. Also included are early-stage testing methods for both consumer and industrial products as well as mathematical and statistical screening models.

BUSINESS STRATEGIES FOR PROBLEM PRODUCTS
David S. Hopkins
1981/51 pp./$30
The Conference Board, Inc.
845 3rd Ave.
New York, NY 10022

This research report studies practices at more than 120 companies in dealing with problem products. The report deals with methods for monitoring product performance and diagnosing problem symptoms such as low profitability or low market share. Also examined is the range of options available as well as measures for heading off product difficulties.

RESOURCES FOR THE INFORMED EXECUTIVE

**CORPORATE STRATEGIES OF THE
AUTOMOTIVE MANUFACTURERS**
John B. Schnapp
1979/196 pp./$24.95
Lexington Books
125 Spring St.
Lexington, MA 02173

A study of the economic impact of federal regulatory programs on the automakers, this book provides a very useful comparison of how the

General Motors—Total Investment as Percentage of Total Revenues, 1968-1977

1968	9.3%
1969	8.9%
1970	9.3%
1971	8.4%
1972	7.8%
1973	7.5%
1974	7.5%
1975	6.3%
1976	6.2%
1977	6.3%

Source: GM annual reports.
Note: These are five-year rolling averages with each year representing the last year of the series. Therefore, the percentage given for 1968 is an average of the percentages for 1964, 1965, 1966, 1967, and 1968.

*Decline in capital investments by General Motors
(from Corporate Strategies of the Automotive
Manufacturers).*

major companies in this industry conduct business. The book reports on American Motors, Chrysler, Ford, General Motors, Toyota, Nissan, Honda and Volkswagen. Separate chapters examine the decision-making process in each of these corporations.

**DOING BUSINESS
WITH THE JAPANESE**
Mitchell F. Deutsch
1983/197 pp./$14.50
New American Library
1633 Broadway
New York, NY 10019

This book is a very valuable resource if you expect to do business with, negotiate with, compete with or take a job with the Japanese. If you have no such expectations, the book will still serve you well as an introduction to a people and their way of living and doing business. It is a practical book, with concrete examples that help show how to understand the mentality of the Japanese. The author is a former advertising executive of the Sony Corp.

MIRACLE BY DESIGN: THE REAL REASONS BEHIND JAPAN'S ECONOMIC SUCCESS
Frank Gibney
1982/239 pp./$15.50
Times Books
3 Park Ave.
New York, NY 10016

Their economic success has stimulated intense interest in the management methods of the Japanese. This book, however, presents a broader view of the Japanese experience. A journalist and businessman who has lived and worked in Japan for many years, the author examines the cultural background of the success story and provides the introductory understanding needed for further reading in this area. He concentrates on such aspects as the work ethic and the society's emphasis on long-term goals, and he maintains that there are indeed many lessons for us to learn from the Japanese.

QUEST FOR SURVIVAL AND GROWTH
Anant R. Negandhi and B. Rajaram Baliga
1979/163 pp./$35.95
Praeger Publishers
383 Madison Ave.
New York, NY 10017

This book is a comparative study of American, European and Japanese multinational corpora-

JAPANESE MANAGEMENT AND HOW IT SUCCEEDED

To begin with, the Japanese were for our time the original practitioners of supply-side economics. They accumulated capital and used it in the classic way—for plant modernization and technology development. They saved prodigiously to provide ever more investment funds. But then they took the standard idea of capital one step further. Western economists tended to think of capital in terms of money, plant, material and technology. This means investing in plants, patents and processes, which will bring a good return when used well. To this, however, the Japanese capitalist adds people. The most conspicuous characteristic of Japanese capitalism is its belief that long-term investment in people—which includes training them, partly educating them and developing them within a company—is fully as important as long-term investment in plant.

From: *Miracle by Design: The Real Reasons Behind Japan's Economic Success*, Frank Gibney (New York: Times Books, 1982)

tions in their relationships with host countries. It covers 124 corporations and their operations in Brazil, India, Malaysia, Peru, Singapore and Thailand. Quoting extensively from interviews, the authors focus on the executives of these companies and how their management policies and practices vary with national backgrounds.

AMERICAN MULTINATIONALS AND AMERICAN INTERESTS
C. Fred Bergsten, Thomas Horst
and Theodore H. Moran
1978/535 pp./$29.95
Brookings Institution
1775 Massachusetts Ave., N.W.
Washington, DC 20036

Noting that in recent years over a fifth of American corporate profits have been earned overseas, this book is a detailed study of multinational operations and their complex effects in the U.S. and in foreign countries. The authors examine such aspects as taxation, competition, exports, employment, raw material supply and foreign policy. Charted data illustrate the text throughout.

FORTUNE

$39/26 issues per year
Time-Life Bldg.
Chicago, IL 60611

Fortune tracks the day-by-day course of business with a reliability that has made the magazine a watchword. It is a storehouse of information, and such measurements as the Fortune 500 company rankings have become standards. In articles that trace failure as well as success, business leaders and their companies come under close study. The magazine reports on economic outlook, business trends, investment markets and an open-ended variety of related subjects.

EIGHT ESSENTIAL PERIODICALS FOR BUSINESS EXECUTIVES

Everyone's list of the top publications for business executives will vary, but the periodicals cited below will be found at the top of most rankings. They are listed alphabetically here.

FINDING EXCELLENCE HERE AT HOME

The findings from the excellent companies amount to an upbeat message. There is good news from America. Good management practice today is not resident only in Japan. But, more important, the good news comes from treating people decently and asking them to shine, and from producing things that work. Scale efficiencies give way to small units with turned-on people. Precisely planned R&D efforts aimed at big bang products are replaced by armies of dedicated champions. A numbing focus on cost gives way to an enhancing focus on quality. Hierarchy and three-piece suits give way to first names, shirtsleeves, hoopla and project-based flexibility. Working according to fat rule books is replaced by everyone's contributing.

Even management's job becomes more fun. Instead of brain games in the sterile ivory tower, it's shaping values and reinforcing through coaching and evangelism in the field—with the worker and in support of the cherished product.

From: *In Search of Excellence: Lessons from America's Best-Run Companies*, Thomas J. Peters and Robert H. Waterman, Jr. (New York: Harper & Row, 1982)

Review entries with subscription data appear elsewhere in these pages (consult index for page numbers):

Business Week	*Harvard Business Review*
Dun's Business Month	*Inc. Magazine*
	The New York Times
Forbes	*The Wall Street Journal*
Fortune	

RESEARCH AND KNOW-HOW FOR MANAGEMENT

The Conference Board is an international association of more than 3,000 companies and organizations. Its staff works with member executives to produce research material in such areas as management practices, planning, marketing, economics, finance and public affairs. Information is shared in bulletins, reports and other publications, as well as in a program of seminars and conferences. For further details, write:

The Conference Board, Inc.
845 3rd Ave.
New York, NY 10022

BUSINESS WEEK

$39.95/51 issues per year
1221 Avenue of the Americas
New York, NY 10020

A newsweekly with a reputation for up-to-date coverage, this publication packs its issues with information about all aspects of business. It reports on economics and the business outlook as well as on finance and investment. Departments and features report on specific industries and individual companies. Cover stories and special reports provide in-depth coverage, and national and international political news is closely covered. Profiles of executives and their companies are regular features.

DAILY UPDATE ON BUSINESS WITH THE NEW YORK TIMES

The business section of *The New York Times* provides national and worldwide news and feature reporting seven days a week. The section is often as large as a separate newspaper. It covers business developments, corporate news, finance and investment markets. The paper is widely available at newsstands across the country. Home and office delivery is offered in some areas. Annual subscription by mail for both weekdays and Sundays is $185 in the northeastern U.S., and at higher rates elsewhere. For further information, write:

The New York Times
229 W. 43rd St.
New York, NY 10036

LIFE AND DEATH ON THE CORPORATE BATTLEFIELD

Paul Solman and Thomas Friedman
1982/242 pp./$13.95
Simon and Schuster
1230 Avenue of the Americas
New York, NY 10020

Aiming for an understanding of the basic workings of American business, this book studies how corporations compete. The authors have been associated with the Public Broadcasting System's documentary television series "Enterprise" and they bring a similar savvy style to their book. They are writing for a general audience, but they penetrate the subject deeply, giving the business executive a fresh perspective on the corporate world. The book focuses on particulars and uses case histories to show how companies and their leaders succeed and fail, tracing decisions and strategies that have built powerful corporations and destroyed others. The book is much like a guided tour, and such stops as the Harvard Business School make for fascinating reading.

ENTERPRISE
$16.50/11 issues per year
1776 F St., N.W.
Washington, DC 20006

A publication of the National Association of Manufacturers, this magazine reports and comments on developments in industry. Areas such as government regulations and international trade are covered regularly. Individual issues feature special sections on such major subjects as unemployment, regulatory reform and international competition. A subscription is included in NAM membership.

CANADIAN BUSINESS
$36/12 issues per year
70 The Esplanade
Toronto, Ont. M5E 1R2
Canada

Here is a resource for following the progress of business across the border. This magazine spotlights companies that are making news and focuses on their top executives. These pages will keep you in touch with trends and new developments.

DUN'S BUSINESS MONTH
$27/12 issues per year
875 3rd Ave.
New York, NY 10022

As well known as its parent, Dun & Bradstreet, this monthly provides broad coverage of the business world. Its articles and regular departments report on money and markets, on economic developments, and on happenings in Washington. In-depth stories spotlight major companies and their executives in the news. (Your management position may qualify you for a free subscription to this controlled-circulation magazine.)

FURTHER UP THE ORGANIZATION
Robert Townsend
1984/254 pp./$15.95
Alfred A. Knopf
201 E. 50th St.
New York, NY 10022

This revised edition updates the 1970 best-seller by an author who was equally successful as a top executive with several major U.S. corporations. His book is common sense and straight talk aimed at organizational routines and rituals. He casts a very hard eye on what is bureaucratic in the organization, seeking to humanize business and urging a participative management. Topic by topic, he examines how the organization works, pointing out the things that stifle people and strangle productivity and profits.

MEGATRENDS
John Naisbitt
1982/290 pp./$15.50
Warner Books
666 5th Ave.
New York, NY 10103

This is a book to stimulate your thinking about the future and challenge your planning, both for your company and for your career. The author focuses on 10 fundamental trends that he believes are transforming our society. In his view of the future, he emphasizes such trends as a shift from industry-based to information-based society, from national to global economy

If you don't do it excellently, don't do it at all. Because if it's not excellent it won't be profitable or fun, and if you're not in business for fun or profit, what the hell are you doing here?

From: *Further Up the Organization*, Robert Townsend (New York: Alfred A. Knopf, 1984)

and from centralized to decentralized organization. The book points out specific changes that are already taking place and envisions changes that will come as the result of the fundamental trends of our time.

WHISTLE-BLOWING: LOYALTY AND DISSENT IN THE CORPORATION
Alan F. Westin, Editor
1981/181 pp./$19.95
McGraw-Hill Book Co.
1221 Avenue of the Americas
New York, NY 10020

This book presents accounts of 10 cases in which employees spoke out publicly to report corporate violations of law, company policy or ethical standards. In his commentary, the editor, an attorney, relates the cases to new legislation and trends in this aspect of corporate management. Included are cases involving airline safety, illegal campaign contributions, false reporting to the government, product safety and employee rights.

Expectations have risen regarding the level of competence of executives and the people who follow them. This means that executives must become leaders who will teach their followers to be more effective. Executives who cannot do so tend to withdraw into paralysis and let their organizations drift—to the dismay of their employees and the loss of their stockholders.

From: *Executive*, Harry Levinson (Cambridge, MA: Harvard University Press, 1981)

IN SEARCH OF EXCELLENCE
Thomas J. Peters and
  Robert H. Waterman, Jr.
1982/360 pp./$19.95
Harper & Row
10 E. 53rd St.
New York, NY 10022

Based on extensive and elaborate survey research with some of the largest and most successful companies in the U.S., this book's lessons in sound management made it a bestseller. The authors identify eight elements that are key factors in well-run companies and they present detailed descriptions of examples of the elements in operation in specific companies. The examples provide both fascinating reading and ready-to-use ideas for executives.

CORPORATE TURNAROUND
Donald B. Bibeault
1982/406 pp./$24.95
McGraw-Hill Book Co.
1221 Avenue of the Americas
New York, NY 10020

The author presents strategies both for averting trouble and for turning the failing company around. A turnaround executive himself, the author has gathered material from 97 other executives and he reports on the experiences of more than 200 companies in trouble. Included are tables of useful statistical data.

SECTION 5

Building Your Career

THE MBA AND OTHER ADVANCED TRAINING

THE HARVARD ADVANCED MANAGEMENT PROGRAM

The Advanced Management Program at Harvard Business School is one of the best known of the training programs for senior executives. It is a 13-week residential program that prepares 160 executives for future responsibilities in top management. Each year the program is offered in three sessions, one in the fall, one in the winter and the third in a split session in which the 13 weeks are divided between two consecutive summers. It is an intensive program in which classes are held six days a week and participants usually work 12 hours a day. The Harvard case method is the major teaching technique in the program, as it also is in the school's MBA program. About one-third of the participants come from abroad. All must be nominated, sponsored and supported financially by their employing organizations. The fee for the program is $18,200, which includes books and materials as well as lodging and meals. There is also a $450 fee for Class Association dues. For literature and further information, write:

Advanced Management Program
George Pierce Baker Hall
Harvard Business School
Boston, MA 02163

EXECUTIVE PROGRAMS AT UC, BERKELEY

The Graduate School of Business at the University of California at Berkeley offers four annual residential programs in executive education. The Executive Program runs for four consecutive weeks in the autumn. It is designed for senior executives and focuses on forces that shape the business and political environment. Enrollment is limited to 35, approximately one-third of whom are from abroad. Management Development is a week-long program in July for middle and upper levels of management and it is focused on the latest developments in management training and thinking. Enrollment is limited to 45, about 10 percent of whom are from abroad. Business Public Affairs is held in June and is a

While the number of MBA graduates continues to rise, the demand for MBA's in general is slackening. It is, therefore, becoming increasingly important to get an MBA from one of the top ten business schools.

From: *The Insider's Guide to the Top Ten Business Schools*, Tom Fischgrund, Editor (Boston: Little, Brown & Co., 1983)

one-week program for senior executives in areas such as public affairs, government relations, community affairs and social policy. It is limited to 30 participants. Applicable Capital Market Theory is a seminar held in June. It is designed for investment professionals and deals with the application of Capital Market Theory. Enrollment is limited to 35. For literature and information about fees, write:

Executive Education Programs
Graduate School of Business
350 Barrows Hall
University of California
Berkeley, CA 94720

EXECUTIVE TRAINING
AT CARNEGIE-MELLON

The Graduate School of Industrial Administration at Carnegie-Mellon University conducts an annual six-week residential Program for Executives. Limited to 50 participants, the program provides intensive training for mid-career executives in senior general-management and specialist positions. Participants must be sponsored by their firms. A tuition fee of $6,750 covers books and materials as well as on-campus facilities and meals. Room charges of $2,200 cover accommodations at the Pittsburgh Hyatt during the six-week program. Facilities available include computer equipment. A unique feature of the program is the Man-

agement Game, a computer simulation in which a team of students act as the top officers of a corporation, reporting regularly to a board of directors and senior executives. This same computer simulation is used in the graduate school's MBA program, a two-year program leading to the degree of Master of Science in Industrial Administration (MSIA). For literature and further information, write:

Graduate School of Industrial Administration
Carnegie-Mellon University
Schenley Park
Pittsburgh, PA 15213

COLUMBIA'S MS DEGREE
FOR EXECUTIVES

Also well known for its nondegree executive programs held at the Arden House conference center in upstate New York, the Columbia Graduate School of Business offers its Master's Degree Program for Executives in a two-year part-time schedule. Participants continue in their positions with their firms while attending a full day of classes every Friday for four terms. In addition, each term begins with a one-week, full-time residential program at a conference center. The program totals 36 credit hours and earns the degree of Master of Science in Business Policy. Participants must have at least 10 years of organizational experience as well as several years in a managerial or senior professional position. A bachelor's degree or equivalent preparation is required and participants must be sponsored by their firms. Tuition and living expenses are $5,500 for each of the four terms; this includes books and materials as well as lodging and meals during the four residential weeks. For literature and further information about this program and others at Columbia, write:

Executive Program in Business Administration
Columbia University
Graduate School of Business
New York, NY 10027

change and marketing and financial management. The all-inclusive fee for the seminar programs is $3,700. Also offered is a nine-month full-time program leading to a Master of Science in Management degree. The program is designed for mid-career executives who have at least eight years of experience and are sponsored by their firms. For literature and further information, write:

Stanford Executive Program
Graduate School of Business
Stanford University
Stanford, CA 94305

EXECUTIVE PROGRAMS AT STANFORD UNIVERSITY

The Graduate School of Business at Stanford offers a selection of several nondegree programs for executives during the summer weeks. Its eight-week program in advanced management is designed for executives at or near the highest levels of responsibility and with more than 10 years of experience. Participants live on campus and take part in a full schedule of classes and study. Participants are sponsored by their firms and pay a fee of $12,000, which includes books and materials as well as lodging and meals. Several other programs are offered as two-week seminars. One is designed for chief or senior executives of smaller companies and deals with general management, while others specialize in such areas as organizational

WORKING EXECUTIVES AND THE MBA PROGRAM

It may seem curious that an institution established to give experience also requires it. But business schools are looking for well-qualified applicants who not only can benefit from the MBA program but can also contribute to it. Someone who has had a few years of work experience is more likely to be able to do this. In addition, business schools prefer students who are more mature and more likely to have developed a sense of who they are and where they are going. And, an applicant with work experience can make a better case on his or her application when asked to state his or her three greatest accomplishments and career goals.

From: *The Insider's Guide to the Top Ten Business Schools*, Tom Fischgrund, Editor (Boston: Little, Brown & Co., 1983)

COMPREHENSIVE DIRECTORY TO BUSINESS SCHOOLS

The American Assembly of Collegiate Schools of Business is recognized as the accrediting agency for bachelor's and master's degrees in business. The organization's annual membership directory ($3.50) lists addresses and telephone numbers and identifies all accredited schools. Write:

American Assembly of Collegiate
  Schools of Business
605 Old Ballas Rd.
St. Louis, MO 63141

FINDING YOUR WAY TO GRADUATE SCHOOL

The Graduate Management Admission Council is a resource for information about graduate programs at business schools. The organization's directory is a useful guide to degree programs. Write:

Graduate Management Admission Council
Box 2886
Princeton, NJ 08541

AN MBA PROGRAM FOR EXECUTIVES

The Wharton School at the University of Pennsylvania offers its Executive MBA Program in a format tailored for working execu-

A GUIDE FOR EVALUATING PART-TIME MBA PROGRAMS

There are many part-time evening MBA programs. It is an unfortunate fact that often the differences between the full-time and the part-time programs are larger than the day and night differences in their schedules. In theory, of course, there is no reason why a school cannot offer an excellent program on a part-time basis. Indeed the programs (at least as far as the classes are concerned) could be the same. The part-time student simply proceeds at a slower pace. In practice, however, it often isn't that way at all. In considering a particular school, you should ask:

1. Do both programs use the same faculty or is there a new night crew of practitioners?
2. Are the admissions standards the same?
3. Are the degree requirements the same?
4. Can you automatically transfer from one program to the other depending on your time constraints and cash flow?

From: *The MBA Degree*, Gary D. Eppen, Dennis B. Metcalfe and Marjorie E. Walters (Chicago: Chicago Review Press, 1979)

tives. In a two-year schedule, classes meet all day Friday and Saturday on alternate weekends, continuing through the summers. There are also four full weeks of classes during the schedule. Overnight residence on campus is required for both the Fridays and the four full weeks of classes. The program begins in June of each year. It is designed for men and women with a minimum of 10 years of work experience that includes at least seven years in a managerial position. Participants must be at least 30 years old, have a college degree or its equivalent, be headed for senior management and be endorsed by the employer. The program includes a series of executive lecturers as well as a week-long trip to a foreign country to study international business practices. Courses are taught through lectures, case studies, group and research projects as well as computer simulation. The cost of the program is $15,000 for each of the two years, including books, lodging and meals. The Wharton School also conducts a wide variety of seminar programs for executives around the country. For literature and further information, write:

The Wharton Executive Program
204 Vance Hall/CS
University of Pennsylvania
Philadelphia, PA 19104

THE MBA DEGREE

Gary D. Eppen, Dennis B.
   Metcalfe and Marjorie E. Walters
1979/153 pp./$5.95
Chicago Review Press, Inc.
213 W. Institute Pl.
Chicago, IL 60610

This handbook is an excellent resource for advice and information about the MBA degree. Associated with the University of Chicago's Graduate School of Business, the authors begin with guidance in the decision to seek the degree. They offer very specific suggestions for evaluating schools and examine costs and the process of admission. An especially useful chapter studies the advantages of the MBA in specific career fields.

Having an options policy means quietly staying in circulation in the job market for your particular field, checking now and then to see what other possibilities may exist and occasionally entertaining an offer from another organization. Although very few people realize it, a politically conscious, career-minded professional needs to have options *in good times*, just as much as in hard times.

From: *Executive Tune-Up*, Karl Albrecht (Englewood Cliffs, NJ: Prentice-Hall, Inc., 1981)

THE INSIDER'S GUIDE TO THE TOP TEN BUSINESS SCHOOLS

Tom Fischgrund, Editor
1983/316 pp./$8.95
Little, Brown & Co.
34 Beacon St.
Boston, MA 02106

This book actually focuses on the top 10 MBA programs in the country. In alphabetical order, this selection of schools is Chicago, Columbia, Harvard, Michigan, Northwestern, Sloan, Stanford, Tuck, UCLA and Wharton. Each program is presented in detail, with extensive quotes from graduates to provide insider perspectives and advice. Especially useful is a series of charts comparing many aspects of the 10 MBA programs, including such factors as fees and average starting salaries after completing the programs.

Any executive who seriously wants to reach the top must broaden his range of interests and familiarize himself with business and economic matters far beyond the realm of his own immediate field.

From: *How to Be a Successful Executive*, J. Paul Getty (New York: Playboy, 1981)

THE MBA: 20 MAJOR GRADUATE SCHOOLS

MBA degree programs are widely available in graduate schools across the country. Generally speaking, the degree involves 60 credit hours in a program of two years of full-time study or a longer span of part-time study. Some schools offer part-time programs designed for working executives (see examples in these pages). If you contemplate pursuing the MBA, below is a listing of 20 major graduate schools from which you might seek literature.

Arizona State University
College of Business Administration
Tempe, AZ 85281

Carnegie-Mellon University
Graduate School of Industrial Administration
Schenley Park
Pittsburgh, PA 15213

Columbia University
Graduate School of Business
New York, NY 10027

Cornell University
Graduate School of Business and Public Administration
Ithaca, NY 14853

Dartmouth College
Amos Tuck School of Business Administration
Hanover, NH 03755

Harvard Business School
Soldiers Field
Boston, MA 02163

Indiana University
Graduate School of Business
Bloomington, IN 47405

Massachusetts Institute of Technology
Sloan School of Management
Cambridge, MA 02139

Northwestern University
Graduate School of Management
2001 Sheridan Rd.
Evanston, IL 60201

Stanford University
Graduate School of Business
Stanford, CA 94305

Tulane University
Graduate School of Business Administration
New Orleans, LA 70118

University of California at Berkeley
Graduate School of Business Administration
350 Barrows Hall
Berkeley, CA 94720

University of California at Los Angeles
Graduate School of Management
Los Angeles, CA 90024

University of Chicago
Graduate School of Business
1101 E. 58th St.
Chicago, IL 60637

University of Florida
College of Business Administration
Gainesville, FL 32611

University of North Carolina
Graduate School of Business Administration
Chapel Hill, NC 27514

University of Michigan
Graduate School of Business Administration
Ann Arbor, MI 48109

University of Pennsylvania
The Wharton School
Vance Hall
Philadelphia, PA 19104

University of Texas
Graduate School of Business
Austin, TX 78712

University of Virginia
Colgate Darden Graduate School
  of Business Administration
Box 6550
Charlottesville, VA 22906

GROOMING YOURSELF FOR THE TOP JOB

TUTORING YOUR SKILLS IN PUBLIC SPEAKING AND BUSINESS WRITING

A management consulting firm, Communispond, Inc., specializes in communications training for executives. The firm offers its workshop courses in major cities around the country and it also conducts customized programs for its corporate clients. Training in public speaking makes use of videotape in the learning process. The firm also provides coaching in TV and radio skills. For further information, write:

Communispond, Inc.
485 Lexington Ave.
New York, NY 10017

WRITING FOR DECISION MAKERS
Marya W. Holcombe and
   Judith K. Stein
1981/257 pp./$16.95
Lifetime Learning Publications
10 Davis Dr.
Belmont, CA 94002

The authors offer sophisticated coaching in a very useful manual on effective writing. The book's approach is analytical, showing, to begin with, how to identify and evaluate your primary reader in order to determine what and how you will write. The authors provide valuable guidance in researching, analyzing and or-

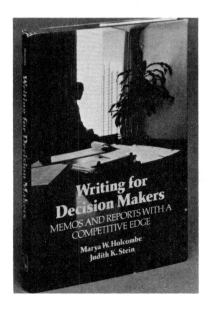

ganizing content, with directions for use of outlines, diagrams and storyboards for working out strategy. Included are chapters on style and the use of graphics such as tables and charts. Especially helpful are chapters on revising and editing of material. A valuable bonus feature of the book is the use of two case studies in each of which the communications situation and content are spelled out, and then the actual writing process is worked out in a sample that follows.

Writing Evaluation Checklist

1. Is it structurally sound?
   —is the thought logically developed?
   —do paragraphs and headings clearly reflect that development?
   —are there any constructions that don't make sense?
   —do the connecting phrases show correct relationships between ideas?

2. Does it answer all the questions it raises?

3. Is it concise?
   —does it tell the reader the facts he or she needs to know and no more?
   —are all unnecessary words and phrases deleted?

4. Is it appropriate in tone and language?
   —is the tone appropriate for the reader to whom it is aimed?
   —is the language adaped to the vocabulary of the reader?
   —are all technical terms and abbreviations explained?
   —is the writing free of sexist words or phrases?

5. Are there errors of grammar, spelling, or punctuation?

6. Summary evaluation: Is the memo or report effective? (Use the scale below.)

   Superior   Acceptable   Unacceptable

This checklist provides a basis for a review of written material (from Writing for Decision Makers*).*

THE EXECUTIVE'S GUIDE TO HANDLING A PRESS INTERVIEW
Dick Martin
1977, 1981/39 pp./$3.95
Pilot Books
103 Cooper St.
Babylon, NY 11702

The author offers detailed guidance for handling interviews with the press. He makes suggestions about preparation, content, technique and style, and gives tips for handling difficult questions and situations. Included is specific guidance for phone, radio and television interviews and news conferences. (If ordering by mail, add $1 for postage and handling.)

GROOMING FOR THE TV INTERVIEW

Jack Hilton, Inc., specializes in training executives for media interviews, as well as in producing TV programming for both corporate and broadcast use. The firm also offers training in public-speaking skills. Its TeleCounsel course grooms the executive for media appearances. It is presented in a two-day format for six participants, for a fee of $12,000, and in a one-day format for two participants, for a fee of $3,500. Both formats involve an additional charge for production expenses. For further information, write:

Jack Hilton, Inc.
60 E. 42nd St.
New York, NY 10165

EXECUTIVE SPEAKING

J. Lewis Powell
1972, 1980/163 pp./$15
BNA Books
1231 25th St., N.W.
Washington, DC 20037

With the premise that skill in public speaking is crucial in projecting an image of executive competence, the author offers coaching in all aspects of speech presentation. His advice ranges from sizing up the audience to preparing and delivering the speech. He emphasizes style and points out the common pitfalls that face the speaker.

POLISH FOR PUBLIC SPEAKING

Whether you address sales meetings and industry conventions or participate on TV talk shows, Speech Dynamics, Inc., offers coaching designed to make you a confident and persuasive speaker. The program is headed by Dorothy Sarnoff, author of *Speech Can Change Your Life* and *Make the Most of Your Best.* Courses are given both in individual sessions and for small groups (12 to 14 participants). The fee for a typical two-day group course is $700, and a three-part audiocassette coaching course ($72) provides a means of sampling the program. For further information, write:

Speech Dynamics, Inc.
111 W. 57th St.
New York, NY 10019

TIPS FOR HANDLING VISUALS IN A SPEECH

A visual aid must be visible to your whole audience or it is worse than useless. A visual aid that can't be seen negates the whole purpose of a visual aid. To prevent such visibility problems, you must know in advance how many people will be in your audience, the size of the room and the type of lighting. Check out your aid in that room beforehand so that you know it can be seen by everyone. If the audience is small (up to 15 people) and your visual aid is a chart, it needn't be the size of a billboard to be seen. On the other hand, if your audience is large and scattered across a large auditorium, you will have to put your chart on a slide and project it if your audience is to see it.

If you are going to show a slide, videotape or film in a darkened room, be sure that you, the speaker, are not in the dark. You are a living visual aid, the most important one; you must not be upstaged by whatever other aid you are using. You can prevent this by arranging for a small light to shine on you so your voice is not disembodied. You must remain visible to retain your authority.

From: *Speak for Yourself—With Confidence*, Elayne Snyder with Jane Field (New York: New American Library, 1983)

SPEAK FOR YOURSELF— WITH CONFIDENCE

Elayne Snyder with Jane Field
1983/213 pp./$7.95
New American Library
1633 Broadway
New York, NY 10019

A speech teacher and consultant, the author presents expert coaching on the writing and delivery of speeches. She provides step-by-step directions, with an emphasis on techniques that build confidence. Included is coverage of impromptu public speaking as well as handling media interviews, meetings, seminars and question and answer sessions.

WOMEN EXECUTIVES AND THE MENTORING PROCESS

As more women enter management careers, cross-sex mentoring will become more important in business. Women managers are working in what is still mainly a man's world. They need male mentors who can help them appreciate and master the fine points of male psychology. Women are often baffled, for instance, by the dynamics of team play that most men take for granted. Good male mentors can explain the subtle blend of competitiveness and cooperation that characterizes so many male relationships. When women are more attuned to male psychology, they will be able to participate in the real sources of power and influence—the informal relationships and social contacts through which men have traditionally established their careers and won their promotions. Similarly, women mentors can help men understand the fine points of women's traditionally nurturing roles. With sensitive cross-sex mentoring, managers can break down some of the sex barriers that inhibit understanding and cooperation. It is a way to map out territory so that men and women will not be so alien in one another's worlds.

From: *Executive*, Harry Levinson (Cambridge, MA: Harvard University Press, 1981)

HOW TO HANDLE SPEECHWRITING ASSIGNMENTS
Douglas P. Starr
1978/39 pp./$3.95
Pilot Books
103 Cooper St.
Babylon, NY 11702

This manual on writing speeches for others provides a useful resource for the executive in that role or writing for his or her own use. The author presents careful guidelines for preparing the ghostwritten speech, including detailed guidance for dealing with the speaker. (If ordering by mail, add $1 for postage and handling.)

PREPARING EFFECTIVE PRESENTATIONS
Ray J. Friant, Jr.
1982/32 pp./$3.50
Pilot Books
103 Cooper St.
Babylon, NY 11702

This manual gives directions for preparing visual material for oral presentation. The author gives detailed and illustrated guidance for organizing material that has visual impact and coordinates with the speaker's commentary. (If ordering by mail, add $1 for postage and handling.)

3M AUDIOVISUAL PRODUCTS, SERVICES AND EXPERTISE

The 3M Audio Visual Division is a useful resource for ideas for effective presentations. Its catalog, *Products to Serve Your Audio Visual Needs*, shows a wide variety of equipment and materials. Among the overhead projectors represented, for instance, are those of the model 6200 series, which fold up into a briefcase unit for easy traveling. Another source of ideas for your presentations is the 3M Meeting Graphics Service, which sells customized graphics via a telephone link with your computer or word processor. This service offers a free seminar program that is conducted around the country.

Circulate your report in draft form to others in your division or department, asking for comments and suggestions both about the information and the way it is presented. Don't merely learn to accept constructive criticism—learn to solicit it actively.

From: *Writing Effective Business Letters, Memos, Proposals and Reports*, Samuel A. Cypert (Chicago: Contemporary Books, Inc., 1984)

A similar free program, the Communication Seminar for Management, focuses on the use of audiovisual techniques for meetings and presentations. For literature and further information, write:

3M Audio Visual Division
Box 33600
St. Paul, MN 55133

AUDIOVISUAL RESOURCES FOR EFFECTIVE PRESENTATIONS

The Visual Horizons catalog is well stocked with products and ideas for making your presentations stronger. The firm offers a wide variety of items for slide projection, including customizing of your slide programs and selections of slide graphics. Among the special services available are color slides from your computer graphics. Audio equipment includes portable sound units. Write:

Visual Horizons
180 Metro Park
Rochester, NY 14623

SELF-DEVELOPMENT THROUGH AUDIOCASSETTE PROGRAMS

Tape-recorded material offers a time-efficient advantage. You can listen and learn while driving your car to or from work, or while simply sitting back in your chair to relax. Execu-Time Systems, Inc., markets a wide selection of cassettes. The Leadership Management series, for instance, consists of 11 tapes prepared by such authorities as George S. Odiorne and James K. Van Fleet ($11.95 per tape, or $115 for the complete series). Other cassettes (priced at $10.95 each) deal with personal motivation, success skills, sales techniques, physical fitness and health. For a mail-order catalog, write:

Execu-Time Systems, Inc.
Box 631
Lake Forest, IL 60045

PROS WHO PACKAGE MEETINGS, PRESENTATIONS, BROCHURES

The Chartmakers, Inc., offers a wide range of professional services in the preparation of meeting programs, presentations and printed materials. The firm specializes in audiovisuals and the use of varied media for small groups as well as large audiences. Presentations range from sales and marketing programs to meetings for employees and shareholders. The firm also produces charts and easel presentations as well as brochures and other printed materials. For introductory literature, write:

The Chartmakers, Inc.
33 W. 60th St.
New York, NY 10023

If, as a working woman, you are going to realize career advancement and the personal fulfillment you seek as a human being, you must overcome the male dominance of executive row. To do that, you must be one part job expert, one part psychologist and one part guerrilla fighter. For starters, you must stop playing the role of victim and start getting control of the sexual signals you send. Even though you may not be aware of it, subconsciously, you may be playing out a role, a life-orienting script which you have been taught to act out since childhood.

From: *Womaning: Overcoming the Male Dominance of Executive Row*, Dean B. Peskin (Port Washington, NY: Ashley Books, Inc., 1982)

ACROSS THE BOARD

$30/11 issues per year
845 3rd Ave.
New York, NY 10022

This magazine is a publication of The Conference Board, Inc., an association for information sharing among member companies and their executives (if your firm is a member, your subscription will cost $15). The magazine covers a broad range of subjects, including economics, business trends and public affairs. It also offers a variety of articles of personal interest to executives in such areas as health and career development.

EXECUTIVE ESSENTIALS

Mitchell J. Posner
1982/627 pp./$8.95
Avon Books
959 8th Ave.
New York, NY 10019

This book provides a valuable reference resource, with information and advice on a wide variety of topics. There are sections on time management, information-gathering skills and

sources, executive health, management skills and executive education. The author also deals with career planning, executive compensation, office automation and business travel.

TEACHING YOURSELF SPEED READING

Xerox Learning Systems markets an audiocassette program that will help you cut down on the time demands of your reading. Called *Speed Reading Self-Taught*, the program is designed to double or triple reading speed and increase comprehension after approximately 10 hours of study and practice. It is priced at $95 (plus $4.95 for shipping and handling). Write:

Xerox Learning Systems
Box 944
Hicksville, NY 11802

MANAGEMENT TRAINING ON VIDEOTAPE

The Business of Management is a training program of 26 half-hour videotapes. Along with documentary footage, the tapes present interviews with guests from corporations and business schools. The program is organized in six modules that cover such aspects as planning, staffing and trends and issues in management. Individual tapes can be rented for $225 for 15 days of use, while the whole program can be purchased for $5,250. Any one tape may be previewed for the special price of $100. Write for brochure:

Wadsworth, Inc.
10 Davis Dr.
Belmont, CA 94002

SHARPENING YOUR MANAGEMENT SKILLS ON YOUR COMPUTER

Thoughtware, Inc., offers a library of management-training programs based on software to be run on the IBM Personal Computer or compatible computers. There are two training series, one on management training and one on management diagnostics. Individual programs are priced from $350 to $450 each and deal with such subjects as leadership, time manage-

ment and conducting meetings. Programs include diskettes and such other materials as training manuals, work sheets, review questions and bibliographies. For literature and further information, write:

Thoughtware, Inc.
2699 S. Bayshore Dr.
Coconut Grove, FL 33133

LEARNING AND MOTIVATION ON AUDIOCASSETTE TAPES

Nightingale-Conant Corp. is a major producer of motivational and self-teaching programs on audiocassette tapes. With tapes, you can listen to a best-selling author while you jog or commute to your office. The firm's catalog offers such books as *The Art of Negotiating* by

The Thoughtware library of management training is based on computer software.

The Nightingale-Conant Corp. markets a wide se-lection of motivational and self-teaching programs on audiocassette tapes.

Gerard I. Nierenberg (12 cassettes, $90). Mo-tivational programs include *The Psychology of Winning* by Dr. Denis Waitley (six cassettes, $45) and *How to Be a No-Limit Person* by Dr. Wayne Dyer (six cassettes, $45). There are programs on time management as well as such subjects as memory training. For mail-order ca-talog, write:

Nightingale-Conant Corp.
7300 N. Lehigh Ave.
Chicago, IL 60648

AMA TRAINING PROGRAMS: OPTIONS FOR BUILDING AN EXECUTIVE CAREER

The American Management Associations of-fer for both members and nonmembers an ex-tensive selection of training programs covering all aspects of management. The Management Course, for instance, provides broad training in

four one-week units that are presented through the year at various locations in the U.S. and Canada (fee for tuition and course materials is $2,750, or $2,400 for AMA members). The AMA's catalog of courses presents more than 100 pages of training programs that range through management methods and skills, information systems, office automation, human resources and personnel management and manufacturing and technology management. At the highest levels of management training is the Presidents Association, a program of courses, forums and roundtables for top executives. Many of the training programs can be brought into a company for groups of executives. The AMA also offers a variety of self-study material through its Extension Institute. For catalogs and brochures with fees and further information, write:

American Management Associations
135 W. 50th St.
New York, NY 10020

A NEWSPAPER TECHNIQUE FOR BUSINESS WRITING

Newspaper writers use a technique they call the *inverted pyramid* style of writing. This means simply your beginning, or lead, sentence should capsulize the entire message, or the most important fact should be presented first and the rest of the facts in descending order of importance. This strategy allows the reader to get the gist of the story by reading only the first few paragraphs. Of course, in the newspaper business there is an added benefit of ending the story with the least important information: layout artists can cut the story from the bottom up to make it fit the page without drastically altering the story.

Leading with your best material dictates that you spend the necessary time polishing the lead until it virtually leaps off the page at the reader. Whatever you say afterward will be enhanced by your first sentence.

From: *Writing Effective Business Letters, Memos, Proposals and Reports,* Samuel A. Cypert (Chicago: Contemporary Books, Inc., 1984)

RESOURCES FOR
THE JOB SEARCH

At one time job-hopping, reflected by one's résumé, was regarded as a negative recommendation. Today the picture is changed. The market value for proven executive ability and intelligence is rated high. A young man who is a "comer" is expected to be a "mover."

From: *Corporate Etiquette*, Milla Alihan (New York: New American Library, 1974)

THE PERFECT RÉSUMÉ
Tom Jackson
1981/208 pp./$8.95
Doubleday & Co.
245 Park Ave.
New York, NY 10017

A broad selection of sample résumés for various work situations makes this how-to book a very useful resource. While it is not tailored specifically for the executive, the book is a storehouse of advice and ideas for résumés that are effective. The author presents various résumé approaches and develops each one with specific directions.

THE COMPLETE RÉSUMÉ GUIDE
Marian Faux
1980/175 pp./$6.95
Simon and Schuster
1230 Avenue of the Americas
New York, NY 10020

An effective résumé is an essential career tool. To keep your résumé effective you will have to update it and revise it from time to time. This book is a practical guide to that process, providing detailed directions and suggestions. A selection of 69 model résumés presents a wide variety of useful approaches.

HOW TO TURN AN INTERVIEW INTO A JOB
Jeffrey G. Allen
1983/111 pp./$5.95
Simon and Schuster
1230 Avenue of the Americas
New York, NY 10020

The author presents detailed counsel on how to handle oneself in a job interview. He emphasizes various practical ways that positive atti-

Compensation elements	Impact on individual executive		
	Attract	Retain	Motivate
Salary	High	High	Moderate
Employee benefits	Low	Moderate	Low
Perquisites	Low	Moderate	Low
Short-term incentives	High	Moderate	High
Long-term incentives	Moderate	High	Moderate

The impact of compensation elements on individual executives (from Executive Compensation: A Total Pay Perspective*).*

tude reinforces interview techniques and he gives step-by-step directions that begin with pre-interview research. Especially useful is a selection of questions commonly asked by interviewers, with suggestions for answering them.

EXECUTIVE COMPENSATION: A TOTAL PAY PERSPECTIVE
Bruce R. Ellig
1982/343 pp./$29.95
McGraw-Hill Book Co.
1221 Avenue of the Americas
New York, NY 10020

This book is a comprehensive study of all aspects of executive-compensation programs. A specialist in the field, the author details the five basic elements of compensation: salary, employee benefits, perquisites, short-term incentives and long-term incentives. While also providing a complete background on specific tax factors, the author examines the relative value of various compensation devices, from the perspective both of the executive and of the corporation.

EXECUTIVE COMPENSATION: RESEARCH FINDINGS

The Conference Board, Inc., studies various aspects of executive compensation. *Top Executive Compensation,* for instance, is an annual report of its survey of U.S. companies. Other reports cover such subjects as compensation for

---

ATTRACTING THE ATTENTION OF THE HEADHUNTERS

A headhunter conducts a particular search with a pretty clear idea in mind of the credentials of the ideal candidate. If he has a large square vacant hole, he wants a large square peg to fit it. Generally, he has no use for carrying a lot of extra large round pegs in his back pocket. He works almost exclusively for corporate clients and isn't equipped to serve the individual executive looking to make a career change.

One day, however, the headhunter may be looking around for a peg just about your size. In that case, *you want to make yourself as visible as possible.* When trying to attract the attention of a headhunter, the trick is, *don't* be coy. If you expect to lure him with your extraordinary qualities, first he has to notice you.

- *Publish* in professional journals or even in popular periodicals.
- *Make speeches* at your trade or professional associations.
- *Be newsworthy.* Be active in social and civic affairs. Make a good name for yourself.
- *Cultivate professional contacts.* Headhunters are plugged into the corporate grapevine.

From: *Executive Essentials,* Mitchell J. Posner (New York: Avon Books, 1982)

THREE TYPES OF BONUSES IN COMPENSATION PLANS

Cash and Carry Bonuses. This is the simplest type. Generally, it is given annually, and is based on the company's profit or the executive's productivity. There may or may not be a written agreement between the executive and the company. Cash bonuses are taxable as ordinary income in the year they are received. They are thus not true estate builders, but more like a salary raise; they provide additional spendable income, theoretically available for investment.

Stock Bonuses. A stock bonus gives an executive a personal stake in the future appreciation of the market value of his company's stock and thus is often a greater incentive to him. It also has an advantage over other stock plans in that the executive doesn't have to pay out any money for his investment.

A word of caution about stock bonuses. They are taxable as ordinary income; so it's wise to arrange for a part payment in cash to pay the tax.

Deferred Bonuses. One way to overcome the tax impact on a lump sum bonus is to arrange to have your bonus paid out on the installment plan. This is a particularly good idea if the bonuses are tied to profits and so are liable to be high in some years, low in others.

From: *The Complete Estate Planning Guide*, Robert Brosterman (New York: New American Library, 1982)

sales executives and executives serving overseas. Also available are reports on stock options for executives as well as such benefits as financial planning. Of related interest is the report *Corporate Directorship Practices: The Compensation Committee*, which surveys the function of the compensation committee in various companies. For further information, write:

The Conference Board, Inc.
845 3rd Ave.
New York, NY 10022

A MANUAL FOR MAKING THE RIGHT MOVES

Whether you are negotiating terms of employment for a new position or you are establishing a relocation plan for your company's employees, a corporation's moving policy needs careful consideration. The *Corporate Moving Policy Manual* provides a guide for studying and setting policy. It covers all the elements in relocating an executive with family and household, including international moves, and it examines the options open to the employer and employee. The 44-page manual is free, as is the firm's *Annual Survey of Corporate Moving Practices*. Also available is a series of brochures with how-to information about moving. Write:

Atlas Van Lines, Inc.
1212 St. George Rd.
Evansville, IN 47711

EXECUTIVE RECRUITERS AND OUTPLACEMENT SERVICES

> The person who gets hired is not necessarily the one who can do that job best, but the one who *knows the most about how to get hired.*
>
> From: *What Color Is Your Parachute?*, Richard Nelson Bolles (Berkeley, CA: Ten Speed Press, 1984)

tive Recruiting Firms ($2), a concise listing showing only name, address and phone number.

Consultants News
Templeton Rd.
Fitzwilliam, NH 03447

EXECUTIVE RECRUITERS: TALENT SCOUTS FOR TOP MANAGEMENT

The *Directory of Executive Recruiters* provides more than 2,000 listings of firms and their affiliates and branch offices. There is a separate category of firms that operate on a contingency rather than retainer basis (that is, charge a fee only if the firm places its candidate). Listings show minimum salary as well as professional affiliations, functions covered and industries served. The directory also indexes the listings by functions, industries and geographical location. Priced at $15, the directory includes a glossary of terms as well as guidance for companies and individuals dealing with recruiters. The publisher also markets *50 Leading Execu-*

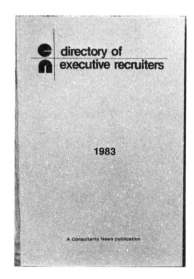

TAKING A SPIRAL VIEW OF YOUR CAREER PATH

One idea that facilitates choosing is to view the career as a spiral path rather than a linear path. Take for example the engineer who has explored both the technical and managerial aspects of his work. He feels a deep need now to choose one path or the other. Both are tempting to different aspects of himself—he is conflicted. But he feels more and more that in order to succeed, he must commit himself to one path or the other. If he views the career as a linear path, this is a paralyzing decision. Yet if he recognizes that a career can be a spiral path, the choice is less painful. He can pursue one path intently well into the future, building later on his skill and experience to turn off into the other—or to alternatives that he has not envisaged, that only opportunity will bring.

From: *Must Success Cost So Much?*, Paul Evans and Fernando Bartolomé (New York: Basic Books, Inc., 1981)

12 MAJOR EXECUTIVE RECRUITING FIRMS

Whether you seek an executive recruiter to help you fill a position for your company or to help you find a new position with another company, you have hundreds of firms to choose from. The wide choice narrows, however, if you limit your selection to those specialists who operate solely on the basis of retainer fees paid by the hiring company. Listed here are 12 major recruiters, a sampling from among the best-known firms around the country. Each of them has branch offices in major cities. An inquiry letter will yield information about services and fees.

Billington, Fox & Ellis, Inc.
20 N. Wacker Dr.
Chicago, IL 60606

Boyden Associates, Inc.
260 Madison Ave.
New York, NY 10016

William H. Clark Associates, Inc.
330 Madison Ave.
New York, NY 10017

Eastman & Beaudine, Inc.
111 W. Monroe St.
Chicago, IL 60603

Heidrick and Struggles, Inc.
125 S. Wacker Dr.
Chicago, IL 60606

Ward Howell International, Inc.
99 Park Ave.
New York, NY 10016

Lamalie Associates, Inc.
101 Park Ave.
New York, NY 10022

Paul R. Ray & Co., Inc.
1208 Ridglea Bank Bldg.
Fort Worth, TX 76116

Russell Reynolds Associates, Inc.
245 Park Ave.
New York, NY 10167

Paul Stafford Associates, Ltd.
45 Rockefeller Plaza
New York, NY 10111

Staub, Warmbold & Associates, Inc.
655 3rd Ave.
New York, NY 10017

Spencer Stuart & Associates
55 E. 52nd St.
New York, NY 10055

THE DOUBLE PURPOSE OF OUTPLACEMENT SERVICES

Outplacement counseling, the domain of a rising number of specialized consulting firms, has a double-edged function. Under contract to a particular corporation, the outplacement counselors provide their clients with advice and strategies for use in terminating both individuals and groups of employees. Then, in turn, the counselors are commissioned to provide employment counseling as well as moral support to dismissed personnel for the duration of their job search. The purpose of outplacement is to re-place the terminated employee.

From: *Executive Essentials*, Mitchell J. Posner (New York: Avon Books, 1982)

THE MARKET FOR EXECUTIVE TALENT
Edward L. Kaufman
1978/277 pp./$115
McGraw-Hill Book Co.
1221 Avenue of the Americas
New York, NY 10020

This report on executive compensation practices combines guidelines for designing compensation programs with findings from an elaborate survey. The survey was drawn from a sampling of 740 privately held companies of all sizes. It shows compensation for key executives by level, by size and earnings of company and by type of company. The report examines all aspects of compensation packages, including bonus plans and various perquisites.

PERKS AND PARACHUTES
John Tarrant
1985/448 pp./$19.95
The Linden Press/Stonesong
1230 Avenue of the Americas
New York, NY 10020

This comprehensive guide covers all aspects of the executive employment contract. It provides the background and know-how for effective negotiation of compensation, benefits, bonuses, perks, severance pay. The author presents case

ON BEING FORCED OUT AND MAKING A GRACEFUL EXIT

If at all possible, *leave of your own volition*, in an atmosphere of parting amicably with the organization. Minimize the significance of the conflict with the other person, rely on your existing political relationships to cast you in a positive light, and don't burn any bridges. In all likelihood, the person upstairs will find this a satisfactory resolution, since, after all, he or she really only wants you gone rather than dead. You save face for

yourself by saving face for the other person. In any case, your colleagues who remain will probably spread the word subtly that the person upstairs unfairly forced you out of the organization and that they've lost a valued associate. You live to fight another day.

As the old expression goes, as they run you out of town, grab a flag and wave it. Make it look like a parade, with you out in front leading it.

From: *Executive Tune-Up*, Karl Albrecht (Englewood Cliffs, NJ: Prentice-Hall, Inc., 1981)

Interviewing should be considered nothing more than packaging yourself for sale. The only difference between selling yourself and selling something else is that you are both the goods and the salesperson. In this sense, the interviewing process is unique and your success can be really exciting.

From: *How to Turn an Interview into a Job,* Jeffrey G. Allen (New York: Simon and Schuster, 1983)

histories as well as specimen contracts and draws on interviews with compensation analysts, executive recruiters and attorneys. Included are such subjects as golden-parachute and golden-handcuff contracts.

THE 100 BEST COMPANIES TO WORK FOR IN AMERICA
Robert Levering, Milton Moskowitz
  and Michael Katz
1984/372 pp./$17.95
Addison-Wesley Publishing Co.
Jacob Way
Reading, MA 01867

The authors present brief but detailed profiles of their selection of 100 U.S. companies. Based on interviews with present and former executives and employees, the profiles give an insider's perspective on everything from salaries and perks to management style and corporate "ambiance." The book is a valuable resource for the executive contemplating a move.

JOB-CHANGE RESOURCES FOR EXECUTIVES

In addition to directories of management consultants, executive recruiters and outplacement services, this publisher offers two monthly newsletters and a mail-order selection of related books and self-study material. These publications are directed to consultants as well as to

their clients. The newsletters are *Consultants News* ($66 per year) and *Executive Recruiter News* ($54 per year). Two self-study programs are available. Priced at $24.95, *Get That Job!* combines two 30-minute cassettes with a 45-page booklet to dramatize interviewing techniques. *Job Marketing,* priced at $195, is a 10-part program of cassettes, booklets and sample letters and résumés. For further information, write:

Consultants News
Templeton Rd.
Fitzwilliam, NH 03447

SO YOU ARE LOOKING FOR A NEW JOB . . . NOW WHAT?
George D. Moffett, Jr.
1983/99 pp./$6
Exposition Press, Inc.
Box 2120
Smithtown, NY 11787

A specialist in executive outplacement, the author presents step-by-step guidance for the search for a new position. The book organizes the process in a campaign format, providing practical advice on the many elements involved. Included is counsel on setting strategy, preparing résumés, handling interviews and negotiating the job offer. Also included is a very useful listing of information sources about potential employers and a sample employment agreement.

OUTPLACEMENT: EASING THE STRAINS FOR THE EXECUTIVE OUT OF A JOB

The *Directory of Outplacement Firms* presents 81 listings, a growing number of firms specializing in services for executives searching for new jobs. There are two separate categories of listings. One category presents firms that are paid exclusively by the executive's former employer. Firms in the second category also accept payment from the individual executive. Listings include a brief profile of the firm and its services, names of principals, salary minimum and fee formula. Priced at $13, the directory is also indexed by geographical location and names of principals. Introductory material gives an overview of outplacement services as well as guidelines for evaluating outplacement firms.

Consultants News
Templeton Rd.
Fitzwilliam, NH 03447

14 SPECIALISTS IN OUTPLACEMENT

As more and more companies provide assistance to their departing executives, the number of consulting firms that specialize in outplacement services continues to grow. Typical services are based on counseling and administrative support during the job search. The 14 firms listed below concentrate on outplacement and are a sampling of programs that are available around the country. If you contemplate such a program for your company, an inquiry letter will bring you detailed information.

Breitmayer Associates
30 Broad St.
Stamford, CT 06901

Challenger, Gray & Christmas, Inc.
11 S. LaSalle St.
Chicago, IL 60603

Compass, Inc.
10 S. 5th St.
Minneapolis, MN 55401

Craigie Associates
220 Lenox Ave.
Westfield, NJ 07090

Darmody & Associates, Inc.
1776 S. Jackson St.
Denver, CO 80210

De Recat & Associates, Inc.
150 Post St.
San Francisco, CA 94108

Drake Beam Morin, Inc.
277 Park Ave.
New York, NY 10172

Executive Group, Inc.
4950 W. Kennedy Blvd.
Tampa, FL 33609

J. J. McNabb, Inc.
645 Madison Ave.
New York, NY 10022

Arnold Menn & Associates
1600 W. 38th St.
Austin, TX 78731

Patrick-Douglas Outplacement
1218 Superior Bldg.
Cleveland, OH 44114

Payne-Lendman, Inc.
5500 Greenwich Rd.
Virginia Beach, VA 23462

Troy Associates, Inc.
4310 Prudential Tower
Boston, MA 02199

Univance
2029 Century Park East
Los Angeles, CA 90067

INGREDIENTS FOR SUCCESS: PERFORMANCE, IMAGE, POWER

Competence and *performance* are obviously necessary over the long haul in any case, but performance is often diminished and sometimes even prevented because of image problems and the under-use or misuse of power.

Image is the perception other people have of you. The "others" you should be concerned about are those who can either help or hinder your performance, support or sabotage your project, accept or reject your proposal, and so forth. You should take the time to identify those people and give some serious thought to how they see you in your role as a manager. Perhaps the most important pair of image holders are your boss and his or her boss.

Power is the ability to influence other people, to get what you want from them, and to get them to do things they would not do if it were not for your "presence," physical or psychological. Paradoxically, one need not have real power in order to use it. It is the other person's *perception* of your power that counts.

From: *Practical Management Skills for Engineers and Scientists*, William C. Giegold (Belmont, CA: Lifetime Learning Publications, 1982)

GUIDANCE FOR CAREER GROWTH

MOVING UP
Eli Djeddah
1971, 1978/178 pp./$4.95
Ten Speed Press
Box 7123
Berkeley, CA 94707

A career counselor, the author offers coaching for making job moves, both within the company and outside it. His advice is detailed and ranges from preparing the right résumé to techniques for setting up interviews. He gives tips on all aspects of the process, illustrating with specific examples.

HOW TO MAKE THINGS GO YOUR WAY
Ralph Charell
1979/186 pp./$5.95
Simon and Schuster
1230 Avenue of the Americas
New York, NY 10020

Focusing on essential aspects of attitude and self-awareness, the author writes about succeeding. He bases his advice on his own experiences of success and failure in his careers as investment advisor, television executive and writer. The author emphasizes outlook on life and the practical steps that can alter it positively. Included are chapters on such subjects as negotiating and decision making as well as his approach to investments.

WHAT COLOR IS YOUR PARACHUTE?
Richard N. Bolles
1970, 1984/387 pp./$8.95
Ten Speed Press
Box 7123
Berkeley, CA 94707

Steering a career requires much sound thinking as well as action and this author has become a best-seller with his guidance in both areas. The book focuses on job hunting and career changing, but it is more than a how-to manual. The author's success lies in helping the reader find new perspectives through careful self-evaluation. The book is a very valuable resource.

Many younger women have come into business expecting too much too soon and have been disappointed at their seemingly slow progress. We must pay our dues too. It takes from 15 to 25 years for a manager to become a top executive. Establish high goals, but be realistically patient about achieving them. Business success rarely happens overnight.

From: *The New Executive Woman*, Marcille Gray Williams (New York: New American Library, 1977)

THE MAGIC OF THINKING BIG
David J. Schwartz
1959, 1982/192 pp./$3.95
Simon and Schuster
1230 Avenue of the Americas
New York, NY 10020

The author offers guidance for personal growth and career success. His basic premise is that self-motivation is the key mechanism in success and he traces its function through a variety of circumstances in business and personal life. The author also examines interpersonal relationships and the part they play in individual success.

CHECKLIST FOR DRAFTING EMPLOYMENT CONTRACTS

1. Identification of the parties.
2. Term, or time, of the contract.
3. The place, or places, where the contract is to be performed.
4. Duties of employee; hours of employment; best efforts to be devoted to employment; maintaining outside job or interests.
5. Working facilities.
6. Maintaining trade secrets.
7. Inventions and patents: discovery in the course of employment; use of employer's facilities; relation of discovery to employer's business.
8. Compensation: wage, salary or commission; overtime work or night work; pay while unable to work due to illness; effect of termination by either party or failure to complete the employment undertaking for any other reasons.
9. Special compensation plans: deferred compensation; percentage of sales or profits; incentive bonus; profit sharing; stock options; pension and retirement plans.
10. Expense account: travel; meals, lodging.
11. Covenant not to compete after leaving employment; length of time; geographical limitations; irreparable harm suffered by employer; hardship not greater than necessary on employee; agreement not injurious to public interest.
12. Employee benefits: life and disability insurance; health insurance; workmen's compensation.
13. Termination of employment: right of either party to terminate on proper notice; discharge of employee for cause.
14. Remedies for breach of contract: liquidated damages.
15. Arbitration of disputes.
16. Vacations and holidays.
17. Assignability of contract by employer or employee.
18. Modification, renewal or extension of contract.
19. Complete agreement in written contract.
20. Law to govern interpretation of contract.
21. Date of contract.
22. Signatures.
23. Witnesses and acknowledgment, if any.

From: *The Complete Guide to Business Contracts*, John C. Howell (Englewood Cliffs, NJ: Prentice-Hall, Inc., 1980)

THE THREE BOXES OF LIFE: AND HOW TO GET OUT OF THEM

Richard N. Bolles
1978, 1981/466 pp./$8.95
Ten Speed Press
Box 7123
Berkeley, CA 94707

The author of *What Color Is Your Parachute?* takes a very broad view of the life/work experience in this book and offers counsel for success. The three boxes of the title are the life stages: education, work, retirement. The author urges that the stages be transformed into aspects of life that are continuously integrated with one another. This is a book of ideas as much as advice and it will provoke you to some very rewarding thinking.

WHERE DO I GO FROM HERE WITH MY LIFE?

John C. Crystal and
   Richard N. Bolles
1974/253 pp./$9.95
Ten Speed Press
Box 7123
Berkeley, CA 94707

If you are in the midst of reassessing your career, this book could be a very valuable resource for you. If you have read author Bolles in his book *What Color Is Your Parachute?* you will already know much about this book from that best-seller. Here Bolles and Crystal present a workbook to take the reader through the process of life/work planning. It is a process for charting a career as well as for changing it.

A CAREER STRATEGY FOR WOMEN EXECUTIVES

Once you *really* know your talents, abilities and interests, you may well be able to identify a new and more significant role for yourself in your present organization or in a different organization that needs what you can offer (whether or not they know it before you approach them). Or you may identify a job you would like to have but for which you lack a requisite skill, perhaps money management. In this case, you can move quickly to pick up that skill and then go after the job. The need you find may even offer you a chance to go on your own and start an entirely new business. The point is this: Do not sit and wait for the decision-making opportunities to come to you. Create them.

From: *Management Strategies for Women*, Ann McKay Thompson and Marcia Donnan Wood (New York: Simon and Schuster, 1982)

CONFESSIONS OF A WORKAHOLIC

Wayne Oates
1971, 1978/146 pp./$1.50
Abingdon Press
Box 801
Nashville, TN 37202

This self-help book offers counsel for those whose work compulsion brings problems in

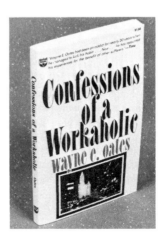

Replenish the male ego, don't threaten it. Because you are a special person, a woman executive, your attention to his ego is even more meaningful. Just as women are drawn to successful men, so men are drawn to creative and productive women, provided they do not deliberately or unconsciously belittle them. You will find yourself a very popular person, a politically wise thing to be.

From: *The New Executive Woman*, Marcille Gray Williams (New York: New American Library, 1977)

WORKAHOLICS
Marilyn Machlowitz
1980/198 pp./$3.50
New American Library
1633 Broadway
New York, NY 10019

The author, a psychologist, reports on her study of workaholism based on extensive interviews with men and women from varied occupations. She spells out both negative and positive aspects of the phenomenon and she concludes that, while addicted, workaholics basically love their work. Suggesting ways to live with and capitalize on this trait, the author offers counsel for the workaholic as well as family, friends and co-workers.

personal life. Tracing the psychological and cultural aspects of what he calls work addiction, the author examines such issues as the work ethic and its meaning in everyday life. His advice combines the practical and the inspirational and focuses on solutions.

SECTION 6

Executive Money Management

FINANCIAL SERVICES

To be financially successful in the 1980's you must be fully familiar with the financial and economic environment. You must understand it on a firsthand basis in its essentials in order to make your own decisions. It's not good enough to have a gut feeling that something's wrong with the world, and then react on the basis of whim or intuition. Nor can you rely on the advice of others without understanding the causes of the economic events that will shape the future. Acting on gut feelings is no better than gambling; and acting on advice that you don't understand is even worse.

From: *Strategic Investing*, Douglas R. Casey (New York: Simon and Schuster, 1982)

SHEARSON'S FULL RANGE OF FINANCIAL SERVICES

One of the giants, Shearson Lehman/American Express offers a complete selection of financial services including stocks and bonds, commodity futures, options, mutual funds, municipal bonds, tax shelters, life insurance and annuities. The firm's Financial Manage-

ment Account offers services that include a choice of three money market funds, an investment account, credit card and checking privilege. Shearson also provides investment management services for corporations and individual executives. The firm is active in investment banking, including the areas of acquisitions and divestitures. For literature and further information, contact a local office or write:

Shearson Lehman/American Express, Inc.
2 World Trade Center
New York, NY 10048

COMPLETE INVESTMENT SERVICES AT DREXEL BURNHAM LAMBERT

A major investment banker as well as provider of investment services for individuals, Drexel Burnham Lambert, Inc., and its subsidiaries are a leading financial resource for the executive. The firm is a leader in managing stock offerings and merger transactions. Its individual services are handled by more than 900 account executives in over 50 offices around the world. Included are stocks, bonds, government securi-

ABOUT THE PITFALLS OF SELECTING STOCKS

In the 1960's, the great economist Paul Samuelson testified before the U.S. Senate that mutual funds perform no better than random portfolios. He then promptly papered a wall with a listing of all 1,200 companies listed on the New York Stock Exchange and selected his portfolio by throwing darts at the list. Over the next decade, his random portfolio outperformed the average mutual fund; it even outperformed those funds dedicated to reducing risk and maximizing long-term capital appreciation.

Several years later, the top brass of *Forbes* magazine pasted the *New York Times* stock pages to the wall, also made ten stock selections by throwing darts, and invested $1,000 in each. A decade later their portfolio had outperformed most of the world's money managers. Yet to this day, *Forbes* continues to publish various investment columns and advice.

From: *Life and Death on the Corporate Battlefield*, Paul Solman and Thomas Friedman (New York: Simon and Schuster, 1982)

ties, municipal bonds, mutual funds, commodities, gold, options, tax shelters, life insurance. The firm also offers investment management for corporations and institutions as well as financial planning for individuals. For literature and further information, contact the firm's local office or write:

Drexel Burnham Lambert, Inc.
60 Broad St.
New York, NY 10004

PAINE WEBBER: A FULL RANGE OF PRODUCTS AND SERVICES

Paine Webber deals in stocks, bonds, options, futures, mutual funds, tax-shelter investments, government securities and municipal bonds. The firm also provides individual annuity and life insurance products as well as various corporate services. Its Resource Management Account offers consolidated service to the customer, combining a brokerage account with money fund option and check-writing and MasterCard credit privileges. Its investment-research facilities include the Portfolio Dynamics service, a computerized portfolio analysis. For literature and further information, contact a local office or write:

Paine Webber Jackson & Curtis, Inc.
140 Broadway
New York, NY 10005

MERRILL LYNCH: A LONG LIST OF FINANCIAL SERVICES

One of the best-known names on Wall Street, Merrill Lynch offers a full range of investment services that includes stocks, bonds, mutual funds, government securities, certificates of deposit, money market funds, municipal bonds and municipal bond funds. The firm's Financial Pathfinder service provides individual financial planning. Services for corporations include investment programs and employee

More than ever, you must stay smart, safe and liquid in a volatile, hostile world: alert to the possibilities that falling prices offer, but ready to move fast to protect your money if inflation resurfaces. Common sense, and an understanding of how we got here, still can see you through. The hazards are greater than ever—but they aren't insurmountable, even now.

From: *Financial Survival in the Age of New Money*, Gordon Williams (New York: Touchstone Press, 1982)

benefit plans as well as business financing. A valuable resource for the investor is the firm's booklet *How to Read a Financial Report.* Another very useful booklet is *Double Income*

Couples: What They Need to Know About Personal Finance and Investing. Contact a company office in your area, or write:

Merrill Lynch Pierce Fenner
 & Smith, Inc.
1 Liberty Plaza
New York, NY 10080

WHEN TO SELL A FALLING STOCK

The most usual method, followed indeed by some quite successful investors, is to sell any stock that goes down 10 percent from the price you paid for it. This is usually refined to state that if the stock advances after you buy it, you then should sell any time it drops 10 percent from its high point. When the stock reacts, you act. Rid yourself of all ego and all emotion; do it by the book. This method is based on the (absolutely correct) theory that most investors will try to talk themselves out of a sale, that they will tend to dither and rationalize as the stock descends. The automatic rule is designed to avert the negative investment results of this variety of inner turmoil by forcing you to cut your losses before they become so large as to be disabling.

From: *How to Make Money in Wall Street*, Louis Rukeyser (New York: Dolphin Books, 1976)

A MUNICIPAL BOND FUND FOR TAX-FREE INVESTING

John Nuveen & Co., Inc., specializes in municipal bonds, and its Nuveen Tax-Exempt Bond Fund offers individual investors a way to buy into a nationally diversified portfolio. The minimum investment is 50 $100 units, or $5,000. Earnings are reinvested or paid out monthly, quarterly or semi-annually. The firm has offices in 15 major cities across the country. For literature, write:

John Nuveen & Co., Inc.
209 S. LaSalle St.
Chicago, IL 60604

The 30 stocks that comprise the Dow Jones Industrial Average are widely regarded as prominent pillars of the market. This is unquestioned—in terms of earnings, uninterrupted dividends and sufficient stability price-wise, they may be held indefinitely with minimal danger of any serious loss. Yet these are primarily stocks with histories of relatively moderate growth, so those selected by any enterprising investor should outperform the Dow Jones Industrial Average by at least two-to-one when the average is rising, and during such times the aggressive growth investor is unwilling to settle for anything less than a 50 percent annual increase.

From: *Stock Market Strategy for Consistent Profits*, Raymond R. Righetti (Chicago: Nelson-Hall, Inc., 1980)

IDS: FINANCIAL PLANNING FOR INDIVIDUALS AND COMPANIES

Investors Diversified Services, a subsidiary of American Express, is one of the major firms offering financial planning services for individuals and companies. The firm's representatives are based in almost 200 divisional offices across the country. IDS sells face-amount investment certificates, mutual funds, life insurance and annuities. It also provides investment and administrative services for corporate and institutional group-pension customers. For literature, write:

Investors Diversified Services, Inc.
IDS Tower
Minneapolis, MN 55402

COMPREHENSIVE SERVICES AT PRUDENTIAL-BACHE

Combining both investment and insurance facilities, Prudential-Bache offers a broad range of services. A long list of investment services includes stocks, bonds, mutual funds, money market funds, government securities, precious metals, retirement plans. The firm's planning services are described in the booklet *Total Financial Planning*, which is available with a separate section to be used for a personal financial inventory. Also available is the Command Account, which coordinates financial components in a single service, for either an individual or a company. For literature and local branch information, write:

Prudential-Bache Securities, Inc.
100 Gold St.
New York, NY 10292

FINANCIAL PLANNING FOR EXECUTIVES

**PERSONAL FINANCIAL
PLANNING FOR EXECUTIVES**
Paul A. Randle and
    Philip R. Swensen
1981/298 pp./$17.95
Lifetime Learning Publications
10 Davis Dr.
Belmont, CA 94002

The authors offer a useful guide that covers all aspects of personal financial planning. After

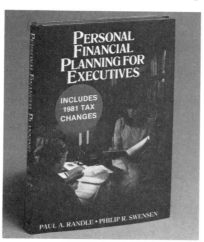

an opening section that presents a broad introduction to basics, the authors deal with such areas as retirement plans, insurance selection, Employee Stock Ownership Plans, income-tax considerations. The book provides detailed guidance on investments ranging from conventional options to tax shelters. A separate chapter offers advice on estate planning. Especially helpful is a series of work sheet formats for use by the reader.

**THE COMPLETE ESTATE
PLANNING GUIDE**
Robert Brosterman
1964, 1982/359 pp./$3.95
New American Library
1633 Broadway
New York, NY 10019

This handbook gives a thorough review of all phases of programs for building your personal estate. Along with capital investments in stocks, bonds, annuities, insurance and real estate, the author explains the profitable use of

BASIC CONSIDERATIONS IN PLANNING A TAX HAVEN

To understand the planning of a tax haven company, you as a corporate executive or your tax counsel should have a working familiarity with the tax laws of the country of residence or citizenship, and with the tax laws of the tax haven countries, as they apply to the particular enterprise being planned. Certain tax haven countries are best suited for certain enterprises. Hong Kong, for example, would in many cases be a viable choice for a manufacturing enterprise, since its tax laws favor manufacturing for a world market; furthermore, a Hong Kong–based plant has access to a vast pool of local labor, as well as Eastern markets. As another example, a Panamanian-based distribution company can benefit from Panama's tax laws that favor such enterprises, as well as from Panamanian shipping facilities and proximity to Latin American consumer markets. In any case, the tax haven company should be planned in accordance with the financial goals that it hopes to achieve. This also means that the tax haven country should impose little or no taxes on the particular activity being planned. Further, if there are tax treaties in existence between the tax haven country and your country of citizenship or residence, the effects of these treaties should be carefully studied.

From: *Tax Havens for Corporations*, Adam Starchild (Houston: Gulf Publishing Co., 1979)

corporate fringe benefits for executives. The book is a valuable introduction to estate management, with careful counsel on the selection of professional advisors and the services they can provide. Throughout the book, tax factors are clearly explained.

TAX SHELTERS
Robert and Carol Tannenhauser
1978, 1982/242 pp./$3.95
New American Library
1633 Broadway
New York, NY 10019

Don't let your plans be formulated by those who sell financial products and services. Remember, they have a strong vested interest in selling those products—that is how they make their living. Their advice may be excellent, but you have no way to judge unless you have previously defined your objectives.

From: *Personal Financial Planning for Executives*, Paul A. Randle and Philip R. Swensen (Belmont, CA: Lifetime Learning Publications, 1981)

The authors present a comprehensive introduction to the benefits as well as the risks of tax-shelter investments. Beginning with the basics and emphasizing a clear understanding, the book shows how to evaluate both profit potential and tax benefits in a venture. Tax laws and their application are explained in detail and risk factors are fully spelled out. Included are such investment ventures as real estate, oil and gas, coal, movies, equipment leasing and precious metals.

TAX HOTLINE

$37.95/12 issues per year
500 5th Ave.
New York, NY 10110

This guide to business and personal tax situations covers the broad range of tax laws, rules and regulations. It is written for the nonexpert, and the reporting is specific and detailed. The tax information and advice includes such areas as investments, tax shelters, executive compensation and retirement planning.

PERSONAL TAX STRATEGIST

$79/12 issues per year
10076 Boca Entrada Blvd.
Boca Raton, FL 33433

This monthly newsletter is a detailed guide to minimizing your income taxes. It provides directions for managing income as well as advice in financial and estate planning.

TAX SHELTER INSIDER

$124/12 issues per year
10076 Boca Entrada Blvd.
Boca Raton, FL 33433

This newsletter presents a monthly update on IRS and tax-court rulings as well as detailed assessments of tax-shelter investment opportunities. The newsletter offers cautionary advice where it finds legal or financial risk to the investor.

FINANCIAL PLANNING STRATEGIST

$48/12 issues per year
10076 Boca Entrada Blvd.
Boca Raton, FL 33433

This monthly newsletter provides advice for personal financial planning. It covers investments, taxes, insurance, credit, retirement and estate planning. The emphasis is on retirement planning and taxes.

MAKING SUCCESSFUL INVESTMENTS

HIGH-TECH: HOW TO FIND AND PROFIT FROM TODAY'S NEW SUPER STOCKS
Albert Toney and Thomas Tilling
1983/399 pp./$16.95
Simon and Schuster
1230 Avenue of the Americas
New York, NY 10020

This investor's guide covers more than 250 companies in 14 different high-tech industries. It offers a comprehensive and practical introduction to this field and it is packed with such specific information as company addresses and long lists of information sources. Among the 14 industries covered are genetic engineering, robotics, cellular mobile radio, fiber optics, applications software, personal computers, medical and military technology. The book includes an appendix section with a personal computer program for charting and evaluating investment information.

American industry in the last decades has increasingly turned to executives with financial or legal backgrounds to fill top management slots. . . . In technology, look for marketing and engineering people. The worst thing you can discover when you are investigating the management of a company is a collection of lawyers.

> From: *High-Tech: How to Find & Profit from Today's New Super Stocks*, Albert Toney and Thomas Tilling (New York: Simon and Schuster, 1983)

SUCCESSFUL INVESTING
Staff of United Business Service Co.
1983/446 pp./$10.95
Simon and Schuster
1230 Avenue of the Americas
New York, NY 10020

A useful reference resource for both newcomer and experienced investor, this book is a broad introduction to investment alternatives as well as the bases for making choices. There are individual chapters on each of the basic investment categories as well as on such subjects as how to read an annual report. The book covers all aspects of its subject, including tax considerations and financial planning.

STRATEGY FOR MAKING HIGH-TECH INVESTMENTS

There are two ways to approach the problem of selecting promising high-tech candidates. Either you can study and concentrate on the prospects for an individual company, or you can do the same for the entire industry and then buy the shares of two or three companies that appear certain to participate in the new industries' bright future.

The latter approach is probably more dependable, since the flow of capital into and out of entire industries is much more predictable than for a single company.

From: *High-Tech Investing*, Rodger W. Bridwell (New York: Times Books, 1983)

MERRILL LYNCH MARKET LETTER

$44/24 issues per year
165 Broadway
New York, NY 10080

A publication of the brokerage house of the same name, this twice-monthly newsletter provides an update on the market and the economy. It concentrates on profiles of individual companies and their potential as investments.

DYNAMIC INVESTING

Jerome Tuccille
1981/155 pp./$2.50
New American Library
1633 Broadway
New York, NY 10019

A broker, the author explains his strategy for systematically shifting investments to profit from changing market conditions. He focuses on a set of cues that determine automatic trading decisions and he applies his strategy to a wide range of investments that include stocks, treasury bills, precious metals and real estate.

BARRON'S

$63/52 issues per year
22 Cortlandt St.
New York, NY 10007

Barron's update on business and finance provides broad coverage that ranges from news stories to comprehensive financial statistics.

There are charts of market performance as well as various indicators and stock indexes. This tabloid offers the investor a concise review of the week combined with previews of what is to come.

THE PROFESSIONAL TAPE READER

$250/24 issues per year
Box 2407
Hollywood, FL 33022

Using a system that traces stocks as they progress through cyclic stages, this newsletter charts the markets in two issues each month. A telephone advisory service is included in the subscription, and a three-issue trial subscription ($30) is available.

REAL ESTATE INVESTING LETTER

$72/12 issues per year
757 3rd Ave.
New York, NY 10017

Whether you are new to such investments or are already established in real estate, this monthly newsletter offers both basic guidance and trend reporting. It covers such subjects as property selection, financing and tax considerations.

PERSONAL FINANCE
$78/24 issues per year
Box 9665
Arlington, VA 22209

Twice a month this newsletter offers its perspectives on the changing economy. Based on its findings and predictions, the newsletter offers financial counsel and investment suggestions.

WEEKLY INSIDER REPORT
$85/52 issues per year
Box 59
Brookside, NJ 07926

This newsletter lists transactions reported to the Securities and Exchange Commission by major shareholders, directors and officers of publicly held corporations. The listings show the number and price of shares traded as well as the number of shares held by the insider. If your research takes you further in this direction, Vickers Stock Research also publishes a newsletter that lists stock options exercised by insiders (*Insiders' Options*, $85/26 issues per year).

SYSTEMS & FORECASTS
$140/24 issues per year
185 Great Neck Rd.
Great Neck, NY 11021

Reporting on market trends and offering investment advice, this newsletter bases its suggestions on a variety of indicators. The subscription includes a telephone advisory service. Along with its own forecasting, the newsletter reviews assessments being made by other advisory services.

INDUSTRY FORECAST
$100/12 issues per year
Box 26
Chappaqua, NY 10514

This newsletter provides a monthly update on economic conditions and outlook for use in business and investment decisions. The subscription includes a quarterly report on profits and stock prices as well as a guide for using the newsletter in making investments.

UNITED BUSINESS & INVESTMENT REPORT
$170/52 issues per year
210 Newbury St.
Boston, MA 02116

This 12-page newsletter offers the reader weekly reporting and investment advice. Investment recommendations are specific, with detailed commentaries on individual companies. There is extensive coverage of business, financial, economic and political news. The newsletter maintains a list of more than 150 common stocks, follows them and makes recommendations from week to week.

TRIAL OFFERS
FOR NEWSLETTERS

Select Information Exchange is a clearinghouse that specializes in investment newsletters. Its catalog lists a wide variety of publications and features trial offers for a broad selection of newsletters. The offers permit you to select a fixed number of newsletters for short trials at a package rate (for example, 20 publications for a total of $11.95). For catalog, write:

Select Information Exchange
2095 Broadway
New York, NY 10023

BRENNAN REPORTS
$145/12 issues per year
Box 882
Valley Forge, PA 19482

This newsletter presents very readable reporting and counsel on tax-shelter investments and tax-planning strategies. Investments range from real estate to equipment leasing, oil and gas drilling, cattle feeding and cable TV. Reports of court decisions provide helpful guidance.

DOW THEORY FORECASTS
$148/52 issues per year
7412 Calumet Ave.
Hammond, IN 46324

Along with its commentary on the week's activity in the market, this newsletter makes specific predictions and recommendations for the weeks to come. It maintains a list of recommended stocks, and the subscription includes a consultation service.

THE LOW PRICED STOCK SURVEY
$62.50/26 issues per year
7412 Calumet Ave.
Hammond, IN 46324

The focus of this newsletter is low-priced stock that has potential for substantial growth. Recommendations are spelled out in detailed data about individual companies.

EMERGING GROWTH STOCKS
$225/26 issues per year
7412 Calumet Ave.
Hammond, IN 46324

The emphasis in this newsletter is on companies with less than $120 million is sales and fewer than 20 million shares outstanding. Recommendations are highlighted in reports that profile companies in extensive detail.

COMMODEX: COMMODITIES ADVISORY BY MAIL OR ON-LINE COMPUTER

The main element in this advisory service for traders in commodity futures is a bulletin computed from market statistics and mailed daily. Annual subscription is $450. It includes a 120-page manual, which explains the advisory's system, as well as 24-hour access to telephone information. An on-line computer service offers expanded coverage for an additional annual subscription of $1,200. Write:

Commodex
114 Liberty St.
New York, NY 10006

SILVER & GOLD REPORT
$144/24 issues per year
Box 40
Bethel, CT 06801

This guide for investors in precious metals reports on price trends and news developments in the field. It offers detailed assessments and advice about investment opportunities.

GOLD NEWSLETTER
$65/12 issues per year
4425 W. Napoleon Ave.
Metairie, LA 70001

Published by the National Committee for Monetary Reform, this newsletter closely tracks the gold market. It reports on political and economic developments, emphasizing trends that relate to gold prices. Along with providing a source of specific information, the newsletter offers a means of observing the mood of the gold-buying public.

THE PROFESSIONAL INVESTOR
$125/24 issues per year
Box 2144
Pompano Beach, FL 33061

Among the features of this investment newsletter is a review of the current market assessments being made by 55 other advisory services. Along with a summary of market activity, the newsletter reports on a variety of indicators and investment statistics. It offers a trial subscription of six issues for $15.

FINANCIAL SURVIVAL REPORT
$69/48 issues per year
Box 25
Pleasanton, CA 94566

This financial newsletter is published by Howard Ruff and is the successor to his earlier *Ruff*

A CAUTIONARY TALE ABOUT INVESTING IN GOLD

A significant portion of the demand for gold is not for current industrial or artistic use but rather is motivated by psychological considerations—in particular, by fear regarding an uncertain social and economic future. Gold has traditionally been thought of as a hedge against inflation; when consumer prices threaten to rise rapidly the private demand for gold expands, but when inflation subsides that demand often vanishes overnight. This sort of demand typically fluctuates erratically on short notice, and rather small changes in supply or demand can produce wide price swings.

Thus gold is a highly speculative investment in which the warning *caveat emptor* is particularly appropriate. Large gains can occasionally be made, but large losses are just as likely on the basis of the historical record over the past hundred years.

It is appropriate to end . . . with a story. A man on a sinking ship ran to fetch his gold hoard before jumping overboard. When he landed in the water, the weight of the gold made floating impossible, so down he went. The crucial question is: Did he have the gold, or did the gold have him?

From: *Money*, Lawrence S. Ritter and William L. Silber (New York: Basic Books, Inc., 1981)

Times. Its perspective on business cycles and investment emphasizes inflationary factors and such hedges as gold and silver. The newsletter offers specific recommendations and gives example portfolios. A toll-free telephone advisory service is available for an additional $30 annual subscription.

CREATING WEALTH
Robert G. Allen
1983/304 pp./$14.95
Simon and Schuster
1230 Avenue of the Americas
New York, NY 10020

The author continues here where he left off in his earlier best-seller, *Nothing Down*. He pre-

sents a systematic investment program that is based on real estate holdings acquired through purchases leveraged with borrowed funds. The system is spelled out in step-by-step detail, with careful explanation of background information and potential pitfalls. Proceeding from the real estate holdings, the author develops four stages in his program. Included in this portfolio are proportioned investments in rare coins, money market funds, discounted mortgages and limited partnerships.

PERSONAL WEALTH DIGEST
$48/12 issues per year
10076 Boca Entrada Blvd.
Boca Raton, FL 33433

This newsletter summarizes material from more than 100 financial publications. Included is information on the equity markets, real estate investment, taxes and tax shelters.

EXECUTIVE WEALTH ADVISORY
$48/26 issues per year
589 5th Ave.
New York, NY 10017

Published by the Research Institute of America, this newsletter offers wealth-building information and advice. It covers a wide range of areas having to do with managing personal finances, including investments, taxes and money-saving ideas.

USING A BUSINESS PLAN WHEN RAISING CAPITAL

The objective of your business plan, which tells your story to potential lenders/investors, is to compile tangible proof of your financing readiness. Anyone willing to put up cash for your company will want a comprehensive picture of what your business is all about.

Granted, veteran entrepreneurs with long histories of successes sometimes approach a potential lender/investor equipped simply with their latest financial statements. But that is the exception. More often, even the veteran business person (as well as the new entrepreneur or the owner of a business experiencing problems) gets better results with an all-inclusive "biography" of the business. In your case, such a presentation would include a thorough description of both you and your operation, with an indication of how much money you need. You should also explain how you intend to pay it back if your financing takes the form of a loan or what kind of return you anticipate if it's an investment.

The more documentation you can supply with your presentation, the better, particularly during times of tight money, when lending institutions are more than usually selective. A case in point may be seen during the inflation/recession period of the late seventies and beginning eighties, when the Federal Reserve Bank tightened the money supply and all member banks reacted accordingly. Although money was still available, it was hard to come by and a lot more expensive, with the trend started by the banks creating a ripple effect that touched every financial institution. Thus those businesses whose houses were in order were still able to get financing.

From: *Raising Cash*, Sol Postyn and Jo Kirschner Postyn (Belmont, CA: Lifetime Learning Publications, 1982)

REAL ESTATE INVESTMENT DIGEST
$48/12 issues per year
10076 Boca Entrada Blvd.
Boca Raton, FL 33433

Digesting material from a wide range of publications, this newsletter covers all aspects of real estate investment. Included are reports on market conditions, financing, government regulation and tax aspects.

GREEN'S COMMODITY MARKET COMMENTS
$240/26 issues per year
Box 174
Princeton, NJ 08540

This newsletter specializes in the markets for precious metals, concentrating largely on gold and silver. It closely follows world economic and monetary developments and it gives detailed reports on trading activity.

THE HOLT INVESTMENT ADVISORY
$180/24 issues per year
290 Post Rd. W.
Westport, CT 06880

This newsletter presents detailed reporting of investment activity and trends as well as studies of individual companies and their potential as investments. The newsletter uses graphs extensively to illustrate its statistical reporting.

DONOGHUE'S MONEYLETTER

$87/24 issues per year
360 Woodland St.
Holliston, MA 01746

This guide for investors reports both on mutual funds and on money market funds. The newsletter presents a twice-monthly update on fund activity and it tracks a selection of funds as a basis for comment and recommendations.

DONOGHUE'S MONEY FUND DIRECTORY

$24/annual
360 Woodland St.
Holliston, MA 01746

This directory presents 100 pages of data on money market funds. Information is presented in easy-to-read tables and includes addresses, telephone numbers, services and minimum investments. Listings include each fund's yield for the previous two years.

DONOGHUE'S MUTUAL FUNDS ALMANAC

$25/annual
360 Woodland St.
Holliston, MA 01746

More than 600 mutual funds are covered in this 200-page directory, which includes the money market funds. Listings show fund performance statistics as well as investment objectives. Addresses and phone numbers are included. An introductory section combined with appendices provides the reader with a guide to fund investment.

THE WALL STREET DIGEST

$150/12 issues per year
101 Carnegie Center
Princeton, NJ 08540

This monthly newsletter presents commentary and recommendations for investors and features advice drawn from other advisory services. It offers a trial subscription of two issues for $18.

TRENDLINE DAILY ACTION STOCK CHARTS

$390/52 issues per year
25 Broadway
New York, NY 10004

A publication of Standard & Poor's, this weekly report for investors charts the daily fluctuations of securities trading. More than 700 stocks are regularly charted, in addition to various market indicators. The subscription fee does not include postage. The report is also available every other week ($239) and monthly ($124).

FINANCIAL AND BUSINESS INFORMATION IN DEPTH

Standard & Poor's is a name that is synonymous with in-depth financial and business information. The firm's reports for investors total many thousands of pages each year. Priced at $48 each and updated semi-annually, its series of handbooks cover such subjects as growth stocks, over-the-counter stocks and options. One of the best known of the firm's directories is *Poor's Register of Corporations, Directors and Executives* ($298), which lists more than 38,000 companies and more than 400,000 company officials. For a detailed catalog, write:

Standard & Poor's Corp.
25 Broadway
New York, NY 10004

FINANCIAL SURVIVAL IN THE AGE OF NEW MONEY
Gordon Williams
1981/382 pp./$6.95
Simon and Schuster
1230 Avenue of the Americas
New York, NY 10020

The new money of this book's title refers to inflation. The author traces the growth of inflation and how it has transformed the financial system, presenting both an understanding of the system and a basic guide to today's investment opportunities. The book's clear style makes it a valuable resource for anyone who does not have a professional background in the subject.

STRATEGIC INVESTING
Douglas Casey
1982/445 pp./$15.95
Simon and Schuster
1230 Avenue of the Americas
New York, NY 10020

With the premise that there will be economic depression in the 1980s and that this financial collapse is inevitable, the author spells out his strategy for profiting from such circumstances. He projects economic conditions and prescribes specific measures to prepare for and exploit a crash. Along with various steps to ensure liquidity and increase financial resources, he advises stockpiling food supplies and holding gold and silver for security. For the years of depression, he recommends a variety of investment opportunities that he believes will produce substantial profits. While the book's concept may appear extreme, it offers a useful perspective on investment strategy.

GROWTH THROUGH MERGERS AND ACQUISITIONS

Our new age of high technology, led by the computer and genetic-engineering revolutions, will produce unimagined prosperity by the end of the century. It follows that investors who correctly anticipate the coming drastic changes in our industrial and social institutions will profit to an equally unimaginable extent.

From: *High-Tech Investing*, Rodger W. Bridwell (New York: Times Books, 1983)

ing and the target companies. An attorney, the author examines the basic legal factors involved in various acquisition methods as well as IRS and SEC considerations. In separate chapters he traces the process of identifying and evaluating the target company and then negotiating and closing on the acquisition. More than half the book is devoted to such background material as statutes, rulings and sample agreements of various types.

BUSINESS ACQUISITIONS DESK BOOK

F. T. Davis, Jr.
1981/414 pp./$65
Institute for Business Planning, Inc.
IBP Plaza
Englewood Cliffs, NJ 07632

Designed to give the executive a comprehensive background, this book serves as both a working guide and a reference resource for all aspects of acquisitions. The book provides specific guidance for executives in both the acquir-

DATA ON MERGERS AND ACQUISITIONS

W. T. Grimm & Co., consultants and intermediaries in mergers and acquisitions, annually publishes the *Mergerstat Review*. Priced at $125, the review presents more than 100 pages of statistics, charts, graphs, analyses and commentary. Included are both mergers and acquisitions and both publicly and privately held companies. For further information, write:

W. T. Grimm & Co.
135 S. LaSalle St.
Chicago, IL 60603

A SUPERSOURCE FOR BUSINESS DATA

Perhaps best known for its bond ratings, Moody's Investors Service annually publishes thousands of pages of business information. Of major interest is the firm's library of seven manuals with accompanying news reports. The manuals cover more than 20,000 U.S. and foreign corporations and more than 14,000 municipal and government entities, providing valuable data for business management and investing. Among the firm's other publications are three handbooks for investors. The quarterly *Handbook of Common Stocks* covers 944 major stocks with one-page company reviews. *The Handbook of OTC Stocks,* updated quarterly, details 550 over-the-counter stocks. The *Handbook of Dividend Achievers* focuses on more than 400 growth companies. For brochures and price information, write:

Moody's Investors Service
99 Church St.
New York, NY 10007

DIRECTORY INFORMATION ON LEADING U.S. COMPANIES

B. Klein Publications markets three directories that provide detailed information on leading companies in the U.S. *The Top 1,500 Companies* (256 pages, $120) includes both pub-

ACQUISITION AS A STRATEGY FOR CORPORATE GROWTH

Acquisition has been and will continue to be a part of the growth strategy of corporations. Only the degree to which businesses emphasize this form of corporate development has varied over time. A number of economic and other forces help account for the cyclical nature of merger activities. These forces make this approach, rather than internal development or joint ventures, more appropriate for more companies at certain times. However, acquisition is a viable strategy for many firms under any particular set of prevailing economic conditions. Therefore, it is an approach that should always be viewed as a corporate-development alternative.

Reliance on internal development as the preferred route to corporate growth has been a recent rule for many firms—both large, technically sophisticated corporations and smaller, more traditional firms. Now, however, companies increasingly weigh the costs and risks of internal-development programs against renewed opportunities for acquisitions, which can often provide more rapid . . . and predictable results for corporate growth. Recent research indicates, for example, that an average eight years are required before new ventures of major U.S. corporations become profitable.

From: *Acquisition and Corporate Development,* James W. Bradley and Donald H. Korn (Lexington, MA: Lexington Books, 1981)

licly and privately held companies, and the listing is continued in a companion directory titled *The Second 1,500 Companies* (250 pages, $120). A third directory, *The Top 1,500 Private Companies* (250 pages, $120), focuses exclusively on privately owned firms. For catalog, write:

B. Klein Publications
Box 8503
Coral Springs, FL 33065

SEMINARS ON STARTING AND BUILDING THE SMALL-TO-MEDIUM BUSINESS

The Ted Nicholas Institute specializes in seminar programs for small-to-medium businesses. A five-day progam on starting a business covers such areas as raising venture capital, management methods, legal and tax aspects. A two-day program concentrates on building an existing business, covering such aspects as financing expansion and new products. For a brochure, write:

Ted Nicholas Institute
725 Market St.
Wilmington, DE 19801

THE ENTREPRENEUR'S MANUAL
Richard M. White, Jr.
1977/419 pp./$17.50
Chilton Book Co.
Chilton Way
Radnor, PA 19809

The author provides a very detailed and practical how-to manual for business start-ups and spin-offs. The directions are specific and they are illustrated by more than 50 brief case histories drawn largely from the author's work as a management consultant. The author covers such aspects as identifying potential markets and products as well as attracting cofounders and key employees. Especially useful is a listing of 250 venture-capital groups.

35 MAJOR SOURCES OF VENTURE CAPITAL

Listed below is a sampling of major venture-capital sources in the U.S. These firms are sources for smaller as well as medium and larger ventures. Many of them are associated with large banks and diversified corporations. Inquiry letters will bring detailed information.

Aetna Life & Casualty Co.
151 Farmington Ave.
Hartford, CT 06115

Allstate Insurance Co.
Allstate Plaza
Northbrook, IL 60062

American Express
    Investment Management Co.
550 Laurel
San Francisco, CA 94022

American Research
    & Development Co.
1 Beacon St.
Boston, MA 02108

Bank of the Commonwealth
719 Griswald
Detroit, MI 48231

Bay Equities, Inc.
555 California St.
San Francisco, CA 94104

Business Development
  Services, Inc.
570 Lexington Ave.
New York, NY 10022

Capital Corporation
  of America
1521 Walnut St.
Philadelphia, PA 19102

Chase Manhattan Capital Corp.
1 Chase Manhattan Plaza
New York, NY 10005

Citicorp Venture Capital, Ltd.
399 Park Ave.
New York, NY 10022

Crocker Capital Corp.
2 Palo Alto Square
Palo Alto, CA 94304

Data Science Ventures, Inc.
221 Nassau St.
Princeton, NJ 08540

Diamond Shamrock Corp.
1100 Superior Ave.
Cleveland, OH 44114

Drexel Burnham & Co.
60 Broad St.
New York, NY 10004

Eagle Management & Trust Co.
1206 River Oaks Bank Tower
Houston, TX 77019

Employers Insurance of Wausau
2000 Westwood Dr.
Wausau, WI 54401

EMW Ventures, Inc.
277 Park Ave.
New York, NY 10017

Exxon Enterprises, Inc.
1251 Avenue of the Americas
New York, NY 10020

First Capital Corp. of Boston
100 Federal St.
Boston, MA 02110

First Century Partnership
345 Avenue of the Americas
New York, NY 10019

First Chicago Investment Corp.
1 First National Plaza
Chicago, IL 60670

First Southern Capital Corp.
821 Gravier St.
New Orleans, LA 70112

GTE New Ventures Corp.
1 Stamford Forum
Stamford, CT 06904

Inno Ven Capital Corp.
Park 80 Plaza West
Saddle Brook, NJ 07662

IRV-New England
157 High St.
Portland, ME 04101

Lehman Bros.
42 Wall St.
New York, NY 10005

Loeb, Rhodes & Co.
42 Wall St.
New York, NY 10005

Motorola New Venture Development
8201 E. McDowell Rd.
Scottsdale, AZ 95235

Paine, Webber, Jackson & Curtis
140 Broadway
New York, NY 10005

Prudential Insurance Co.
Prudential Plaza
Newark, NJ 07101

Robinson-Humphrey Co., Inc.
2 Peachtree St., N.W.
Atlanta, GA 30303

Salomon Bros.
1 New York Plaza
New York, NY 10024

Small Business Enterprises Co.
555 California St.
San Francisco, CA 94104

Techno-Ventures, Inc.
8100 W. Florissant Ave.
St. Louis, MO 63301

Wells Fargo Investment Co.
475 Sansome St.
San Francisco, CA 94111

MERGERS
Peter O. Steiner
1975/359 pp./$9.95
University of Michigan Press
Box 1104
Ann Arbor, MI 48106

This study focuses on the legal and economic aspects of the many conglomerate mergers of the 1960s. The author examines mergers that produced some of today's major corporations. He concentrates on identifying and evaluating the motives involved and traces the effects of mergers, in terms both of economic theories and of legal controls.

DISCLOSURE AND ITS IMPACT ON CORPORATE MERGERS

In overview, the problem is that, because much of the time a tender offer occurs in an adversary setting, the desire to protect the investor must be balanced by the sure knowledge that the more the disclosure, the greater the scope for harassing actions by those opposed to the merger. Even though courts have proven unsympathetic to flimsy assertions of improper conduct, the mere bringing of a law suit may serve to create conditions that lead the merger to fail. For, while all mergers are costly, the cost of a contest can greatly expand the total cost. Thus, while disclosure and antifraud provisions contribute to making intelligent choices possible, to weakening some illegitimate motives for merger and to making more difficult the self-serving behavior of one group at the expense of another, they also weaken some legitimate incentives to merge, and warn and arm some of those who would delay, stop or subvert the merger for self-serving (and socially unworthy) reasons.

From: *Mergers,* Peter O. Steiner (Ann Arbor: University of Michigan Press, 1975)

CORPORATE ACQUISITIONS
Gordon Bing
1980/248 pp./$19.95
Gulf Publishing Co.
Box 2608
Houston, TX 77001

This handbook details a systematic approach to the acquisition process. Its objective is either the single acquisition or a continuous program of acquisitions. The author covers all aspects of the subject, including such areas as financing, identifying target companies, evaluation of prospects, negotiating the purchase and the transition process. Included are extensive checklists for gathering and organizing data.

A CHECKLIST GUIDE TO SUCCESSFUL ACQUISITIONS
Victor Harold
1973, 1980/45 pp./$3.50
Pilot Books
103 Cooper St.
Babylon, NY 11702

The author identifies 268 points of information as essential to sound decision making in the acquisition process. This concise manual provides both a workable format for research and an introduction to the varied aspects of acquisitions. (If ordering by mail, add $1 for postage and handling.)

PRIMER ON THE LAW OF MERGERS
Earl W. Kintner
1973/530 pp./$16.95
Macmillan Publishing Co.
866 3rd Ave.
New York, NY 10022

Written for the lay reader, this introduction to the legal aspects of mergers is a valuable resource for the executive. The author, an attorney, first examines the merger process and explains in detail how legislation affects the process. Included are chapters on enforcement as well as a selection of texts of federal legislation.

AN ANTITRUST PRIMER
Earl W. Kintner
1964, 1973/325 pp./$19.95
Macmillan Publishing Co.
866 3rd Ave.
New York, NY 10022

This introduction to antitrust and trade regulation is a very useful survey of a complex subject. The author, an attorney, writes for the lay reader. His book is comprehensive yet entirely readable. Included are such aspects as price fixing, mergers and acquisitions, Federal Trade Commission enforcement as well as state antitrust enforcement. Two chapters are devoted to advertising and how regulation affects deceptive practices. The author includes a selection of FTC guides as well as summaries and texts of the principal antitrust statutes.

ACQUISITION AND CORPORATE DEVELOPMENT
James W. Bradley and Donald H. Korn
1981/252 pp./$28.95
Lexington Books
125 Spring St.
Lexington, MA 02173

Building your company by acquiring another has risks as well as rewards. This handbook can guide you through the process. It provides checklists for decision-making evaluations and detailed listings of information sources that include computerized data bases. The authors discuss general principles and examine acquisition strategies and legal considerations. A separate chapter covers valuation of target companies.

FINANCING INDUSTRIAL INVESTMENT
John C. Carrington and George T. Edwards
1979/283 pp./$41.95
Praeger Publishers
383 Madison Ave.
New York, NY 10017

The authors present a comparative analysis of how industrial investment is financed in France, Japan, West Germany, Britain and the U.S. Increasing concern about industrial growth in the U.S. makes this study a useful resource. While the authors are British and write from that point of view, their research findings have broad applications.

GOLDMAN, SACHS: BANKER TO THE CORPORATE WORLD

Goldman, Sachs & Co. is an investment banker of the first rank, a leading manager of industrial debt and equity financings. It is one of the major block-trading firms on the New York Stock Exchange. The firm works with both U.S. and foreign clients to raise equity and debt capital around the world. It is also a leading manager of municipal bond and real estate financings. Active in the field of mergers and acquisitions, the firm's *Annual Review* provides a listing of its clients in this area as

Strategic long-term planning may play a role, but for most companies divestitures are a singular event associated with failure. Few companies have a well-defined, continuous program for systematic evaluation of operations that will routinely lead to early profitable divestment decisions, let alone an established procedure for implementation.

From: *Corporate Divestment*, Gordon Bing (Houston: Gulf Publishing Co., 1978)

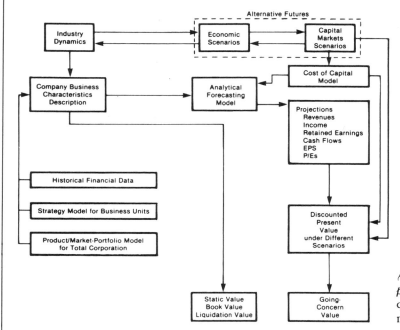

A *diagram tracing the valuation process for acquisitions (from* Acquisition and Corporate Development).

well as in its other areas of operation. For a copy of the review and further information, write:

Goldman, Sachs & Co.
85 Broad St.
New York, NY 10004

MERGERS & ACQUISITIONS
$95/4 issues per year
229 S. 18th St.
Philadelphia, PA 19103

This quarterly journal will keep you thoroughly informed on mergers and acquisitions in the U.S. as well as overseas. There are detailed reports on major mergers, takeovers, divestitures and joint ventures. Feature articles focus on specific subject areas. An especially useful section of the journal presents rosters of all completed transactions for the previous quarter valued at $1 million or more, with prices and terms of the transactions.

CORPORATE DIVESTMENT
Gordon Bing
1978/167 pp./$19.95
Gulf Publishing Co.
Box 2608
Houston, TX 77001

The author presents a guide to the complex transactions involved in selling subsidiaries, divisions and product lines. He examines alternatives as well as major problems that must be taken into account. Included are chapters on defining and pricing the unit that is to be sold as well as on employee relations and negotiating with the prospect.

RAISING CASH

Sol Postyn and
    Jo Kirschner Postyn
1982/309 pp./$26
Lifetime Learning Publications
10 Davis Dr.
Belmont, CA 94002

Written primarily for use in smaller and medium-size companies, this handbook is a thorough guide to raising money for launching a new business or maintaining or expanding an existing operation. The authors present direc-

tions for locating and negotiating with cash sources as well as a review of the elements of financial management. An especially useful section of the book covers the process of designing a business plan for use with potential lenders. A fully developed sample business plan is included.

ACQUISITION SEARCH PROGRAMS

Jerold L. Freier
1981/32 pp./$3.95
Pilot Books
103 Cooper St.
Babylon, NY 11702

An acquisition specialist, the author outlines basic strategies for identifying and evaluating target opportunities. He describes specific techniques and includes a detailed listing of information sources. (If ordering by mail, add $1 for postage and handling.)

LEVERAGED FINANCE: HOW TO RAISE AND INVEST CASH

Mark Stevens
1980/228 pp./$19.95
Prentice-Hall, Inc.
Englewood Cliffs, NJ 07632

This book is largely for the entrepreneur raising money to launch a new business operation. The author focuses on smaller companies and

SIX KEY QUESTIONS BEFORE DIVESTITURE

When the subsidiary to be divested is a significant part of the total corporation, the impact of the sale will change the corporation's nature and many questions should be addressed prior to sale:

1. What will remain of the corporation?
2. In what direction is the corporation going after the sale?
3. Will a divestment reduce the momentum and synergy of the corporation?
4. Will it reduce the spread of risks over the entire corporation?
5. Will it remove from the product line a key segment making it impossible to provide a "complete package"?
6. Will divestment create hostile reactions and attitudes that will adversely affect other operations of the company?

From: *Corporate Divestment*, Gordon Bing (Houston: Gulf Publishing Co., 1978)

spells out financing strategies that range from government loans to private banks and venture-capital organizations. Included is detailed advice on identifying cash sources and dealing with them.

BUSINESS FINANCING AT BARCLAYSAMERICAN

BarclaysAmerican/Business Credit services include business financing, machinery and equipment financing and intermediate-term lending. Typically used for acquisition, buy-out or as a bridge to permanent financing, intermediate-term lending can provide financing for two to ten years for $1 million or more. The firm has offices in 20 locations across the U.S. For further information, write:

BarclaysAmerican/Business Credit
111 Founders Plaza
Hartford, CT 06101

WORLDWIDE FINANCIAL SERVICES FROM HELLER

With offices throughout the U.S. and Canada as well as 23 countries overseas, the Heller company is a major supplier of financial services to businesses. The firm's activities include commercial banking, asset-based lending, factoring and equipment leasing and lending. It is foremost among international factoring companies and it specializes in financial services for exporters. For literature and listing of branch offices, write:

Walter E. Heller & Co.
105 W. Adams St.
Chicago, IL 60603

DIRECTORY INFORMATION FOR CAPITAL SOURCES

Guide to Venture Capital Sources (340 pages, $75) lists more than 500 firms in the U.S. and Canada that offer investment capital and indicates their investment preferences. Included in the directory are 26 articles written by professional venture capitalists. A second directory, *Business Capital Sources* (150 pages, $25), lists firms, banks, mortgage lenders and other sources of business loans. For catalog, write:

B. Klein Publications
Box 8503
Coral Springs, FL 33065

WHEN YOUR NAME IS ON THE DOOR
Earl D. Brodie
1981/264 pp./$24.95
Books in Focus, Inc.
160 E. 38th St.
New York, NY 10016

The onetime owner of a family-founded manufacturing business that he took public, the author offers his personal advice to business owners. The book is targeted to small and medium-size companies, and the author focuses on specific and practical situations that face the owner-manager.

TAX HAVENS FOR CORPORATIONS
Adam Starchild
1979/176 pp./$19.95
Gulf Publishing Co.
Box 2608
Houston, TX 77001

The author reports on more than 20 countries with tax legislation designed to attract foreign corporations. This book is a comprehensive introduction to such tax havens. While it is written for the layperson, it presents detailed background information on all aspects of the subject. Some of the tax-haven locations covered are Bermuda, the Bahamas, Hong Kong, Gibraltar, Liechtenstein and Switzerland.

TAKING CASH OUT OF THE CLOSELY HELD CORPORATION: TAX OPPORTUNITIES, STRATEGIES AND TECHNIQUES
Lawrence Silton
1980/330 pp./$59.50
Institute for Business Planning, Inc.
IBP Plaza
Englewood Cliffs, NJ 07632

A CPA and attorney, the author offers comprehensive guidance for tax management in small to medium companies. The book is directed to both the accountant and the corporate principals. Along with a very readable text, the author includes checklists and sample minutes and other documents. He spells out strategies for reduction of tax as well as tax-favored use of cash flow. All aspects are covered, from pre-incorporation planning to termination of the corporation, and case-study examples are used extensively.

D&B REPORTS
$20/6 issues per year
99 Church St.
New York, NY 10007

This magazine provides the Dun & Bradstreet perspective on smaller businesses (less than $25 million in sales). Articles and departments are tailored to top management. "Dun & Bradstreet Looks at Business," a special section in each issue, presents statistical findings gathered by D&B's several divisions.

OPPORTUNITIES IN INTERNATIONAL TRADE

BUSINESS AMERICA
$55/26 issues per year
Superintendent of Documents
U.S. Government Printing Office
Washington, DC 20402

Published by the U.S. Dept. of Commerce, this journal of the International Trade Administration covers foreign trade policy and reports on world markets and trade opportunities. Features highlight economic trends and business opportunities in selected countries. Coverage includes international trade exhibitions.

EXPORT: TAPPING WASHINGTON'S EXPERTS ON FOREIGN TRADE

The International Trade Administration provides a wide range of services to U.S. firms pursuing export business. The agency's Trade Opportunities Program (TOP) offers a notice service that sends foreign-trade leads directly to the subscribing firm ($25 registration fee, plus $37.50 for each block of 50 leads). The weekly *TOP Bulletin* ($175 per year) lists all current trade leads, which include direct sales opportunities, overseas representation opportunities and tenders by foreign governments. A variety of other surveys, reports and services are available. For further information, write:

U.S. Dept. of Commerce
Trade Information Services
Box 14207
Washington, DC 20044

International finance is a game with two sets of players: the politicians and bureaucrats of national governments, and the presidents and treasurers of giant, large, medium-large, medium, medium-small and small firms. The government officials want to win elections and secure a niche in the histories of their countries. The corporate presidents and treasurers want to profit—or at least avoid losses—from changes in exchange rates, changes that are inevitable in a world with more than 100 national currencies.

From: *The International Money Game*, Robert Z. Aliber (New York: Basic Books, Inc., 1983)

THE AMERICAN EXPORT MARKETER

$68/12 issues per year
10076 Boca Entrada Blvd.
Boca Raton, FL 33433

This monthly newsletter reports on economic trends, business conditions and governmental actions as they affect exporting. Included is information on marketing opportunities around the world.

JOURNAL OF COMMERCE: THE NEWSPAPER OF WORLD TRADE AND TRANSPORTATION

The *Journal of Commerce* is published daily except Saturdays, Sundays and holidays. Annual subscription is $145. The paper covers the world of business from the perspective of international trade, with particular focus on the transportation industry. Here you can keep yourself posted on the movement of goods by sea, air and surface carriers. The newspaper also offers such allied publications as the *Directory of United States Importers* ($175), which indexes more than 25,000 firms and their products. The *Exporters Directory/U.S. Buying Guide* ($225) is a two-volume reference on more than 37,000 exporters. For information, write:

Journal of Commerce
110 Wall St.
New York, NY 10005

AMERICAN IMPORT EXPORT MANAGEMENT

$25/12 issues per year
401 N. Broad St.
Philadelphia, PA 19108

This newsmagazine reports on foreign trade operations, covering the handling and transportation of goods as well as trade opportunities around the world. Included is coverage of U.S. and foreign ports, trade services, economics and finance as well as government regulations.

DIRECTORY RESOURCES FOR EXPORT BUSINESS

B. Klein Publications markets a wide variety of directories, three of which provide valuable resources for exporters. *American Export Register* (2 volumes, 3,000 pages, $95) lists more than 40,000 U.S. exporters and importers classified by products. Also listed are banks doing business in world trade and customhouse brokers. The *Global Guide to International Business* (600 pages, $50) lists private and governmental resources for information and services. *Industrial Reps of Overseas Countries* (50 pages, $20) lists more than 400 agencies, trade missions, consular offices and firms representing 106 foreign countries. For a catalog, write:

B. Klein Publications
Box 8503
Coral Springs, FL 33065

EXPORT-IMPORT REFERENCE RESOURCES

The North American Publishing Co. markets two annual reference resources for foreign trade. The *Custom House Guide* ($259) consists of a hardcover volume plus a binder to hold update material. It covers all aspects of U.S. Customs, including detailed information about Customs ports and their facilities and services. The *Official Export Guide* ($259) consists of a hardcover volume and a binder of regulatory material. The guide provides information about the ports of the world as well as export documentation and international financing. For brochures, write:

North American Publishing Co.
401 N. Broad St.
Philadelphia, PA 19108

WASHINGTON INTERNATIONAL BUSINESS REPORT
$288/24 issues per year
1625 Eye St., N.W.
Washington, DC 20006

This newsletter reports on developments and trends in government policies, programs and regulations that affect international trade and investment. Included in the subscription are two additional publications. An organizational guide issued 12 times per year reports on federal agencies, congressional committees and international organizations. A second guide, also issued 12 times per year, covers major policymakers and key staff members.

FRANCHISING

HANDBOOK OF SUCCESSFUL FRANCHISING
Mark Friedlander, Jr.,
   and Gene Gurney
1981/458 pp./$13.95
Van Nostrand Reinhold Co.
135 W. 50th St.
New York, NY 10020

This directory of franchising companies organizes its listings in 43 categories of business types. Beyond the basic data of the listings, each category is described in a brief profile based on surveys of franchisers and franchisees.

Included are sections with guidance for franchisees as well as background statistics and information sources.

THE BIG BUSINESS OF FRANCHISING

Franchise Opportunities ($9.95) is a comprehensive directory of a segment of the economy that accounts for approximately one-third of all retail sales in the U.S. annually. The 15th edition of the directory contains 356 pages of de-

Now, to most people, a french-fried potato is a pretty uninspiring object. It's fodder, something to kill time chewing between bites of hamburger and swallows of milk shake. That's your ordinary french fry. The McDonald's french fry was in an entirely different league. They lavished attention on it. I didn't know it then, but one day I would, too. The french fry would become almost sacrosanct for me, its preparation a ritual to be followed religiously.

   From: *Grinding It Out*, Ray Kroc (Chicago: Regnery Gateway, Inc., 1977)

tailed information, listing more than 900 companies that offer franchise opportunities in the U.S. and overseas. This resource provides a handy survey of a field that offers opportunities both to corporations and to individual executives.

Sterling Publishing Co.
2 Park Ave.
New York, NY 10016

A GUIDE TO FRANCHISE INVESTIGATION AND CONTRACT NEGOTIATION
Harry Gross and Robert S. Levy
1967, 1979/48 pp./$2.50
Pilot Books
103 Cooper St.
Babylon, NY 11702

This handbook for the prospective franchisee provides guidance in evaluating franchise opportunities. The authors are an accountant and an attorney and they present detailed guidelines and advice. The book is a useful brief introduction to the workings of a franchise operation. (If ordering by mail, add $1 for postage and handling.)

THE ESSENTIAL ELEMENTS IN SUCCESSFUL FRANCHISING

To be successful, the firm must have a product (or service) whose qualities satisfy at least some people (termed the target market), a product which is available where and when the target group wants it (place), one which has its qualities and availability communicated (promoted) to them, and one which is priced in line with their expectations. If properly conducted, the franchising of retailers and wholesalers to sell the product or service aids in getting it where and when the target customers may want it, that is, it aids in achieving the place objective; but if the target group does not know about the product, or if the product is priced out of line with customers' expectations, or if the product qualities themselves just do not satisfy customer desires, the franchising of retailers or distributors to fulfill the place requirements will have been virtually useless. Similar statements, of course, may be applied to other types of distribution or channel arrangements, but the other marketing mix variables can assume critical importance to the prospective franchisee who may spend his entire life savings to acquire the franchise, or even to the poorly capitalized and perhaps overzealous franchisor. If the franchise program does not provide proper balance among all four elements of the market mix, the whole endeavor may fail.

From: *Franchising*, Charles L. Vaughn (Lexington, MA: Lexington Books, 1979)

FUTURE OPPORTUNITIES IN FRANCHISING
Nancy Suway Church
1979/47 pp./$3.50
Pilot Books
103 Cooper St.
Babylon, NY 11702

This guide to franchising offers a concise introduction to the subject. The author outlines current practices and legal aspects of franchising and assesses business opportunities in the field. (If ordering by mail, add $1 for postage and handling.)

Achievement must be made against the possibility of failure, against the risk of defeat. It is no achievement to walk a tightrope laid flat on the floor. Where there is no risk, there can be no pride in achievement and, consequently, no happiness. The only way we can advance is by going forward, individually and collectively, in the spirit of the pioneer. We must take the risks involved in our free enterprise system. This is the only way in the world to economic freedom. There is no other way.

From: *Grinding It Out*, Ray Kroc (Chicago: Regnery Gateway, Inc., 1977)

GRINDING IT OUT: THE MAKING OF McDONALD'S
Ray Kroc with Robert Anderson
1977/201 pp./$9.95
Contemporary Books, Inc.
180 N. Michigan Ave.
Chicago, IL 60601

While this is a very personal recounting of the building of the McDonald's franchise system, it is a useful resource for tracing the stages in the process. Ray Kroc tells his story in detail, spelling out the parts that he and many others played in the steady growth of a company that became a model and standard for other franchise systems. The book provides a valuable perspective on both franchising and entrepreneurship.

FRANCHISING
Charles L. Vaughn
1974, 1979/281 pp./$24.95
Lexington Books
125 Spring St.
Lexington, MA 02173

This comprehensive introduction to franchising covers all aspects of the subject, beginning with a detailed review of the history and scope of this segment of the economy. The author shows how franchising works as a marketing system and examines its advantages and disadvantages to franchiser and franchisee. He then describes the process of starting and running a franchise system, with chapters on selecting and training franchisees and financing the system. Also covered is international franchising. The author makes extensive use of examples of existing franchise operations, making the book a valuable study of current practices in this field.

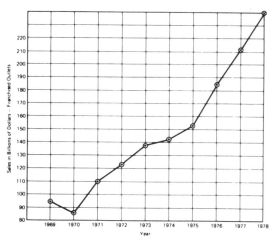

The growth in sales of franchise businesses, 1969–1978 (from Franchising*).*

GUIDANCE FOR EXECUTIVE WEALTH-BUILDING

FINANCIAL WORLD
$41.95/26 issues per year
1450 Broadway
New York, NY 10018

This newsmagazine reports on developments in business and industry from the investor's perspective. Its articles, departments and columnists provide background and analysis of trends and change. Each month the magazine presents a special section charting 1,600 stocks listed on the New York and American stock exchanges.

WEALTHBUILDING
$23.40/12 issues per year
402 W. Interstate 30
Garland, TX 75043

Here is a monthly source of information and ideas for your personal investment program. The magazine focuses on financial planning, with emphasis on tax-sheltered investments. The advertising offers a variety of investment opportunities, many of them syndications in such areas as energy, Thoroughbred horses and real estate.

STOCK MARKET STRATEGY FOR CONSISTENT PROFITS
Raymond R. Righetti
1980/163 pp./$17.95
Nelson-Hall, Inc.
111 N. Canal St.
Chicago, IL 60606

Dismissing predictive formulas and hunches, the author presents a strategic approach to the stock market. He focuses on buying only those stocks that are rising in price and have particular growth characteristics. Along with examining these characteristics, the author identifies specific cues that dictate selling stock holdings. Included are chapters on selecting and working with a broker as well as specific investment pitfalls.

THE NEW YORK TIMES BOOK OF MONEY
Richard E. Blodgett
1971, 1979/223 pp./$8.95
Times Books
3 Park Ave.
New York, NY 10016

This book is a basic guide to managing personal finances. It provides useful information in a broad variety of areas. Included is coverage on banking, insurance, investment, retirement and taxation. There are also sections on such subjects as home mortgages and educational expenses. The book is well organized and presents quick answers to common questions.

HIGH-TECH INVESTING
Rodger W. Bridwell
1983/283 pp./$17.65
Times Books
3 Park Ave.
New York, NY 10016

The author reports on the present and future of high technology and the investment opportunities it offers. Along with identifying specific companies and their prospects, the author concentrates on providing a clear but detailed background on the technology itself. He goes into computer-related industries, genetic engineering and energy-related technology. The premise is that the more you know about the technology, the sounder your investment decisions will be. This approach provides fascinating reading along with profit potential.

USING FACTORING TO RAISE CASH

Commercial factoring, one of the oldest forms of business financing, is another excellent way to get fast cash for business operations. Factoring uses the technique of professional money management to shore up cash flow and to lubricate the financial wheels.

Let's say that you are faced with a familiar but exasperating business problem: many of your accounts are late or delinquent payers. Stubborn collection problems such as these can dry up cash flow, crippling your firm's operations. With so much money outstanding, you may not have the needed cash for growth strategies—for the steps necessary to expand your own business. Factoring can help you raise cash and overcome this problem. To use factoring, you send all sales invoices directly to a commercial factor, who promptly reimburses you for up to 80 percent of the invoice values. The remaining balance is settled by the factor on the average collection date.

The beauty of it is that you are getting most of the money up front—you don't have to hold hands with delinquent accounts. The factor assumes part of your business risks—and as a leveraged entrepreneur, that's exactly what you want. Although factoring is an excellent technique for use by small firms, it is also employed by the corporate giants as well. Even some of the Fortune 500 turn to factoring when they need fast cash for their receivables.

From: *Leveraged Finance*, Mark Stevens (Englewood Cliffs, NJ: Prentice-Hall, Inc., 1980)

THE INTERNATIONAL MONEY GAME
Robert Z. Aliber
1973, 1983/356 pp./$8.95
Basic Books, Inc.
10 E. 53rd St.
New York, NY 10022

The author explains in simple and very readable terms how the international monetary system works. Despite the subject's complexity, the author makes his book lively reading, drawing upon fascinating historical sketches to show how the monetary system has evolved. Included are discussions of international debt problems as well as the economics of the world oil supplies.

MONEY
Lawrence S. Ritter and
    William L. Silber
1970, 1981/340 pp./$7.50
Basic Books, Inc.
10 E. 53rd St.
New York, NY 10022

This guide to monetary theory and policy is clear and comprehensive and has the added value of a sense of humor. Exploring the influence of money on the nation's economy, the authors examine such aspects as the Monetarist-Keynesian views, the impact of interest

The realities of power within the Federal Reserve System (from Money*).*

> Those who insist on treating Wall Street as a casino, in which they are determined to indulge their fantasies of being the highest roller around, should remember to keep careful track both of their risks and their resources. Be aware of the odds each time you take the dice, and always save a quarter for the hatcheck girl.
>
> From: *How to Make Money in Wall Street*, Louis Rukeyser (New York: Dolphin Books, 1976)

rates and Federal Reserve policy. The book's easy reading is made even more pleasant by a selection of cartoons.

HOW TO MAKE MONEY
IN WALL STREET
Louis Rukeyser
1974/276 pp./$6.95
Doubleday & Co.
245 Park Ave.
New York, NY 10017

This book will have much to tell you whether you are a newcomer to Wall Street or an experienced investor. As he has shown on his weekly television program, the author knows how to make clear sense out of the complexities of his subject. He covers the subject thoroughly and brings new perspectives to many aspects of it.

MONEY, BANKING
AND THE ECONOMY
Thomas Mayer, James S. Duesenberry
    and Robert Z. Aliber
1981/755 pp./$25.95
W. W. Norton & Co.
500 5th Ave.
New York, NY 10110

Either as a review resource or as an introduction to the subject, this book is a useful study of how the financial system works. Its style is

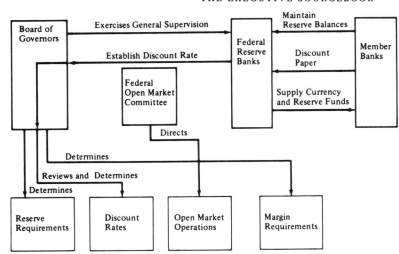

The functions of the Federal Reserve System (from Money, Banking and the Economy).

clear and the material is well organized. A college text, the book's examines the financial structure, money supply, monetary theory, inflation, monetary policy and international finance.

KEEPING UP TO DATE WITH THE WALL STREET JOURNAL

While its primary focus is finance and investment, *The Wall Street Journal* covers all the national and international news that relates to the world of business. The newspaper is published daily except Saturdays, Sundays and general legal holidays. It is available at newsstands in many areas. Annual subscription is $101. For information, write:

The Wall Street Journal
22 Cortlandt St.
New York, NY 10007

MUTUAL FUNDS: A SOURCE OF INVESTMENT INFORMATION

The Investment Company Institute is the national association of mutual funds. The organization offers consumer literature that could be useful if you contemplate investment in mutual funds. Ask for *The Mutual Fund Fact Book* ($2). Write:

Investment Company Institute
1775 K St., N.W.
Washington, DC 20006

A POCKET PROPHET FOR THE STOCK MARKET

William Finnegan Associates, Inc., offers a computer approach to anticipating the performance of the stock market. The firm's Market Forecaster system is designed to predict the Dow Jones average 80 trading days hence. The system is based on a special module programmed with a predictive equation and combined with a Hewlett-Packard programmable calculator. Weekly data published in *Barron's* are punched into the calculator, and the result is a forecast to guide your buy-or-sell decision making. A complete system is priced at $420. For further information, write:

William Finnegan Associates, Inc.
21235 Pacific Coast Hwy.
Malibu, CA 90265

INDEX